with CD-ROM/
Audio CD

face2face

Upper Intermediate Student's Book

Chris Redston & Gillie Cunningham

CAMBRIDGE
UNIVERSITY PRESS

Contents

Listening	Help with Listening and Help with Fluency	Extended Speaking	Writing
		An English learner profile	
Two university students	contractions		A one-minute conversation
Exam stories	sentence stress and rhythm	Exam experiences	
Doing evening classes	**Help with Fluency** sentence stress and rhythm	Conversations about everyday topics	
			Reading and Writing Portfolio 1 WB p64

Listening	Help with Listening and Help with Fluency	Extended Speaking	Writing
Two people's eating habits		Old and new habits	Your eating habits
		Discussion about things that you're used to, etc.	Things your family are used to, etc.
Saving time	linking (1): consonant-vowel links; linking /r/ sounds	How organised are you?	
Problems with young children **Song** Complicated	**Help with Fluency** linking (1): consonant-vowel links; linking /r/ sounds	Discussion about controversial statements	
			Reading and Writing Portfolio 2 WB p66

Listening	Help with Listening and Help with Fluency	Extended Speaking	Writing
		Honesty questions	
Gun crime	third conditional	How life would have been different	Your imaginary past
A lawyer-client meeting	weak forms	Discussion of real-life crimes	
A phone conversation	**Help with Fluency** sentence stress and weak forms (1)	Asking for help	
			Reading and Writing Portfolio 3 WB p68

Listening	Help with Listening and Help with Fluency	Extended Speaking	Writing
Famous urban legends		Two urban legends	
		Completing a story	
A practical joke	predicting what comes next	Telling a true story	Using connecting words in sentences
A nightmare day **Song** I Heard it Through the Grapevine	**Help with Fluency** sentence stress	Good day or bad day	
			Reading and Writing Portfolio 4 WB p70

Listening	Help with Listening and Help with Fluency	Extended Speaking	Writing
		Comparing things	Comparing places, people or things
A trip to the Eden Project		Life in the year 2050	Personal plans and arrangements
The history of perfume	homophones	Designing a new perfume or aftershave	
A conversation about ecological footprints	**Help with Fluency** linking and contractions	Discussions about the environment	
			Reading and Writing Portfolio 5 WB p72

Listening	Help with Listening and Help with Fluency	Extended Speaking	Writing
		Tips for a British tourist in your country	Tips on social codes
A difficult colleague		The next two weeks	The future of people you know
Breaking codes	linking (2): /w/, /j/ and /r/ sounds	Types of code	
A day at the office	intonation: being polite		Two conversations
			Reading and Writing Portfolio 6 WB p74

1 A life of learning

1A A global language

Vocabulary Language ability

 a) Choose the correct words in these phrases. Check in Language Summary 1 **V1.1** p113.

1 (my) *first*/*last* language (is) ...
2 be bilingual *in/at* ...
3 be fluent *at/in* ...
4 be reasonably good *on/at* ...
5 can get *to/by* in ...
6 know a *little/few* words of ...
7 can't speak a word *of/with* ...
8 can *have/make* a conversation in ...
9 speak some ... , but it's a *lot/bit* rusty
10 pick *up/off* a bit of ... on holiday

b) Choose five phrases from **1a)**. Use them to make sentences about yourself or people you know.

My first language is Russian.

c) Work in groups. Take turns to tell each other your sentences. Ask follow-up questions if possible.

Reading and Grammar

 a) How important is learning English in your country? Why?

b) Read the article about learning English around the world. Match headings a)–d) to paragraphs 1–4.

a) Learn English 24 hours a day
b) A changing language
c) An English-speaking world
d) A passport to employment

Who owns English?

1 More people speak English than any other language, but according to English language expert David Crystal, non-native speakers now outnumber native speakers by three to one. "There's never before been a language that's been spoken more as a second language than a first," he says. By the end of last year, the number of adult English speakers in Asia had reached 350 million. And according to the British Council, in ten years' time 2 billion people will study English and about half the world's population will speak it.

2 Why such enthusiasm for English? In a word, jobs. "We always tell students they need two things to succeed – English and computers," says Chetan Kumar, manager of a language school in Delhi. For the middle classes in India, English can mean a prized job in a call centre. And the story is the same in other parts of the world. At a Toyota factory in the Czech Republic, English was chosen as the working language of the Japanese, French and Czech staff. Many other multinational companies, like Samsung and LG.Philips, have started moving towards an English-only email policy. Technology is a big factor in all this change – 80% of the world's electronic information is stored in English.

3 The way that people study English is also changing. In South Korea, for example, the national government has been building English immersion schools all over the country, where teenagers live in an all-English environment for up to four weeks at a time. In these 'English villages', students check into their accommodation, go shopping, order food, go to the bank, take cooking classes or acting lessons – all in English. And they seem to enjoy the experience – when we visited one acting class, a student was pretending to be the film star Orlando Bloom, to the obvious amusement of his classmates.

4 However, these new English speakers aren't just learning the language – they're changing it. There are hundreds of different types of English in the world today, such as 'Hinglish', the Indian mix of Hindi and English. New words are being invented every day all over the world. As David Crystal says, "No one owns English now. What happens to it is on the shoulders of all of us."

Adapted from *Newsweek* 07/03/05

3 Read the article again. What does it say about these people, numbers, things and places?

> native speakers   350 million   2 billion   a call centre
> Toyota   Samsung   80%   South Korea   Hinglish

Help with Grammar The English verb system

4 **a)** Look at the article again. Match the words/phrases in blue to these verb forms.

Present Simple *tell*	Present Continuous
Past Simple	Past Continuous
Present Perfect Simple	Present Perfect Continuous
Past Perfect Simple	Present Simple Passive
	Past Simple Passive

b) Fill in the gaps in these rules with *continuous*, *perfect*, *simple* or *passive*.

- We usually use _____ verb forms to talk about things that are repeated, permanent or completed.

- We usually use _____ verb forms to talk about things that are in progress, temporary or unfinished.

- We usually use _____ verb forms to talk about things that connect two different time periods (the past and the present, etc.).

- We usually use _____ verb forms when we are more interested in what happens to somebody or something than in who or what does the action.

c) Look at the verb forms in pink in the article. Which are activity verbs? Which are state verbs? Then choose the correct word in this rule.

- We don't usually use *activity/state* verbs in continuous verb forms.

d) Check in Language Summary 1 **G1.1** p114.

5 Work in pairs. Name the verb forms in **bold** in these pairs of sentences. Discuss the difference in meaning between a) and b) in each pair.

1. a) They **studied** Portuguese for three years.
   b) They**'ve studied** Portuguese for three years.
2. a) Kemal often **watches** DVDs.
   b) Kemal**'s watching** a DVD at the moment.
3. a) Jo **did** her homework when I got home.
   b) Jo **was doing** her homework when I got home.
4. a) She **teaches** English.
   b) She**'s teaching** English while she's in Berlin.
5. a) When we got there, the class **started**.
   b) When we got there, the class **had started**.
6. a) Antonio **repaired** his car last week.
   b) Antonio's car **was repaired** last week.

6 **a)** Read about Michelle's language learning experiences. Choose the correct verb forms.

I [1](*started*)/*'ve started* studying Spanish after I [2]*went/was going* to Argentina on holiday last year. I [3]*'d never been/never went* to South America before and I couldn't speak a word of Spanish. While I [4]*had travelled/was travelling* around the country, I [5]*picked up/was picking up* enough words and phrases to get by. I [6]*told/was told* that my pronunciation [7]*was/was being* quite good, so when I got home I [8]*decided/was deciding* to learn Spanish properly. A friend [9]*recommended/ was recommended* a school and I [10]*go/'ve been going* there for about six months. I [11]*always enjoy/'m always enjoying* the lessons and the language [12]*teaches/is taught* in a communicative way. I [13]*think/'m thinking* that I [14]*'m learning/'ve learned* a lot since I started. It's not all fun, though – at the moment I [15]*study/'m studying* for my first exam!

b) **R1.1** Listen and check.

Get ready ...
Get it right!

7 Turn to p110. Follow the instructions.

Vocabulary education
Grammar uses of auxiliaries
Help with Listening contractions
Review verb forms

QUICK REVIEW ● ● ●
Think of something you: did last weekend; have done recently; have been doing
for a long time; do every week; were doing at nine o'clock last night. Work in pairs.
Take turns to tell each other about these things. Ask follow-up questions.

Vocabulary Education

1 **a)** Work in pairs. What is the difference between these words/phrases? Check new words/phrases in **V1.2** p113.

1 a state school, a private school
2 a university, a college, a campus
3 an undergraduate, a graduate, a postgraduate
4 a degree, a Master's, a PhD
5 a tutor, a lecturer, a professor
6 a tutorial, a seminar, a lecture
7 fees, a student loan, a scholarship
8 a subject, a course, a career

TIP! ● We only show the main stress (•) in words/phrases.

b) Choose eight words/phrases in **1a)** that are connected to you or people you know.

c) Work in pairs. Take turns to tell each other why you chose those words. Ask follow-up questions.

> I chose 'a lecture' because I went to an interesting lecture yesterday.

> Oh? What was it about?

Mia   *Tim*

Listening and Grammar

2 **a)** Work in groups. Discuss these questions.

1 Have you, or has anyone you know, been to university or college? Did you/they enjoy it? What did you/they study?
2 What problems do you think students have during their first week at university?

b) **R1.2** Look at the photos. Mia and Tim are university students. This is their first week. Listen and tick the things they talk about.

● a lecture ✓   ● transport problems
● food   ● accommodation ✓
● getting lost ✓   ● money ✓
● courses they're doing ✓ ● weekend plans

3 **R1.2** Listen again. Fill in gaps a)–h) with one word.

1 TIM You went to Professor Lee's geography a) _lecture_ yesterday, didn't you?
  MIA Yeah, but I didn't understand very much.
  TIM Neither did I.
2 TIM And it's a huge campus – I keep getting b) _lost_ !
  MIA Yes, so do I. Yesterday I was walking around for ages looking for the c) _bookshop_ .
3 TIM Well, at least you found it in the end. Maybe you should get a d) _map_ .
  MIA I did have a e) _map_ !
4 TIM My brother's done that course. He graduated last f) _July_ .
  MIA Did he? Has he found a job yet?
5 MIA And what are you studying?
  TIM Geography and economics. Most people think economics is really g) _boring_ , but I don't.
6 TIM Anyway, do you live here on campus?
  MIA No, I don't. I was told it was really h) _expensive_

Help with Grammar **Uses of auxiliaries**

4 AUXILIARIES IN VERB FORMS

a) Look again at Tim and Mia's sentences in **3**. Name the verb forms in blue.

didn't understand – Past Simple

b) Which of the verb forms in blue in **3** have auxiliaries? Which two verb forms don't have auxiliaries?

c) Complete these rules with *be, do* or *have*.

- We make all continuous verb forms with: .... + verb+*ing*.
- We make all perfect verb forms with: .... + past participle.
- We make all passive verb forms with: .... + past participle.
- In the Present Simple and Past Simple we use a form of .... to make questions and negatives.

TIP! ● We also use modal verbs (*will, would, can, could,* etc.) as auxiliaries: *I'll* (= will) *do my best.*

d) Check in G1.2 p115.

5 OTHER USES OF AUXILIARIES

a) Look at these other uses of auxiliaries. Match the phrases in pink in **3** to a)–f).

a) a question tag *didn't you?*
b) an echo question to show interest ╱
c) to agree with somebody with *so* or *neither* ╱
d) to avoid repeating a verb or phrase ╱
e) a short answer to a *yes/no* question ✓
f) to add emphasis

b) Check in G1.3 p115.

Help with Listening **Contractions**

- In spoken English we often contract the auxiliaries *am, are, is, have, has, had, will* and *would*. We also contract negatives (*don't, wasn't, won't,* etc.).

6 **a)** R1.3 Listen to these pairs of sentences. Which do you hear first?

1	a) She's made it.	b) She made it.
2	a) He'd started it.	b) He started it.
3	a) You're taught it.	b) You taught it.
4	a) I've lost it.	b) I lost it.
5	a) We'll watch it.	b) We watch it.
6	a) I won't buy it.	b) I want to buy it.

b) R1.4 Listen and write six sentences. You will hear each sentence twice.

c) Work in pairs. Compare sentences. Which auxiliaries are contracted in each sentence?

7 **a)** Mia and Tim meet again in the cafeteria the next day. Fill in the gaps in their conversation with the correct positive or negative auxiliaries. Use contractions where possible.

TIM Hi, Mia. ¹ *Have* you had lunch yet?
MIA Yes, I ² .... But I can stay and chat for a bit.
TIM Great! So, what ³ .... you do last night?
MIA Well, I ⁴ .... going to go out with some friends, but I ⁵ .... in the end. I ⁶ .... catch up on some sleep, though. I was in bed by 10.30!
TIM It ⁷ .... been a busy few days, ⁸ .... it?
MIA Yes, it ⁹ .... And I ¹⁰ .... need my sleep!
TIM Me too. Er, what ¹¹ .... you doing this evening?
MIA Nothing special. Why ¹² .... you ask?
TIM Well, I ¹³ .... going to see a band.
MIA ¹⁴ .... you? That sounds fun!
TIM So ¹⁵ .... you fancy coming along?
MIA Yeah, sure. Call me later. Here's my number.
TIM Thanks. Oh, by the way, ¹⁶ .... you find your lecture yesterday?
MIA Yes, I ¹⁷ .... And I ¹⁸ .... even need a map!

b) R1.5 Listen and check.

8 Change these sentences to avoid repeating verbs or phrases.

1 I don't speak German, but my younger brother ~~speaks German~~. *does*
2 Ian didn't go to college, but his sister went to college.
3 My parents haven't been there, but we've been there.
4 Penny doesn't like golf, but her brothers like golf.
5 We're not going out tonight, but they're going out tonight.
6 Tom enjoyed the play, but I didn't enjoy the play.

Get ready ... Get it right!

9 **a)** Work in pairs. Choose one of these situations or invent your own. Then write a one-minute conversation between the people. Include at least five different uses of auxiliaries from **4c)** and **5a)**.

- two students who are sharing a house
- two friends who are lost on their way to a party
- a couple trying to decide where to go on holiday
- two students talking about their school, college or university

b) Practise the conversation with your partner until you can remember it.

10 **a)** Work in groups of four with another pair. Take turns to role-play your conversations. Guess the relationship between the people.

b) Role-play one of your group's conversations for the class.

1C Making the grade

Vocabulary verb patterns (1)
Skills Reading: Under examination;
Listening: Exam stories
Help with Listening sentence stress
and rhythm
Review verb forms; echo questions

QUICK REVIEW ● ● ●
Write four interesting things about yourself or people you know. Work in pairs. Take turns to say your sentences. Respond with an echo question and a follow-up question. A *I've been scuba diving a few times.* B *Have you? Where did you go?*

Reading and Vocabulary

1 a) Work in pairs. Discuss these questions.

1 Do you think exams are a good way to test students' knowledge? Why?/Why not?
2 What do you think is the best way to revise for exams?

b) Read the article. Is Jeremy Harris for or against exams? Why?

2 a) Read the article again. Tick the true sentences. Correct the false ones.

1 He didn't sleep the night before his maths exam.
2 The writer talked to his classmates before his maths exam.
3 He thinks children have to do too much writing in exams.
4 He doesn't think that everything children learn at school is useful.
5 He wants his daughters to leave school at 16.
6 He uses his knowledge of maths a lot in his daily life.

b) Work in pairs. Compare answers.

Under examination

Jeremy Harris looks back on his experiences of school exams.

It's been years since I last did an exam, but the memories of my O Levels* are still disturbingly fresh. I remember staying up all night before my maths exam, trying to learn dozens of equations by heart. The next day I avoided sitting next to my friends on the school bus and refused to talk to anyone outside the exam hall in case they made me forget everything I'd learned. When the teacher finally allowed us to pick up our pens, I immediately wrote down the equations in case I might need them during the exam. I didn't, of course, but I still have nightmares about the whole experience.

Back then I never stopped to think if exams were a good idea, but now that my twin daughters are doing their GCSEs*, I'm beginning to wonder whether exams are actually worth doing at all. Why do we still force kids to sit in an overheated gym and write until their arms fall off?

Is a three-hour memory test really a good way to find out how much children know? Kids always end up forgetting almost everything they learn at school anyway. (Can you remember the second law of thermodynamics or who invented the light bulb? I thought not.) Personally I regret spending so much time at school learning things I've never needed to know since – and these days you can find out everything on the Internet anyway.

Of course, I still encourage my daughters to take their GCSEs seriously and I expect them both to continue studying next year. Emily hopes to become a journalist and I'm trying to persuade Julia to go to medical school. They're both very bright, but they find it hard to concentrate. They usually study for half an hour and then stop to call their friends or watch TV. However, we all know that qualifications help people get jobs, and a graduate in the UK will earn nearly

twice as much as someone who left school at 16. So I pretend to believe that exams are a good idea, and I always remember to wish my daughters luck before each one.

By the way, I did manage to pass my maths O Level, but since then nobody's ever asked me to do calculus or draw a graph. The way I see it, if you need to add up a few numbers, try using a calculator. So maybe it's time to stop testing how much children remember and teach them to be better human beings instead.

*O Levels = exams that 16-year-olds in the UK took before 1988
*GCSEs = exams that 16-year olds in the UK take now

Help with Vocabulary Verb patterns (1)

3 **a)** Look at the verbs in blue in the article. Write the infinitive forms of these verbs in the table.

avoid	+ verb+ing
refuse	+ infinitive with to
make	+ object + infinitive
allow	+ object + infinitive with to
might	+ infinitive

b) Write these verbs in the table in **3a)**. Some verbs can go in more than one place.

> could   would rather   prefer   keep   let   start
> seem   should   don't mind   continue   finish
> forget   love   had better   like   pay   hate
> plan   convince   miss   enjoy   decide

c) Look at the verbs in pink in the article. Match the verb forms to the meanings.

1 *remember* + verb+ing
2 *remember* + infinitive with *to*
a) remember something that you did before
b) make a mental note to do something in the future

3 *stop* + verb+ing
4 *stop* + infinitive with *to*
c) stop something that you were doing
d) stop doing one thing in order to do something else

5 *try* + verb+ing
6 *try* + infinitive with *to*
e) make an effort to do something difficult
f) do something in order to solve a problem

d) Check in **V1.3** p113.

4 Work in pairs. Student A → p104. Student B → p107. Follow the instructions.

Listening

5 **a)** Check these words with your teacher or in a dictionary.

> cuffs   cheat   pocket money   an oral exam

b) Work in pairs. Look at pictures A and B. What do you think is happening in each one?

c) **R1.6** Listen and check your answers to **5b)**.

6 **a)** **R1.6** Listen again. Write six words/phrases to help you remember each story.

b) Work in new pairs. Take turns to tell each other one of the stories. Include as much detail as possible.

Help with Listening Sentence stress and rhythm

• In spoken English we usually only stress the words that give the main information. This gives English its natural rhythm.

7 **a)** **R1.6** Listen to the beginning of the first exam story. Notice the stressed words.

My worst exam moment happened when I was caught cheating by my mum after a history exam. I really liked history classes, but I didn't have a very good memory.

b) Work in pairs. Look again at **7a)**. Which parts of speech are usually stressed? Which are usually unstressed?

adjectives – stressed   possessive adjectives – unstressed

c) Look at the next part of the story. Which words do you think are stressed?

So on the morning of the exam I wrote loads of important facts and figures on the insides of my shirt cuffs. I made sure that I got to the exam room really early so I could sit at the back.

d) **R1.6** Listen and check.

e) Look at R1.6, p143. Listen to the stories again. Notice the sentence stress and rhythm.

8 Work in groups. Discuss these questions.

1 What was the last exam you did? How did you feel before, during and after it?
2 What was the hardest exam you've ever taken?
3 Have you ever done an oral exam? What was it like?
4 Do you know any other interesting or funny stories about exams? If so, tell the group.

Henry

Yvonne

1D Evening classes

Real World keeping a
conversation going
Help with Fluency sentence
stress and rhythm
Review verb patterns; echo
questions; question tags

QUICK REVIEW ●●●

Choose five of these verbs and write sentences about yourself: *stop; avoid; persuade; remember; refuse; try; help; end up; hope; encourage; pretend.* Work in pairs. Take turns to say your sentences. Ask follow-up questions. A *I stopped smoking last year.* B *Well done. How did you manage it?*

BC Barnwell College
of Further Education
Grove Street London W6 3SW
www.bcfe.ac.uk

1 Work in groups. Discuss these questions.

1 Where can you do evening classes in your town/city?
2 Have you, or has anyone you know, ever done any evening classes? If so, which ones?
3 Look at the advert. Which two evening classes would you like to do? Why?

2 a) [R1.7] Listen to a conversation between two friends, Kim and Sue. Tick the evening classes that Kim is doing.

b) Listen again. Answer these questions.

1 How long ago did Kim and Sue last meet up?
2 What did Kim have to do in her last creative writing class?
3 What did she get for her birthday?
4 Which class does she find difficult?
5 Why does she find the evening classes helpful?
6 Who does she go to her dance class with?
7 How long is Sue going to be in the USA?

Evening classes October 2nd – December 15th
Register online or call us on 020 8741 2099.
All classes are 6.30 p.m. – 8.00 p.m.

DAY	CLASS
Monday	● Thai cookery ● Digital photography ● Yoga – beginners
Tuesday	● Computer skills – intermediate ● Pottery ● Salsa – intermediate
Wednesday	● Painting with watercolours ● Creative writing ● Yoga – intermediate
Thursday	● Ballroom dancing ● Creative photography ● Computer skills – beginners
Friday	● Jewellery making ● Film studies ● Salsa – beginners

Real World Keeping a conversation going

● We often use short questions to keep a conversation going and to show interest.

3 a) Fill in the gaps in short questions 1–10 with these words.

~~going~~ what mean that like else sort way come as

1 How's it _going_ ?
2 Why's _____ ?
3 Like _____ , exactly?
4 How do you _____ ?
5 What's the teacher _____ ?
6 What _____ are you doing?
7 Such _____ ?
8 How _____ ?
9 In what _____ ?
10 What _____ of dancing?

b) Fill in the gaps in these parts of the conversation with a preposition.

KIM I go every week.
SUE Really? Who _____ ?

SUE I'm off to the USA on Sunday.
KIM Are you? How long _____ ?

TIP! ● We also use echo questions (KIM *It's really difficult, actually.* SUE **Is it**?) and questions with question tags (*It's been ages,* **hasn't it**?) to keep a conversation going.

c) Check in [RW1.1] p115.

4 a) [R1.8] Listen to eight sentences. For each sentence you hear, complete these short questions with a preposition.

1 What _about_ ?
2 Where _____ ?
3 Who _____ ?
4 What _____ ?
5 Who _____ ?
6 Who _____ ?
7 How long _____ ?
8 Who _____ ?

b) [R1.9] Listen and check. Are prepositions in short questions stressed or unstressed?

a) Read the next part of Sue and Kim's conversation. Fill in the gaps with one word.

s First, I'm going to my cousin's wedding in Seattle.
k ¹ *Are* you? Who ² _____ ?
s My brother, Frank. I'm rather nervous about the whole thing, though.
k Really? How ³ _____ ?
s Frank and I don't really get on particularly well.
k How do you ⁴ _____ ?
s Er, we tend to argue quite a lot.
k Yes, families can be difficult, ⁵ _____ they? And what ⁶ _____ are you doing?
s After the wedding I'm going on a trip that my friend Brad's organised.
k ⁷ _____ you? What ⁸ _____ of trip?
s We're going walking in the Rockies.
k How long ⁹ _____ ?
s Five days. Oh, I can't wait!

b) R1.10 Listen and check.

Help with Fluency
Sentence stress and rhythm

6 **a)** R1.10 Look at R1.10, p144. Listen again. Notice the sentence stress and rhythm.

b) P Work in pairs. Practise the conversation in R1.10, p144 until you can remember it. Then close your books and have the conversation again. Try to use natural sentence stress and rhythm.

TIP! ● P = pronounciation.

7 Work in new pairs. Have two conversations. Use these ideas or your own. Ask each other questions to keep the conversations going.

● your work or studies
● a problem you have
● a place you love going to
● something interesting you've done lately
● your plans for next weekend
● something you are/aren't looking forward to

---

1 Review

Language Summary 1, p113

1 **a)** Fill in the gaps with these words. Then use phrases 1–7 to make true or false sentences about yourself. **V1.1**

~~in~~ bit few up by of in

1 I'm fluent _in_ …
2 I only know a _____ words of …
3 I'd like to be bilingual _____ …
4 I can't speak a word _____ …
5 I used to speak some … , but it's a _____ rusty now.
6 I can get _____ in …
7 I picked _____ a bit of … when …

b) Work in pairs. Tell your partner your sentences. Guess which sentences are true.

2 Work in pairs. Underline and correct the incorrect verb forms in these sentences. **G1.1**

1 Yesterday I've spent an hour in the park. It was very relaxing.
2 I'm needing a new dictionary. I lost mine last month.
3 My English is quite good. I learn it since 2004.
4 I lost my English book last week, but it handed in at reception last night.
5 Kim was back from Italy since Monday. She had a great time.
6 I realised that I meet Samir before.
7 My sister phoned while I talked to John.

3 **a)** Write the words connected to education. **V1.2**

1 **ttilauor**	t _utorial_
2 **cpmusa**	c_____
3 **guraated**	g_____
4 **leeructr**	l_____
5 **crhholssiap**	s_____
6 **eeergd**	d_____

b) Work in pairs. Compare answers. Then think of six more words/phrases connected to education.

c) Tell your partner about your education.

---

4 Choose the correct words. G1.2

A ¹*Did/Have* you ever studied a subject you ²*haven't/didn't* like?
B I ³*did/was* study IT for a year, which was a bit boring. You work with computers, ⁴*do/don't* you?
A Yes, I ⁵*am/do*. I write software.
B ⁶*Are/Do* you? ⁷*Didn't/Wasn't* your father work for a software company?
A No, he ⁸*didn't/wasn't* actually, but my brother ⁹*does/is*. I ¹⁰*'m/was* going to work for the same company, but I ¹¹*didn't/wasn't* in the end.

5 Fill in the gaps with the correct verb form. V1.3

1 *to meet/meeting*
  a) He remembers _____ me in 2001.
  b) I forgot _____ Jo at the airport.

2 *to tell/telling*
  a) I expect them _____ me soon.
  b) I regret _____ them about that.

3 *to drink/drinking*
  a) I've stopped _____ coffee.
  b) I persuaded him _____ some water.

4 *to talk/talking*
  a) She refused _____ to me.
  b) I avoided _____ to him.

5 *to be/being*
  a) I pretended _____ asleep.
  b) I kept _____ woken up.

Progress Portfolio

a) Tick the things you can do in English.

☐ I can talk about my language ability.

☐ I can talk about education.

☐ I can ask and answer detailed questions about the present and the past.

☐ I can understand an article which expresses a specific point of view.

☐ I can use short questions to keep a conversation going effectively.

b) What do you need to study again? See CD-ROM ●1A–D.

2 Time for a change

2A It's bad for you!

Vocabulary expressing frequency
Grammar present and past habits, repeated actions and states
Review keeping a conversation going; present and past verb forms

QUICK REVIEW ● ● ●
Work in pairs. Take turns to tell each other what you did last weekend. Ask each other short questions and try to keep each conversation going for two minutes. A *I went camping.* B *Did you? What was it like?*

Reading, Listening and Grammar

1 **a)** Read part of a web page on health. Try to fill in gaps 1–4 with these percentages.

> 25%   33%   50%   70%

b) Work in pairs. Compare answers. Then check on p159.

c) Do you think a similar survey done in your country would produce the same results? Why?/Why not?

2 **a)** Look at the photos of Cassy and Ted, two people who took part in the survey. Who do you think says sentences 1–3 and who do you think says sentences 4–6?

1 Every day when I get home from work, I'**ll have** a coffee and half a packet of chocolate cookies.
2 I **know** what I like and I **eat** what I like.
3 My mom**'s always telling** me what I should and shouldn't eat.
4 But when I was a teenager I'**d get up** in the morning and go straight to the cookie jar.
5 I **used to be** addicted to chocolate chip cookies – my mom **used to hide** them from me.
6 And then I **read** a lot of books about health and nutrition, and I **knew** I had to change.

b) **R2.1** Listen and check. Tick the sentences in 2a) when you hear them.

c) Listen again. Answer these questions.

1 What does Cassy say about French and American eating habits?
2 Has Cassy's attitude to food ever changed?
3 Who is healthier, Cassy or her mother?
4 Does Ted ever eat things that are unhealthy?
5 Why does he check food labels all the time?
6 What does he say about Japanese and American eating habits?

d) Work in pairs. Compare answers. Whose attitude to food is most like yours, Cassy's or Ted's?

http://www.foodstuff.net/diet.html

So what IS good for me?

Many people are confused and worried about something that should be one of life's greatest pleasures – eating. A recent survey done in the USA has shown that:

1 _____ of adults are confused by reports giving dietary advice.

2 _____ believe that healthy eating means giving up food they enjoy.

3 _____ feel guilty when they eat food they enjoy.

4 _____ don't want the government to advise them on what sort of food they should or shouldn't eat.

Cassy

Ted

14

Help with Grammar Present and past habits, repeated actions and states

3 **a)** Look at the verb forms in **bold** in sentences 1–3 in 2a). Complete these rules with *Present Simple*, *will + infinitive* or *Present Continuous*.

- We use the _PRES S_ to talk about present habits, repeated actions and states.
- We often use the _PRES. Cont_ with *always* to talk about present habits and repeated actions that annoy us or happen more than usual.
- We can use _will + inf_ to talk about repeated and typical behaviour in the present. We don't usually use this verb form with state verbs for this meaning.

b) Look at these sentences. Which talks about repeated and typical behaviour? Which talks about a future action?

1 Sometimes I**'ll eat** things I know are unhealthy.
2 Tonight I**'ll** probably **have** a burger. ~Fut

c) Look at the verb forms in **bold** in sentences 4–6 in 2a). Complete these rules with *Past Simple*, *would + infinitive* or *used to + infinitive*.

- We use the _PAST S_ and _USED_ to talk about past habits, repeated actions and states.
- We can use _WOULD + INF_ to talk about past habits and repeated actions. We don't usually use this verb form with state verbs.

TIP! • We don't use *used to* or *would* + infinitive for something that only happened once: *In 2003 I gave up smoking.* not ~~In 2003 I used to give up smoking.~~

d) Check in **G2.1** p116.

4 Look at these sentences. Are both verb forms possible? If not, choose the correct one.

1 Last night *I'd have*/(*I had*) two burgers for dinner and *I used to feel*/*I felt* a bit sick afterwards.
2 I **rarely** drink coffee now, but at one time *it'd be*/ *it used to be* my favourite drink. STATE
3 I **seldom** pay attention to government reports about food because *they'd change*/*they're always* ~ANNOYING *changing* their advice.
4 *I walk*/*I'll walk* to work just for the exercise and I **frequently** *go*/*am going* to the gym.
5 **Occasionally** *I eat*/*I'll eat* vegetables, but only because *I'll know*/*I know* they're good for me.
6 *I always worry*/*I'm always worrying* about my diet.
7 Once *I used to try*/*I tried* not adding salt to my food. It tasted awful! ← 1 time
8 When I was younger, *I didn't use to like*/*I wouldn't like* coffee. STATE

5 **a)** Read about Ted's parents, George and Kath. Fill in the gaps with the correct form of the verbs in brackets. Sometimes there is more than one possible answer.

George   *Kath*

Before we ¹ _got_ (get) married, Kath and I ² _____ (live) in Boston. Then in 1996 we ³ _____ (move) to New York, where we ⁴ _____ (have) a small apartment. Back then **more often than not** we ⁵ _would_ (stay) at home in the evening because we ⁶ _____ (not have) much money. Ted says that I ⁷ _always go_ (always go on) about how poor we ⁸ _____ (be) then, but it's true. For example, **every so often** we ⁹ _____ (buy) Ted a burger as a treat, but Kath and I ¹⁰ _____ (never eat) out. But now that we ¹¹ _____ (have) more money we ¹² _____ (go) to restaurants quite a lot. In fact, **most weeks** we ¹³ _____ (eat) out at least twice. **Most of the time** we ¹⁴ _____ (go) to local restaurants, but **once in a while** we ¹⁵ _____ (drive) up to Boston and go to one of our favourite restaurants there. I really ¹⁶ _____ (love) Boston and **every now and again** I ¹⁷ _____ (think) about moving back there, but Kath ¹⁸ _____ (always tell) me that's unrealistic.

b) Work in pairs. Compare answers.

Vocabulary Expressing frequency

6 **a)** Put the words/phrases in **bold** in 4 and 5a) into these groups. Check in **V2.1** p116.

lower frequency *rarely*   higher frequency *frequently*

b) Write four true and four false sentences about your eating habits. Use words/phrases from 6a).

c) Work in pairs. Tell each other your sentences. Guess which of your partner's sentences are true.

Get ready ... Get it right!

7 Make notes on the differences between your life five years ago and your life now. Use these ideas or your own.

- sleeping habits
- free time activities
- time with friends and family
- sport and exercise
- work or study
- taste in music/films/ TV programmes
- places you have lived
- annoying habits

8 **a)** Work in groups. Discuss how your life now is different from your life five years ago. Use language from 3.

b) Tell the class about the person whose life has changed the most.

Vocabulary feelings and opinions
Grammar *be used to, get used to*
Review present and past habits

QUICK REVIEW ●●●
Write three sentences about your friends' present and past habits or routines. Work in pairs. Take turns to tell your partner about your friends. Ask follow-up questions if possible. Are any of your friends similar? **A** *My friend Maria's always complaining about her job.* **B** *Really? Why's that?*

Vocabulary Feelings and opinions

1 **a)** Look at the adjectives in **bold**. Then choose the correct prepositions. Check in V2.2 p116.

1 I'm **terrified** *for/of* flying.
2 I'm **fascinated** *by/for* other cultures.
3 I always get **excited** *of/about* travelling to new places.
4 I'm usually **satisfied** *for/with* the service I get on planes.
5 I'm **shocked** *by/with* how little some people know about my country.
6 I was quite **disappointed** *in/of* the last place I went to on holiday.
7 I was **impressed** *of/by* the facilities at the last hotel I stayed in.
8 I'm not **aware** *to/of* any dangers for travellers in my country.
9 My country is **famous** *for/about* its historical buildings.
10 I'm very **fond** *of/with* spicy food.
11 I'm not **sure** *about/for* the need for so many security checks at airports.
12 I'm **sick** *of/at* the weather we've been having recently.

b) Tick the sentences in **1a)** that are true for you.

c) Work in pairs. Take turns to say the sentences you ticked. Ask follow-up questions.

> I'm terrified of flying.

> Really? When was the last time you flew?

Reading and Grammar

2 **a)** Look at the photo. Which city do you think this is? Why?

b) Check these words/phrases with your teacher or in a dictionary.

> a foreign correspondent   the rush hour
> ignore   a tortilla   a pedestrian

c) Read the article. What does the writer think is the hardest thing to deal with in this city?

Letter from abroad

by Peter Taylor

I've always been fascinated by Mexico, even as a child. So I was excited about coming here from Canada as a foreign correspondent, and since I arrived I haven't been disappointed in anything. It's such a wonderful country full of colours, sounds and smells that are so different from those back home. Before I came here, I'd read that Mexico had a much slower pace of life than Canada – but I soon realised they weren't talking about Mexico City. Waking up early enough to avoid the 7 a.m. to 11 p.m. rush hour wasn't easy at first, but now ¹**I'm used to getting up at 5 a.m. every day**.

And as for driving here, ²**I'm slowly getting used to it** – but when I first arrived I was absolutely terrified of being in a car. This is a city of 20 million people and it feels like they're all on the road at the same time. But don't get me wrong, I'm really impressed with the way Mexicans drive, they're amazing. And of course there are rules of the road – it just takes a while for ³**a foreigner to get used to them**. For example, I've learned to ignore traffic lights. For months I annoyed every traffic cop in Mexico City by stopping at red lights while they were desperately trying to keep the traffic moving. Also ⁴**I wasn't used to people driving so close to me**. In fact you can't get a Mexican tortilla between one car and another!

Yes, driving in Mexico City is educational and exciting – and it's certainly a lot less dangerous than walking! I have to admit that ⁵**I still haven't got used to being a pedestrian here**. Can you imagine how difficult it is to cross the road in this city? ⁶**I'll never get used to doing that**!

3 a) Read the article again. What does Peter Taylor say about these things?

a) his job
b) the rush hour
c) Mexican drivers
d) traffic lights
e) the distance between cars
f) walking in the city

b) Work in groups. Discuss these questions.

1 How does the traffic in Mexico City compare to the traffic in the capital city of your country?
2 Do you drive in cities very often? If so, do you enjoy it? Why?/Why not?
3 Have you ever driven in a foreign country? If so, where? What was it like?

Marcus – Japan

Erin – Iceland

Help with Grammar *be used to, get used to*

4 a) Look at phrase 1 in the article. Answer these questions.

1 Did Peter find it difficult to get up at 5 a.m. when he first arrived in Mexico?
2 Is it difficult for him now?

b) Look at phrases 1 and 2 in the article. Complete these rules with *get used to* and *be used to*.

- We use _____ to talk about things that are familiar and no longer strange or difficult for us.
- We use _____ to talk about things that become familiar, less strange or less difficult over a period of time.

c) Look at phrases 1–6 in the article. Choose the correct words/phrases in these rules.

- After *be used to* and *get used to* we use the *infinitive/verb+ing*.
- After *be used to* and *get used to* we *can/can't* use a noun or a pronoun.

d) Match phrases 1–6 in the article to these forms of *be used to* or *get used to*.

a) Present Simple *1*
b) Present Continuous
c) Present Perfect Simple
d) Past Simple
e) *will* + infinitive
f) infinitive with *to*

e) What is the difference in meaning between these two sentences?

1 *I used to live in Mexico City.*
2 *I'm used to living in Mexico City.*

f) Check in `G2.2` **p117.**

5 `R2.2` `P` **Listen and practise.**

I'm used to /juːstə/ *getting up at 5 a.m. every day.*

---

6 a) Look at the photos of Peter's colleagues and the places where they work. Then fill in the gaps with the correct positive or negative form of *be used to* or *get used to*. Sometimes there is more than one possible answer.

1 I _'m not used to_ all the customs yet – like it's rude to blow your nose in public.
2 It was hard to _____ just eating rice for breakfast.
3 I _____ sleeping in daylight, so I find it difficult in the summer when it never gets dark.
4 I don't think I'll ever _____ the written language – it has three alphabets.
5 The summers here aren't very warm and I _____ temperatures of about 30°C in the summer.
6 I _____ finding my way around new places using a map, but I can't read the maps here.

b) Work in pairs. Compare answers. Who said the sentences in 6a), Marcus or Erin?

7 a) Make four sentences about your family using *be used to* or *get used to*.

b) Work in pairs. Compare answers. Are any the same?

Get ready … Get it right!

8 Write five of these things on a piece of paper. Don't write them in this order.

Something that you …

- are used to doing during the week
- don't think you'll ever get used to
- will have to get used to in the future
- would find it impossible to get used to
- weren't used to doing at one time, but you are now
- are getting used to at the moment

9 a) Work in pairs. Swap papers. Take turns to ask your partner about the things he/she has written. Ask follow-up questions if possible.

b) Tell the class two things you found out about your partner.

Vocabulary word building (1): suffixes
Skills Reading: Timely tips; Listening: Saving time
Help with Listening linking (1): consonant-vowel links; linking /r/ sounds
Review feelings and opinions

VOCABULARY AND SKILLS

QUICK REVIEW ●●●
Write three true and three false sentences about yourself using these adjectives: *terrified; fascinated; excited; disappointed; fond; sick*. Work in pairs. Swap papers. Guess which of your partner's sentences are true. Ask follow-up questions about the ones that are true: *Why are you so terrified of spiders?*

Reading and Vocabulary

1 Work in pairs. Discuss these questions.

1 How do you remember appointments, things you need to buy, people's birthdays, etc.?
2 Do you usually do everything you plan to do each day? If not, why not?

2 **a)** Check these words with your teacher or in a dictionary.

a priority   an interruption
procrastinate   dread

b) Read the article about how to manage your time efficiently. Match headings a)–i) to tips 1–9.

a) Make lists *tip 1*
b) Listen to your body clock _____
c) Find out how long things take _____
d) Choose your priorities _____
e) Learn to say no _____
f) Combine several activities _____
g) Don't procrastinate _____
h) Allow time for mistakes _____
i) Don't aim to be perfect _____

c) Read the article again. In what way can you:

1 help your memory?
2 prioritise?
3 be sure of what you can achieve in a certain time?
4 avoid doing things that others should do?
5 approach a job that you don't want to do?

d) Work in groups. Discuss these questions.

1 Which of the tips surprised you? Why?
2 Which do you already do?
3 Which would you like to try? Why?
4 Which don't you think would be useful? Why not?

Timely tips

1 Don't rely on your memory alone. Write a 'to do' list for each day, **preferably** the night before or first thing in the morning.

> To Do List
> ① finish Coursework
> ② Launderette
> ③ Shopping
> ④ Phone Dad

2 **Decide** on the best order to do things. You can use colours, numbers or letters to signal which things on your list are the most urgent or important. If there's a deadline, write down the date you need to finish the task by.

3 Things don't always go according to plan. Experts suggest that mistakes and interruptions will take up 50% of the time you have available. This may mean you have to reconsider the number of things you had **originally** hoped to do.

4 When you do routine tasks, time yourself doing them. This allows you to plan your time more **realistically**.

5 If you are really **convinced** that what you have to do is essential, it will be easier to say no to things that you are not **responsible** for and to people who make unexpected demands on your time. Remember, saying no isn't always a **weakness**.

> NO, I'M AFRAID I CAN'T.

6 People's energy levels differ greatly, depending on the time of day. There are morning people and those who work better in the afternoon or evening. Therefore try to do things at a time of day to suit the type of person you are.

7 Putting twice as much effort into a task may only achieve a 1% **improvement** and perfection is unattainable. So don't be too **critical** of yourself and learn to **recognise** when enough is enough. Otherwise you'll just be wasting precious time.

> THIS IS GOOD ENOUGH!

8 Try multitasking. Do the ironing while you watch TV, study for your test while you're travelling on the bus, or just mentally run through things you're trying to learn while you're in the shower.

9 When there's a job you really dread doing, don't keep putting it off. Make 'holes' in it by breaking it into smaller tasks. Do them one at a time and set a time limit. This is called the 'Swiss cheese method'.

Help with Vocabulary Word building (1): suffixes

3 **a)** Work in pairs. Complete the table with the words in **bold** in the article.

verb	noun	adjective	adverb
prefer	preference	preferable	1 ....
2	decision	decisive	decisively
originate	originality origin	original	3 ....
–	realism reality	realistic real	4 .... really
convince	conviction	5 .... convincing	convincingly
–	responsibility	6	responsibly
weaken	7	weak	weakly
improve	8	improved	–
criticise	criticism	9	critically
10	recognition	recognisable	recognisably

b) Look at the table again. Do we use these suffixes for verbs (V), nouns (N), adjectives (ADJ) or adverbs (ADV)?

-ence *N* -able *ADJ* -ly -ion -ive -ate
-ity -al -ism -ic -ally -ed -ing
-ility -ible -en -ness -ment -ise

c) Look at the verbs in the table. Which verbs change their spelling when a suffix is added?

decide → *decision*

d) Check in V2.3 p116.

4 **a)** R2.3 P Listen and practise. Notice how the stress changes.

prefer preference preferable preferably

b) Work in pairs. Take turns to test your partner on the word families in **3a)**.

(responsibility) (responsible, responsibly)

Listening

5 R2.4 Listen to Nancy and Jake. Which three time management tips from the article does each person talk about? Write their names next to the headings in **2b)**. Which tip do they both talk about?

6 **a)** R2.4 Listen again. Tick the true sentences. Correct the false ones.

1 Nancy didn't use to buy all the food at one time.
2 She uses her computer to make lists.
3 She still tries to make the perfect sandwich.
4 Jake found all of the time management course helpful.
5 He doesn't like the idea of multitasking.
6 He agrees that you shouldn't aim for perfection.

b) Work in pairs. Compare answers.

Help with Listening Linking (1): consonant-vowel links; linking /r/ sounds

• We usually link words that end in a consonant sound with words that start with a vowel sound. In British English, when a word ends in -r or -re, we only say the /r/ sound when the next word begins with a vowel sound.

7 **a)** R2.5 Listen to these words/phrases. Notice the linking /r/ sounds.

1 later later ͜/r/͜ on
2 far far ͜/r/͜ away
3 better better ͜/r/͜ idea
4 more more ͜/r/͜ often
5 another another ͜/r/͜ hour
6 sure sure ͜/r/͜ about

b) R2.4 Listen again to the beginning of what Nancy says. Notice the consonant-vowel links and linking /r/.

I've been running͜ a sandwich delivery service͜ in the centre ͜/r/͜ of the city for ͜/r/͜ over ͜/r/͜ a year. When͜ I first started͜ I wasted loads͜ of time because͜ I wasn't͜ at͜ all͜ organised.

c) Work in pairs. Look at what Nancy says next. Draw the consonant-vowel links and linking /r/ sounds.

After I'd started making the sandwiches I'd realise that I hadn't got everything I needed for all the different fillings. That meant I'd have to spend another hour in the supermarket or even a couple of hours sometimes!

d) Look at R2.4, p144. Check your answers.

e) R2.4 Listen again and read what Nancy says. Notice the linking.

8 Look at p111. Follow the instructions.

Nancy

Jake

2D I see your point

Real World discussion language (1):
agreeing and disagreeing politely
Help with Fluency linking (1):
consonant-vowel links; linking /r/ sounds
Review word building (1): suffixes

QUICK REVIEW ● ● ●
Write three verbs that can be made into nouns, adjectives and adverbs.
Work in pairs. Swap papers with your partner. Take turns to tell your
partner what the nouns, adjectives and adverbs are for each verb.

James Jenny Liam Lily Hazel Harriet

1 Work in groups. Discuss these questions.

1 Were your parents strict about food and meal times when you
were a child? If so, in what way?
2 What kind of things do children eat these days? What don't
they eat?

2 **a)** Look at the photo. Where are the people? What are they doing?

b) **R2.6** Listen to James (Jenny's father), Hazel (Harriet's mother)
and Lily (Liam's grandmother) talking about children's eating
habits. Answer these questions.

1 Who thinks that parents should be strict about children's
eating habits?
2 Who doesn't agree with being strict?
3 Who doesn't have a strong opinion on the subject?

c) Work in pairs. Fill in the gaps with James, Lily or Hazel.

1 __J__ is having trouble persuading his/her child to eat.
2 __H__ believes the way to encourage children to eat is to make meal
times fun.
3 __J__ and __L__ don't let their children help them prepare food.
4 __J__ and __H__ agree that letting children help you cook slows
things down.
5 __H__ and __H__ agree it's important that boys learn to cook.

d) Listen again. Check your answers.

Real World Discussion language (1):
agreeing and disagreeing politely

3 **a)** Look at these sentences. Are they
ways of agreeing (A) or disagreeing (D)?

1 I don't know about that. *D*
2 I can't really see the point of *D*
(forcing kids to eat).
3 Oh, do you think so? *D*
4 I see what you mean. *A*
5 Oh, I wouldn't say that. *D*
6 I see your point. *A*
7 I suppose that's true, actually. *A*
8 You might be right there. *A*
9 That's a good point. *A*
10 Well, I'm still not convinced. *D*
11 Well, I can't argue with that. *A*
12 I suppose you've got a point there. *A*

TIP! ● We often follow an agreement
phrase with *but* to challenge the other
person's opinion: *I see what you mean,*
but *I think it's much better to let them eat
when they want.*

b) Check in **RW2.1** p117.

4 a) Fill in the gaps in this conversation between James, Hazel and Lily with words from **3a)**.

L I think children under eight should go to bed at seven.

H ¹......... you think ....? Why not let them go to bed when they're tired?

J I don't ²......... about .... Kids never admit they're tired.

H That's a ³......... ....

L Yes, I think seven o'clock is a good bedtime for all young kids.

J You ⁴......... be .... there.

H Well, I ⁵......... really .... the .... of forcing kids to go to bed.

J But if you don't, parents never have any time on their own.

L I ⁶......... what you ....

H Well, I'm ⁷......... not .... If my kids were all in bed at seven, I'd never see them.

L But if they're up late, they get bad-tempered.

J Yes, you can't ⁸......... with ....

b) R2.7 Listen and check. Who do you agree with most?

Help with Fluency
Linking (1): consonant-vowel links; linking /r/ sounds

5 a) R2.7 Look at R2.7, p145. Listen again and notice the linking.

b) P Work in groups of three. Practise the conversation in R2.7, p145. Take turns to be James, Hazel and Lily. Try to use natural linking and rhythm.

---

6 a) Look at these sentences. Think of at least two reasons why you agree or disagree with them.

1 TV makes children violent.
2 Children under ten shouldn't be allowed to have mobile phones.
3 Friends give the best advice.
4 20 is a good age to get married.

b) Work in groups. Discuss the sentences in **6a)**.

♪ R2.8 Look at the song *Complicated* on p102. Follow the instructions.

---

2 Review

Language Summary 2, p116

1 a) Look at the <u>underlined</u> phrases. Tick the correct phrases. Change the incorrect ones. G2.1

1 I <u>used to go out</u> with friends last night.
2 <u>I'm usually waking up</u> at 7 a.m.
3 <u>I'd have</u> pets when I was a child.
4 Occasionally <u>I'll stay in</u> at the weekends, but I normally <u>go out</u>.
5 <u>I'm always lose</u> things.
6 I <u>didn't use to watch</u> as much TV as I do now.

b) Make sentences 1–6 in **1a)** true for you.

I didn't go out with friends last night.

c) Work in pairs. Tell your partner your sentences.

2 Work in pairs. Find four things that you have in common. Use these words/phrases. V2.1

> rarely   more often than not
> seldom   once in a while
> occasionally   most weeks
> frequently   every now and again

3 a) Fill in the gaps with a preposition. V2.2

1 I'm excited .... moving house.
2 I'm afraid we're not satisfied .... the service.
3 I'm not aware .... any problems.
4 We're very fond .... dogs.
5 He was disappointed .... his results.
6 I'm impressed .... the food.
7 I'm sick .... waiting for her.
8 They're not sure .... the colour.
9 Jon's famous .... being late.
10 I'm shocked .... the price of houses.
11 She's terrified .... the dark.
12 He's always been fascinated .... magic tricks.

b) Work in pairs. Compare answers.

---

4 a) Use phrases 1–7 to write sentences about your friends. G2.2

1 ... is getting used to ...
2 ... will never get used to ...
3 ... has got used to ...
4 ... is used to ...
5 ... will have to get used to ...
6 ... never got used to ...
7 ... took a long time to get used to ...

b) Work in pairs. Tell each other your sentences. Ask follow-up questions if possible.

5 a) Work in pairs. Student A, look at the words in list A. Write all the words in each 'word family' and mark the stress on each word. Student B, do the same for list B.

A	B
responsible	preferably
criticism	recognition
originally	weakness
improve	decide

b) Swap papers with your partner. Do you agree with your partner's answers? V2.3

c) Take turns to make sentences with one word from each 'word family' on your partner's paper.

Progress Portfolio

a) Tick the things you can do in English.

☐ I can talk about the frequency of present and past habits and states.

☐ I can express my feelings and opinions about everyday situations.

☐ I can talk about adapting to strange or difficult situations.

☐ I can understand an article giving advice.

☐ I can agree and disagree politely with others and explain why.

b) What do you need to study again? ● 2A–D

21

3 It's against the law

3A Honesty

Vocabulary types of crime, criminals and crime verbs
Grammar second conditional; alternatives for *if*
Review agreeing and disagreeing politely

QUICK REVIEW ●●●
What is your opinion of these things: computer games; designer clothes; graffiti; mobile phones; reality TV? Work in pairs. Take turns to give your opinions. Agree or disagree with your partner and give your reasons.

Vocabulary Types of crime, criminals and crime verbs

1 **a)** Tick the crimes you know. Check in V3.1 p118.

> robbery theft burglary
> mugging shoplifting
> smuggling kidnapping fraud
> bribery murder arson
> vandalism looting terrorism

b) Write the criminals and the verbs for the crimes in **1a)** if possible. Check in V3.2 p118.

robbery → robber, rob

c) Work in groups. Discuss these questions.

1 Which of the crimes in **1a)** do you think are: very serious, quite serious, not very serious?
2 Which crimes are common in your country? Which aren't very common?
3 Have you, or has anyone you know, been a victim of crime? If so, what happened?

Reading and Grammar

2 **a)** Read the questionnaire. Choose the best answers for you.

b) Work in pairs. Compare answers. Check on p159. How honest are you and your partner?

How honest are you?

If someone asked you if you were honest, you'd probably say yes. But are you really as honest as you think? Answer these questions and find out!

1 Imagine you found some library books that were due back eight months ago, would you return them?

a) **I'd take the books back if I didn't have to pay a fine.**
b) No way. I'd probably try to sell them.
c) I'd take them back, even if I had to pay a fine.

2 Suppose a cash machine gave you twice as much money as you asked for, would you keep it?

a) Yes, I would. **If the bank found out, I could say I didn't count it.**
b) No, I wouldn't. That would be theft.
c) **If I really needed it, I might keep it.**

3 Imagine you saw a ten-year-old boy shoplifting, would you tell a security guard?

a) Yes, I certainly would. It might stop the boy doing it again.
b) I'd tell a security guard as long as he/she agreed not to call the police.
c) Assuming no one else saw the boy, I'd just tell him to return the things he'd stolen.

Help with Grammar Second conditional; alternatives for *if*

3 SECOND CONDITIONAL

a) Look at the sentences in **bold** in the questionnaire. Answer these questions.

1 Are these sentences about real or imaginary situations?
2 Are they about: a) the past? b) the present or the future?
3 How do we make second conditionals?
4 Which modal verbs can we use instead of *would* in the main clause?

TIP! ● *Even if* = it doesn't matter whether the situation in the *if* clause exists or not: *I'd take the books back, **even if** I had to pay a fine.*

ALTERNATIVES FOR *IF* =⟶ SONG

b) Look at the alternatives for *if* in blue in the questionnaire. Fill in these gaps with *provided*, *assuming* and *as long as*.

1 _Providing_ and _as long as_ mean 'only if (this happens)'.
2 _Assuming_ means 'accepting that something is true'.

c) Choose the correct words in these rules.

● *Imagine* and *suppose* have the *same meaning*/different meanings.
● We can use *imagine* and *suppose* as an alternative for *if* in *questions*/positive sentences.

TIP! ● We can say *provided* or *providing* and *suppose* or *supposing*.

d) Check in G3.1 p119.

4 If you needed paper for your printer at home, would you steal it from your school or office?

a) Provided no one was looking, I'd take as much as I needed.
b) No, I wouldn't. I'd be terrified of someone seeing me.
c) Assuming I couldn't buy any on the way home, I might take a bit.

PRIVATE PARKING

5 Supposing you couldn't find a parking space in town, would you park in a private car park?

a) No, I wouldn't. If they clamped my car, I'd be stuck there all day.
b) Of course I would. Wouldn't everyone?
c) Yes, I would, providing I wasn't going to be very long.

4 **a)** Fill in the gaps with the correct form of the verbs in brackets.

1 If someone _offered_ (offer) you a job in the USA, _____ you _____ (accept) it?

2 I _____ (not take) the job if my family _____ (not want) me to.

3 If the pay _____ (be) really good, I _____ probably _____ (accept) the job.

4 I _____ (might go) even if the money _____ (not be) very good.

5 If they _____ (not offer) me full medical insurance, I _____ (not take) the job.

6 If I _____ (get) there and I _____ (not like) it, I _____ (come) straight home.

b) Work in pairs. Compare answers.

5 **a)** Read these questions and answers. Are both words/phrases possible? If not, choose the correct one.

1 A *Suppose/Provided* you found a lottery ticket and it had the winning number, would you collect the money?
  B Yes, I would, *imagine/assuming* I couldn't find the owner.

2 A *Imagine/If* your best friend had nowhere to live, would you let him/her come and live with you?
  B I'd let him/her stay with me *as long as/provided* it wasn't for too long.

3 A *If/Suppose* some friends asked you to look after their four cats for a month, would you agree to do it?
  B No, I wouldn't, *even if/provided* they paid me!

4 A *Imagine/As long as* you saw a man being attacked in the street, would you try to help him?
  B Yes, I might, *suppose/provided* I wasn't alone.

b) Work in pairs. Compare answers. Then take turns to ask each other the questions. Answer for yourself.

Get ready ... Get it right!

6 Work in groups. Group A → p105. Group B → p108. Follow the instructions.

HONESTY IDIOMS

Vocabulary crime and punishment
Grammar third conditional
Help with Listening third conditional
Review types of crime, criminals and crime verbs

QUICK REVIEW ● ● ●
Write a list of five crimes you know. Work in pairs. Take turns to say a crime. Your partner says the criminal and the verb if possible.

Vocabulary Crime and punishment

1 **a)** Work in pairs. Match a verb in A to a word/phrase in B. Check in V3.3 p118.

A	B
commit	somebody to court
arrest	evidence
charge	somebody for a crime
take	a crime
give	somebody with a crime

find	somebody (£500)
acquit/convict	somebody to prison (for 10 years)
send	somebody (not) guilty
sentence	somebody of a crime
fine	somebody to (10 years) in prison

b) Work in pairs. Who normally does the things in **1a**: a criminal, the police, the judge, the jury or a witness?
A criminal commits a crime.

Listening and Grammar

2 **a)** Work in pairs. Look at pictures A and B. What is happening in each picture? What do you think happened next?

b) R3.1 Listen to three friends talking about what happened in the pictures. Check your answers.

3 **a)** Work in pairs. Look again at pictures A and B. Student A, retell story A. Student B, retell story B. Use these words/phrases to help you. Include as much detail as you can remember.

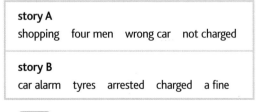

story A			
shopping	four men	wrong car	not charged

story B			
car alarm	tyres	arrested	charged	a fine

b) R3.1 Listen again and check. Were your versions of the story correct?

A

4 **a)** Fill in the gaps in sentences 1–5 with these words. Which stories are these sentences from?

> note   trouble   run   owner   alarm

1 If the woman had shot the men, she'd have been in serious ....
2 If the men hadn't .... away, she could have killed them.
3 I wouldn't have been too happy if the .... had woken me up.
4 If it had been me, I might have left a .... on the car.
5 What would the .... of the car have done if he'd seen him?

b) Work in groups. Discuss these questions.

1 Is gun crime a big problem in your country?
2 Are ordinary people allowed to own guns in your country? Do you think they should? Why?/Why not?

Help with Grammar Third conditional

5 **a)** Look at sentence 1 in **4a**. Answer these questions. Then choose the correct words in the rule.

1 Did the woman shoot the men?
2 Did she get into serious trouble?

● We use the third conditional to talk about *real/imaginary* situations in the *present/past*.

b) Look again at sentence 1 in **4a**. Which verb form is in the *if* clause? Which verb form is in the main clause?

c) Look at sentences 2–5 in **4a**. Answer these questions.

1 Which modal verbs can we use in the main clause to mean 'would perhaps'? *Could / might*
2 Is the *if* clause always first in the sentence? *No*
3 How do we make questions in the third conditional?

d) Check in G3.2 p119.

9 **a)** Read about an unsuccessful robbery. Answer the questions.

In 2005 two men tried to rob a gas station in Poulsbo, Washington. They told the salesgirl to put all the money from the cash register into a bag, but they didn't realise that there were only eight dollars in it. They drove away with the money, but soon got lost because they weren't from that town and they didn't have a map. They finally drove into a gas station to get directions. Unfortunately for them they'd driven back into the same gas station. The salesgirl had called the police, who were interviewing her when the robbers returned.

1 How much money did the robbers steal?
2 Why did they get lost?
3 Where did they end up?
4 Why had they gone there?
5 What do you think happened to the robbers?

b) Look at the text in **9a)** again. Write four sentences about things that would, could or might have happened if things had happened differently.

If the salesgirl hadn't opened the cash register, the robbers might have hurt her.

c) Work in pairs. Compare sentences. Are your partner's sentences correct?

Help with Listening Third conditional

6 **a)** R3.2 Listen to these sentences. Notice the contractions (*I'd, you'd,* etc.) and the weak forms of *have* and *had*.

1 If I'd known about it, I'd have /əv/ come.
2 If you'd told me, I could have /əv/ helped you.
3 She wouldn't have /əv/ been upset if you'd called her.
4 If Fred had /əd/ studied harder, he might have /əv/ passed.

b) R3.3 Listen and write five sentences. You will hear each sentence twice.

7 R3.4 P Listen and practise. Copy the contractions and weak forms.

I wouldn't have /əv/ met her. → *If I hadn't gone to the party, I wouldn't have /əv/ met her.*

8 **a)** Read about Jim's terrible evening. Fill in the gaps with the correct form of the verbs in brackets.

1 It *might have been* (might be) better if I _____ (take) the bus to Juliet's party last night.
2 If Mary _____ (tell) me she was going, I _____ (could ask) her for a lift.
3 I _____ (not park) in the street if I _____ (know) there were car thieves in the area.
4 If I _____ (not leave) my car unlocked, the thieves *might not have staion* (might not steal) it.
5 If Mary _____ (not give) me a lift home, I don't know where I _____ (stay).
6 My parents _____ (be) very worried if I _____ (not come) home last night.

b) Work in pairs. Compare answers. What happened to Jim last night? How did he get home?

Get ready ... Get it right!

10 **a)** Make notes on six interesting things that have happened in your life. Write them in the order they happened.

1998 – passed my medical exams
2002 – met Pedro at my cousin's wedding

b) Make third conditionals to describe how life would have been different if these things hadn't happened.

If I'd failed my medical exams, I might have become a teacher.

11 **a)** Work in pairs. Take turns to tell each other about the things you wrote in **10a)**. Ask follow-up questions if possible.

b) Tell the class two interesting things about your partner's past.

3C Identity theft

Vocabulary verbs and prepositions
Skills Reading: Protect your identity;
Listening: A lawyer-client meeting
Help with Listening weak forms
Review third conditional

QUICK REVIEW ● ● ●
Think of one thing that you did: last year; last month; last weekend; yesterday. Decide what would have happened if you hadn't done these things. Work in pairs. Take turns to tell each other your sentences: *I started university last year. If I hadn't, I might have got a job in a bookshop.*

Reading and Vocabulary

1 Work in groups. Discuss these questions.

1 How many things do you carry with you that have personal information on them?
2 Do you ever use your credit card on the Internet? If so, what for?
3 Do you know anyone whose credit card has been stolen? If so, what happened?

2 **a)** Work in pairs. What do you know about identity theft?

b) Compare ideas with the whole class.

c) Read the advert for a law firm. How many of the things you discussed are in the advert?

d) Work in the same pairs. Compare answers.

3 Read the advert again. Find answers to these questions.

1 How might you find out that you're a victim of identity theft?
2 Why has it become easier over the years to steal someone's identity?
3 What information can someone get about another person from the Internet?
4 How can Cabott & Spencer help prevent identity theft from happening?

Help with Vocabulary Verbs and prepositions

4 **a)** Look at the verbs in pink in the article. Fill in the gaps with the correct prepositions.

1 spend sth _on_ sb/sth
2 insist _on_ sth
3 explain sth _to_ sb
4 worry _about_ sb/sth
5 cope _with_ sb/sth
6 provide sb _with_ sth

b) Look at the verbs in **4a)** again. Which have an object before the preposition? ① ③ ⑥

c) Look at the verbs in blue in the article. Fill in the gaps with the correct prepositions.

1 apply _to_ sb/sth _for_ sth
2 complain _to_ sb _about_ sb/sth
3 talk _to_ sb _about_ sb/sth
4 shout _at_ sb _for_ sth
5 apologise _to_ sb _for_ sth
6 depend _on_ sb/sth _for_ sth

d) Check in **V3.4** p118.

Protect your identity with Cabott & Spencer

One identity theft occurs every six minutes. The criminal doesn't necessarily take money from your bank account and no one steals your wallet or burgles your house. And you know nothing about it until you get a credit card statement showing you have bought a Ferrari, been to Tahiti or spent £2,000 on a Versace suit. You certainly didn't apply to the bank for a new account, but you've got one and someone's been writing bad cheques in your name. This can add up to thousands of pounds, which you haven't got. Who do you complain to and what exactly do you complain about? Someone you don't know has been buying things in your name and left you with the bill, and a very poor credit rating –

but who's going to believe you? You could insist on talking to the police about it, but even if you manage to explain the problem to them, they usually aren't interested until they come to question you about a crime you haven't committed. You contact the bank and credit card companies daily, and end up shouting at everyone for not sorting it out. They apologise to you for the stress you must be experiencing, then tell you not to worry about it – their fraud department's looking into it. Meanwhile you have to cope with more bills and more threatening letters from company lawyers.

In today's world we depend on credit cards for everything. We buy things on the Internet or over the phone and happily give our credit card details. And we rely on the banks and credit card companies to safeguard our accounts from fraud. But just how easy is it to steal someone's identity? Easier than you might think! The traditional way is to steal or make a copy of someone's credit card, driving licence, etc. However, these days hundreds of databases exist online with detailed information about your personal life. Various companies can provide other people with your address, professional history, bank account details and so on. There's even software that will give people access to your personal details within minutes.

17

5 **a)** Fill in the gaps with the correct form of the verbs in brackets and the correct prepositions.

1 Have you *applied for* any store cards recently? (apply).

2 Do you usually .... paying when you and a friend go out for a meal? (insist)

3 What do you .... most? (worry)

4 Have you .... anyone recently? If so, what did you .... ? (apologise)

5 Which person in your life do you .... most? (depend)

6 How do you usually .... people who annoy you? (cope)

7 What do you most like .... money .... ? (spend)

8 When was the last time you .... something? Who did you .... ? (complain)

9 Has anyone .... you this week? (shout)

10 When was the last time someone had to .... something .... you more than once? (explain)

11 Who do you .... on the phone regularly? (talk)

12 What kind of information do people have to .... their bank .... when they open an account? (provide)

b) Work in pairs. Take turns to ask and answer the questions in **5a)**. Ask follow-up questions if possible.

Cabott & Spencer

At Cabott & Spencer we offer comprehensive identity theft protection. We will check all the information held about you on the Internet every day. If we find that anyone has made inquiries about your credit details, opened a new bank account in your name or tried to change your address, we will contact you immediately. Then you can act quickly before you get a huge bill, a bad credit rating – or even end up in prison.

Listening

6 **a)** **R3.5** Listen to Bonnie Mead's conversation with her lawyer. Tick the things that she talks about.

- legal advice
- her friends' reaction
- her parents' reaction
- her work situation
- how the problem started
- how her identity was stolen
- how much money is involved
- how she's tried to deal with the problem

b) Listen again. Answer these questions.

1 Who has been sympathetic to Bonnie's problems?

2 Why did she have to take time off work?

3 How did she first find out that something was wrong?

4 What happened when she went to the police?

5 What happened when she told the bank to close the new accounts?

6 What problem was there when she called the mobile phone company?

Help with Listening Weak forms

7 **a)** Work in pairs. How do you say the strong and weak forms of these words?

can	was	were	has	have	are	do	you	at	for
of	to	from	as	and	that	some	a	the	your

b) **R3.6** Listen and check. The strong form of each word is said first. Notice the schwa /ə/ in the weak forms.

c) Work in pairs. Look at the first part of Bonnie's conversation with the lawyer. Which words do we hear as weak forms?

LAWYER Good afternoon, Ms Mead. Come in and take a seat. Firstly I'd like to say how sorry I am that this has happened.

BONNIE Well, thank you for seeing me so quickly. I've been trying to get some legal advice for ages, but I was getting nowhere.

LAWYER Glad I can be of help.

d) Look at R3.5, p145. Check your answers.

e) **R3.5** Listen to and read the conversation again. Notice how the weak forms and sentence stress give English its natural rhythm.

8 Work in groups of four. Student A → p105. Student B → p108. Student C → p110. Student D → p111. Follow the instructions.

3D Do you need any help?

Real World making, refusing and accepting offers
Help with Fluency sentence stress and weak forms (1)
Review verbs and prepositions

QUICK REVIEW ● ● ●

Write four verbs that are often followed by prepositions. Don't write the prepositions. Work in pairs. Swap papers. Take turns to make a sentence with each of your partner's verbs and a preposition. Are your partner's prepositions correct?

1 Work in groups. Discuss these questions.

1 If you have a problem, who do you usually ask for help?
2 When was the last time you offered to help someone? What was the problem? Did the person accept your help?

Bonnie

Helen

2 a) [R3.7] Listen to Bonnie talking to her sister, Helen. Put these topics in the order they are first talked about.

● a trip to Paris
● Bonnie's filing system
● Helen's children
● a threatening letter
● Bonnie's meeting with the lawyer

b) Listen again. Make notes on the topics in 2a).

c) Work in pairs. Compare notes. Which topics did you both make notes on?

Real World Making, refusing and accepting offers

3 a) Fill in the gaps with the words in the boxes.

making offers

> ~~Would~~ What Let like don't help

¹ *Would* you like me to (come round)?
² _____ me (give them a ring for you).
Would it ³ _____ if I (sorted it out for you)?
Why ⁴ _____ I (look after the kids)?
I'll (make a bed up for you), if you ⁵ _____ .
⁶ _____ if I (picked the kids up from school)?

refusing offers

> better manage easier offering

No, it's OK, but thanks for ⁷ _____ .
No, thanks. I'd ⁸ _____ (phone them myself).
No, don't worry. It'd be ⁹ _____ if (I brought the kids back here).
No, that's OK. I can ¹⁰ _____ .

accepting offers

> be mind don't could

Are you sure you wouldn't ¹¹ _____ ?
Thanks. That'd ¹² _____ a great help.
Well, it'd be wonderful if you ¹³ _____ .
As long as you ¹⁴ _____ mind.

b) Look at the sentences in 3a) again. Which verb forms follow these phrases: *Let me ... , Would it help if I ... , Why don't I ... , What if I ... , thanks for ... , I'd better ...* and *It'd be easier if I ... ?*

c) Check in [RW3.1] p119.

4 **R3.8** **P** Listen and practise. Copy the stress and polite intonation.

Would you like me to come round?

5 **a)** Bonnie is moving house and Helen's husband, Nigel, offers to help. Work in pairs. Write conversations using these prompts. Use language from 3a).

1

N / like me / help / move tomorrow?

Would you like me to help you move tomorrow?

B / sure / not / mind?

N No, of course not.

B Thanks. That / great help.

N Why / I come over this evening and help you pack?

B It / wonderful / could.

2

N Let / help / pack those files.

B No, / worry. I / better do those myself.

N Well, what if / carry / these heavy things downstairs for you?

B / long / you / mind.

N Not at all. Then I / pack up the computer and printer, if / like.

B No, / OK. It / easy / I / sort / those out.

b) **R3.9** Listen and check.

Help with Fluency Sentence stress and weak forms (1)

6 **a)** **R3.9** Look at R3.9, p146. Listen again and notice the sentence stress and weak forms.

b) **P** Work in pairs. Practise the conversations in R3.9, p146 until you can remember them. Then close your book and have the conversations again. Try to use natural sentence stress and weak forms.

7 Work in pairs. Student A → p106. Student B → p109. Follow the instructions.

3 Review

Language Summary 3, p118

1 **a)** Find ten crimes. **V3.1**

```
T B U R G L A R Y M
E M T H E T R V B M
R U W L L H S A L U
R R F O O E O N T G
S D R O T F N D M G
P E A T C T E A P I
Q R U I K M U L D N
K I D N A P P I N G
Z L F G F R A S V H
B R I B E R Y M S X
```

b) Work in pairs. Write the criminals and the verbs for the crimes in 1a) if possible. **V3.2**

2 **a)** Write second conditionals using these prompts. **G3.1**

1 A If you / see / some people robbing a shop, what / you do?
  B As long as the robbers / can't / see me, I / call the police.

2 A Suppose you / can / work for any company in the world, which / you choose?
  B I / like to work for H&M provided I / can / have free clothes.

3 A Imagine you / have / the chance to learn a new skill, what / it be?
  B If I / can / afford it, I / learn to fly.

4 A Supposing you / be / a journalist, who / you most like / interview?
  B I / like / interview Prince William providing I / can / ask him anything.

b) Work in pairs. Compare answers. Then ask each other the questions. Answer for you.

3 Choose the correct verbs. **V3.3**

1 *arrest/take* somebody for a crime
2 *acquit/commit* a crime
3 *find/fine* somebody (£500)
4 *send/acquit* somebody to prison
5 *take/charge* somebody with a crime
6 *find/convict* somebody guilty
7 *give/commit* evidence
8 *give/take* somebody to court

4 Correct the mistakes in these third conditionals. **G3.2**

1 It might be better if you'd left yesterday.
2 If you would flown last Monday, it would have been much cheaper.
3 If you'd asked sooner, I can have helped.
4 What you have done last night if she hadn't given you a lift?
5 I wouldn't come if you hadn't asked me.

5 **a)** Choose the correct preposition. **V3.4**

When was the last time you ...

1 applied *for/to* a new passport?
2 talked *about/to* your job?
3 insisted *to/on* speaking to the manager?
4 worried *for/about* travelling?
5 apologised *for/at* being late?
6 spent a lot of money *to/on* a present?
7 shouted *on/at* somebody?
8 provided somebody *for/with* your bank details?
9 complained *to/about* something?

b) Work in pairs. Ask and answer the questions in 5a). Ask follow-up questions.

Progress Portfolio

a) Tick the things you can do in English.

☐ I can talk about crime and punishment.

☐ I can talk in detail about imaginary situations in the present and future.

☐ I can talk in detail about imaginary situations in the past.

☐ I can understand a text about problems in everyday life.

☐ I can make, refuse and accept offers politely.

b) What do you need to study again? **3A–D**

4 Telling stories

4A Urban legends

Vocabulary phrasal verbs (1)
Grammar narrative verb forms; Past Perfect Continuous
Review making, refusing and accepting offers

QUICK REVIEW ●●●
Work in pairs. Student A is organising a party. Student B is moving house. Take turns to offer to help your partner: A *Would you like me to help you pack up the kitchen?* Decide whether to refuse or accept your partner's offers: B *No, don't worry, I can manage.*

Vocabulary Phrasal verbs (1)

1 **a)** Work in pairs. Guess the meaning of the phrasal verbs in **bold** in these questions. Check in V4.1 p120.

1 Do you always remember to **pass on** messages to other people?
2 Do you ever **make up** excuses to avoid doing things you don't want to do?
3 Have you ever been to a party that **turned out** to be really boring?
4 What would you do if you **ran over** a cat in your street?
5 Has a bomb ever **gone off** in the capital city of your country?
6 If you saw a man **running away** from the police, would you try to stop him?
7 Do you find it easy to **work out** what's happening when you watch a film in English?
8 Do you get nervous just before a plane **takes off**?
9 Do you know anyone who's been **knocked out**? How long did it take this person to **come round**?

b) Work in pairs. Take turns to ask each other the questions in **1a)**. Ask follow-up questions if possible.

Reading, Listening and Grammar

2 Read the beginning of an article about urban legends. Answer these questions.

1 What is an urban legend?
2 Where can people read urban legends?
3 Are urban legends ever true?
4 Why do people change some stories?

It must be true, I read it on the Internet ...

Urban legends are funny, surprising or scary stories that are told again and again, often by people saying that they happened to 'a friend of a friend'. These days they're often passed on by email or collected together on websites. Most urban legends are stories that people have made up, but not always. A few turn out to be completely true, and others are based on actual events, but have been changed to make them sound more interesting or shocking. For example, have you heard the one about the dead kangaroo, the falling cow or the exploding house?

A

B

C

3 **a)** Check these words with your teacher or in a dictionary.

> a yacht   the crew   rescue   sink
> get rid of   a bug   insecticide

b) Work in pairs. Look at pictures A–C of famous urban legends. Guess what happened in each story.

c) R4.1 Listen and check your ideas.

4 a) [R4.1] **Listen again. Fill in the gaps with one word.**

THE DEAD KANGAROO STORY

1 In 1987 the world's best _sailors_ **were competing** in the America's Cup yacht _____ off the coast of Fremantle.
2 One day, one of the _____ **went** for a drive in the outback and accidentally **ran over** a _____ .
3 While the sailor **was taking** some _____ , the kangaroo **came round**.

THE FALLING COW STORY

4 The boat **had been sailing** in calm waters when a _____ **fell** from the _____ .
5 Eventually the pilot of a _____ transport plane **told** the _____ what **had happened**.
6 Before they **took off** from their Siberian airbase, the plane's _____ **had stolen** some _____ .

THE EXPLODING HOUSE STORY

7 A woman from _____ **had been trying** to get rid of all the _____ in her home for years.
8 She **put** all the bug _____ in her house, but unfortunately she **hadn't read** the _____ .

b) Work in pairs. Compare answers. Do you think these stories are true? Look at p159. Check your ideas.

Help with Grammar Narrative verb forms; Past Perfect Continuous

5 a) Look at the verb forms in **bold** in sentences 1–3 in **4a**). Then complete these rules with *Past Simple* or *Past Continuous*.

- We use the _____ for completed actions in the past. These tell the main events of the story in the order that they happened.
- We use the _____ for a longer action that was in progress when another (shorter) action happened.
- We also use the _____ for background information that isn't part of the main story.

b) Look at the verb forms in **bold** in sentences 4–8 in **4a**). Are they in the Past Simple, Past Perfect Simple or Past Perfect Continuous?

had been sailing – Past Perfect Continuous

c) Choose the correct words in these rules.

- We usually use the Past Perfect *Simple/Continuous* for an action that was completed before another action in the past.
- We usually use the Past Perfect *Simple/Continuous* for a longer action that started before another action in the past (and often continued up to this past action).

d) Fill in the gaps with *had*, *'d*, *verb+ing* or *past participle*. How do we make these verb forms negative?

PAST PERFECT SIMPLE
subject + *had* or _____ + _____

PAST PERFECT CONTINUOUS
subject + _____ or *'d* + *been* + _____

e) Check in [G4.1] p121.

6 [R4.2] [P] **Listen and practise. Copy the stress and weak forms.**

The boat had /əd/ been /bɪn/ sailing in calm waters.

---

7 a) **Read another famous urban legend. Choose the correct verb forms.**

A few years ago, Robert Monaghan, from Ballymena in Northern Ireland, [1](had)/had had a very bad day. He [2]crossed/was crossing the road near his home when a van [3]hit/was hitting him. While he [4]was getting/got to his feet, another car [5]ran him over/was running him over and then [6]drove away/had driven away. Some people who [7]walked/had been walking past [8]stopped/were stopping to help Robert. They [9]were calling/had called an ambulance and [10]helped/had helped him to his feet. When the ambulance [11]had been arriving/arrived, everyone [12]stepped/was stepping back – everyone except Robert, who [13]didn't realise/wasn't realising what everyone [14]waited/had been waiting for and was run over by the ambulance.

b) Work in pairs. Compare answers. How many accidents did Robert Monaghan have in one day?

8 **Fill in the gaps with the correct form of the verbs in brackets. Sometimes more than one verb form is possible.**

1 I _knew_ (know) that Rory _____ (try) to find a new job for ages.
2 My brother _____ (call) while I _____ (watch) the football.
3 Robin and Cecilia _____ (not go) out) together for very long when he _____ (propose) to her.
4 When I _____ (get) home, I _____ (realise) that I _____ (leave) my mobile at work.
5 By the time the others _____ (arrive), we _____ (already wait) for over two hours.
6 While Angela _____ (walk) home, she _____ (meet) an old school friend that she _____ (not see) for years.

Get ready ...
Get it right!

9 Work in pairs. Student A → p104. Student B → p107. Follow the instructions.

4B Magical novels

Vocabulary books and reading
Grammar defining, non-defining and reduced relative clauses
Review narrative verb forms

QUICK REVIEW ●●●
Work in pairs. Choose two of the urban legends from lesson 4A. Take turns to tell your partner what you remember about each one.

Vocabulary Books and reading

1 **a)** Tick the words/phrases in **bold** that you know. Check new words/phrases in V4.2 p120.

1 Do you usually read **fiction** or **non-fiction**?
2 What's your favourite **novel**? Have you got a **copy** of it at home?
3 What's more important to you in a novel – the **characters** or the **plot**?
4 Who's your favourite **author** or **novelist**?
5 Have you ever read someone's **biography** or **autobiography**?
6 What's your favourite **literary genre**?
7 Which books are **best-sellers** at the moment?
8 Do you like **browsing** in bookshops?
9 Do you usually buy **paperbacks** or **hardbacks**?
10 Do you ever **flick through** magazines at stations or airports?

b) Work in pairs. Take turns to ask and answer the questions in 1a). Ask follow-up questions if possible.

Reading and Grammar

2 **a)** Look at book covers A and B. Have you read these books? If so, what did you think of them?

b) Check these words/phrases with your teacher or in a dictionary.

> solitude   magical realism   isolated   supernatural
> amnesia   a butterfly   a spirit   a coup

3 **a)** Work in pairs. Student A, read the review of *One Hundred Years of Solitude*. Student B, read the review of *The House of the Spirits*. Find answers to these questions.

1 Where is the story set?
2 Which family is the novel about?
3 How many generations of this family are in the novel?
4 What 'magical' things happen in the novel?
5 How are the author's grandparents connected to the novel?

b) Work with your partner. Take turns to ask and answer the questions in 3a).

c) R4.3 Read and listen to the reviews and check your partner's answers. How many things do the two novels have in common?

(A)

One Hundred Years of Solitude

by the Colombian author Gabriel García Márquez is the novel that made magical realism popular around the world. It tells the story of seven generations of the Buendía family, who live in an isolated South American village called Macondo. This is a place where supernatural happenings are part of everyday life – at one point everyone living in the village suffers from both insomnia and amnesia. Many characters also have magical qualities. One man, whose girlfriend is 'the most beautiful girl ever born', is always followed by hundreds of butterflies, and people who die early in the story often return as ghosts.

The book has dozens of characters, which can make the plot difficult to follow, but a family tree helps you work out who's related to who. This brilliant novel, which Márquez says is based on his childhood memories of living with his grandparents, has sold over ten million copies worldwide.

Gabriel García Márquez

(B)

The House of the Spirits was the

first novel written by the Chilean author Isabel Allende. It tells the story of three generations of women whose lives are changed by their country's politics. The women's story, which takes place in an unnamed South American country, begins when the granddaughter, Alba Trueba, finds some diaries that her grandmother Clara wrote 50 years earlier.

As a child, Clara realises she can see the future and is able to predict almost every event in her life. She marries a powerful landowner named Esteban Trueba, who builds her a large house in the country. The house is full of ghosts and spirits, which advise Clara on how to deal with family problems. The story takes place at a time when political groups are battling for control of the country – a fight that ends in a bloody coup and political chaos. This famous novel, which began as a letter to the author's dying grandfather, is considered a classic of the magical realism genre.

Isabel Allende

Help with Grammar
Defining, non-defining and reduced relative clauses

4 **a)** Look at the defining relative clauses in blue and the non-defining relative clauses in pink in the reviews. Choose the correct words in these rules.

- *Defining/Non-defining* relative clauses tell you which person, thing, etc. the writer or speaker is talking about.
- *Defining/Non-defining* relative clauses add extra non-essential information.

b) Look again at the defining relative clauses in blue. Answer these questions.

1 Which words (*who*, *which*, etc.) can we use for: people, things, possessives, places, times?
2 Do we use commas (,) with these relative clauses?

c) Look at the underlined defining relative clauses in these sentences. Why can you leave out *that* in sentence 2?

1 *It's the novel **that** made magical realism popular around the world.*
2 *She finds some diaries (**that**) her grandmother Clara wrote 50 years earlier.*

d) Look again at the non-defining relative clauses in pink. Answer these questions.

1 Do we use *that* in these relative clauses?
2 Can we leave out *who*, *which*, etc.?
3 Do we use commas with these relative clauses?

e) Look at these underlined reduced relative clauses. What are the verb forms in **bold**? What types of word can we leave out?

1 *... everyone (who **is**) **living** in the village suffers from both insomnia and amnesia.*
2 *... the first novel (that **was**) **written** by the Chilean author Isabel Allende.*

f) Check in G4.2 p122.

5 **a)** Look again at the reviews of books A and B. How many more relative clauses can you find?

b) Work in pairs. Compare answers. Are they defining or non-defining relative clauses?

6 **a)** Look at book cover C. Have you read *The Alchemist*? If so, what did you think of it?

b) Read the review of *The Alchemist*. Fill in the gaps with *who*, *which*, etc. if necessary. One gap doesn't need a word.

c) Work in pairs. Compare answers. Then change two of the defining relative clauses in the first paragraph into reduced relative clauses.

d) Which of the three books would you most like to read (or read again)? Why?

7 Join these sentences using defining, non-defining or reduced relative clauses. Use commas where necessary. Sometimes there is more than one possible answer.

1 Yesterday I met a man. The man owned a bookshop.
Yesterday I met a man who owned a bookshop.
2 This is the room. I wrote my first novel in this room.
3 Clive McCarthy was my English teacher. He writes biographies now.
4 That's the woman. Her first novel became a best-seller.
5 I threw out some paperbacks. I hadn't looked at them for years.
6 I lost my copy of *The Alchemist*. It had been signed by the author.
7 I saw an old lady. She was sitting outside the library.
8 I found some old books. They were hidden behind a cupboard.

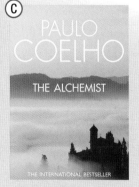

C

The Alchemist by the Brazilian author Paulo Coelho is a story about following your dream. It's about a shepherd boy named Santiago, ¹ *who* travels from his home in Spain to Egypt hoping to find some treasure ² _____ is buried near the Pyramids. He meets many people ³ _____ are travelling along the same road, but nobody knows ⁴ _____ the treasure is hidden. However, Santiago eventually meets the famous Alchemist, the only man alive ⁵ _____ can turn lead into gold.

Finally, the time comes ⁶ _____ Santiago realises that the treasure ⁷ _____ he's been looking for can only be found within himself. This powerful tale, ⁸ _____ has been translated into 61 languages, has sold over 30 million copies worldwide. Its success helped Paulo Coelho, ⁹ _____ other books include *The Fifth Mountain* and *The Valkyries*, to become the best-selling Brazilian author ¹⁰ _____ has ever lived.

Paulo Coelho

Get ready ...
Get it right!

8 Work in groups. Group A → p104. Group B → p107. Follow the instructions.

Vocabulary connecting words: reason and contrast
Skills Reading: April Fool!; Listening: A practical joke
Help with Listening predicting what comes next
Review books and reading; narrative verb forms

VOCABULARY AND SKILLS

QUICK REVIEW ●●●
Write six words/phrases about books and reading that are connected to you in some way. Work in pairs. Take turns to tell your partner why you have chosen these words/phrases: *I chose 'browse' because I love browsing in bookshops.*

Reading and Vocabulary

1 Work in groups. Discuss these questions.

1 Which TV programmes or comedians make you laugh?
2 What's the funniest film you've ever seen?
3 In your country, is there a day when people play practical jokes on each other? If so, when is it?

2 a) Check these words/phrases with your teacher or in a dictionary.

fool   drip   whistle   a hoax   a harvest   a nylon stocking

b) Work in pairs. Look at pictures A–D. What do you think was the April Fool's Day joke for each picture?

c) Read the article. Check your ideas.

April Fool!

Most people know that April 1st is called April Fool's Day **because** people often play practical jokes on each other on this day. **However**, it's not just friends and family you have to beware of – big companies, newspapers and TV stations also do their best to fool the public.

In 1998 Burger King published an ad in *USA Today* announcing a new item for their menu – the left-handed Whopper. This was the same as a normal Whopper, **apart from** one thing – the burger itself was rotated 180° so that the ketchup would drip out of the right side of the burger **instead of** coming out of the left. The ad fooled thousands of people, **despite** being published on April Fool's Day. And in 2002, the British supermarket chain, Tesco, advertised a 'whistling carrot'. The ad explained that the carrot had been genetically engineered to grow with air holes down the side so that it would start whistling when it was fully cooked.

These two adverts are relatively recent, **whereas** Britain's most famous April Fool hoax is much older. In 1957, the BBC documentary series *Panorama* showed Swiss farm workers pulling spaghetti from 'spaghetti trees'. The programme told viewers that the farmers were enjoying an excellent spaghetti harvest **due to** a very mild winter. **As** spaghetti wasn't very common in the UK at that time, many people believed the report. Hundreds of viewers even phoned up to ask where they could buy their own spaghetti trees!

Another famous April Fool's Day joke, this time from 1962, comes from Sweden. It was announced on the news that it had become possible to watch colour programmes on black and white TVs **because of** some new technology the TV station had invented. People were told to pull a nylon stocking over the screen so they would be able to watch the programmes in colour. **Since** almost everyone in Sweden had a black and white TV in those days, hundreds of thousands of people tried to do this, **even though** the news was broadcast on the morning of April 1st.

You might think that people were more easily fooled back in those days. **Nevertheless**, you should be careful next April 1st – this time the April Fool might be you!

3 **a)** Read the article again. Answer these questions.

1 Would the left-handed Whopper have tasted the same as a normal Whopper?
2 Where did the BBC say spaghetti was grown?
3 Why did so many British people believe the spaghetti story?
4 Why did so many people phone the BBC?
5 How many Swedish people tried to convert their black and white TVs to colour?

b) Which story do you think is the funniest? Do you know any other April Fool's Day stories that have been in the newspapers or on TV?

Help with Vocabulary
Connecting words: reason and contrast

4 **a)** Look at the words/phrases in **bold** in the article. Write them in the table.

giving reasons	*because*
expressing contrast	*however*

TIP! ● We can also use these words/phrases for expressing contrast: *except for* (= *apart from*), *in spite of* (= *despite*), *although* (= *even though*).

b) Which words/phrases in **4a)** are followed by:

1 a clause (subject + verb + ...)? *because*
2 a noun or verb+*ing*? *apart from*

c) Check in V4.3 p120.

---

5 Rewrite these sentences using the words/phrases in brackets. Change other words in the sentences if necessary.

1 I love motor-racing. My wife thinks it's boring. (whereas)
   I love motor-racing, whereas my wife thinks it's boring.
2 Joe paid for everything. He didn't pay for the taxi. (apart from)
3 We wanted to go to Canada. The flight was too expensive. (However)
4 Ann went out for a run. It was raining. (despite)
5 I went for a walk. I didn't watch TV. (instead of)
6 He stayed up late. He didn't have to work the next day. (as)
7 The match was called off. The weather was bad. (due to)
8 Most people don't understand. I'll explain it again. (since)
9 We enjoyed the film. It was very long. (even though)

Listening

6 **a)** Check these words/phrases with your teacher or in a dictionary.

> drill   a stunt   dig up   the local council

b) R4.4 Listen to two friends, Kevin and Dave, discussing a practical joke. Make notes on these things.

a) when and where the practical joke took place
b) the people who played the practical joke
c) the other groups of people involved
d) how the practical joke worked

c) Listen again. Tick the true sentences. Correct the false ones.

1 Dave's brother Alan went to Birmingham University.
2 During Rag Week children raise money for charity.
3 Alan and his flatmates had only had four hours' sleep.
4 They called the police from their home phone.
5 When the police arrived, the workmen ignored them.
6 When the workmen and the policemen realised what had happened, they were very angry.
7 Alan and his friends didn't get caught.

Help with Listening Predicting what comes next

7 **a)** Work in pairs. Match words/phrases 1–8 to meanings a)–h).

When we hear ...	we know that the speaker is going to ...
1 Actually,	a) say something that he/she is not certain is true
2 Anyway,	b) say something that someone else told him/her
3 Apparently,	c) correct something that the other person said
4 According to (Alan),	d) return to the main topic
5 Meanwhile,	e) tell you something good or fortunate
6 In the end,	f) move on to a different/new topic
7 Luckily,	g) tell you the conclusion of the story
8 By the way,	h) introduce something happening at the same time, but in a different place

b) R4.4 Look at R4.4, p147. Listen again and <u>underline</u> the words/phrases from **7a)**. Notice what the speaker says after each word/phrase.

---

8 Turn to p110. Follow the instructions.

Vocabulary ways of exaggerating
Real World saying you're surprised
or not surprised
Help with Fluency sentence stress
Review narrative verb forms

QUICK REVIEW ● ● ●
Think of an interesting or funny story about something that happened to you, or to someone you know, at school or on holiday. Work in pairs. Take turns to tell your stories. Try to keep talking for at least two minutes.

1 a) Guess the meaning of these informal sentences for exaggerating. Then do the exercise in V4.4 p120.

1 I'm speechless.
2 I'm dying for a drink.
3 I'm over the moon.
4 I'm scared stiff.
5 I'm starving.
6 I'm going out of my mind.
7 It costs a fortune.
8 It's a nightmare.
9 It's killing me.
10 It drives me crazy.
11 It takes forever.
12 It weighs a ton.

b) Choose five sentences from **1a).** Think of a present or past situation in your life for each sentence.

c) Work in pairs. Take turns to tell each other about your situations. Ask follow-up questions.

I don't usually have lunch, so I'm always starving when I get home.

I got stuck in a traffic jam last night. It took forever to get home.

2 a) R4.5 Listen to Ellen telling her husband, Steve, about her day. Tick the things she talks about.

● their holiday plans
● something they've bought recently
● Ellen's computer
● car repairs
● a problem with their son
● a doctor's appointment
● Ellen's brother
● the garden

b) Listen again. Make notes on the things in **2a)** that Ellen talks about.

c) Work in pairs. Compare notes. Who has the most information?

Ellen   Steve

Real World Saying you're surprised or not surprised

3 a) Fill in the gaps with these words/phrases.

saying you're surprised	saying you're not surprised
believe earth must news kidding	no wonder honest bet wouldn't imagine

I don't ¹ *believe* it!
You ² _____ be joking!
You're ³ _____ !
Why on ⁴ _____ (doesn't he listen to me)?
Wow, that's fantastic ⁵ _____ !

I'm not surprised, to be ⁶ _____ .
I ⁷ _____ you were.
Well, ⁸ _____ (you've got a virus).
Well, he would say that, ⁹ _____ he?
Yes, I can ¹⁰ _____ .

b) Look at Steve's questions a)–d). Then answer questions 1 and 2 and choose the correct word in the rule.

a) *Hadn't they promised to be here today?*
b) *Didn't you install that anti-virus software?*
c) *Have you had a good day?*
d) *Did you ask him round this weekend?*

1 In which questions does Steve not know the answer?
2 In which questions does he think he knows the answer?

● We often use *positive/negative* auxiliaries in questions when we think we know the answer.

c) Check in RW4.1 p122.

4 R4.6 P Listen and practise the sentences in **3a).** Copy the surprised intonation in the first five sentences.

I don't believe it!

5 **a)** Look again at **1a)** and **3.** Then fill in the gaps in the rest of Steve and Ellen's conversation.

S   Guess ¹ *what* ? I've been promoted!

E   Wow, that's fantastic ² _____ !

S   Yes, I'm over the ³ _____ about it.

E   I ⁴ _____ imagine. ⁵ _____ wonder you look so happy. I'm really pleased for you.

S   Thanks. And I get a 40% pay rise!

E   You're ⁶ _____ ! Anyway, ⁷ _____ they going to give the job to Stuart?

S   Yes, they were. But I'm not ⁸ _____ they didn't, to be ⁹ _____ . He was really angry when he found out, though.

E   I ¹⁰ _____ he was.

S   And we're going to Florida this weekend to celebrate.

E   You ¹¹ _____ be joking! That'll cost a ¹² _____ !

b) R4.7 Listen and check.

Help with Fluency
Sentence stress

6 **a)** R4.7 Look at R4.7 p148. Listen again and notice the sentence stress.

b) P Work in pairs. Practise the conversation in R4.7, p148. Take turns to be Steve and Ellen. Try to use natural rhythm and sentence stress.

7 **a)** Imagine you've had a very good or a very bad day. Make notes on what happened.

b) Work in pairs. Take turns to tell each other about your day. Use language from **1a)** and **3.**

 R4.8 Look at the song *I Heard it Through the Grapevine* on p102. Follow the instructions.

---

4 Review
Language Summary 4, p120

1 Fill in the gaps with the correct form of these phrasal verbs. V4.1

run away	run over	come round
knock out	take off	work out	go off
make up	pass on	turn out

1   I nearly _____ a dog today.
2   Please _____ this message to her.
3   He used to _____ lots of excuses for being late.
4   He was _____ in a fight. It was five minutes before he _____ .
5   What time does your plane _____ ?
6   The bomb _____ at 9 a.m.
7   Stop that man. He's _____ !
8   I can't _____ how to turn it on.
9   The party _____ well in the end.

2 **a)** Read the story. Find eight more incorrect verb forms and correct them. G4.1

got
When I ~~get~~ home last night I was feeling tired so I decided to stay in. While I was watching TV I was hearing an explosion nearby. I'd run out to see what happen. As soon as I was getting outside, I had been seeing a lot of smoke coming from a neighbour's garden. I went round to see if he'd been alright and luckily he was fine. Apparently, he'd been burning some rubbish and he hasn't realised that there was an aerosol can in one of the bags. Of course, when it was hitting the fire, it exploded.

b) Work in pairs. Take turns to say a sentence from the corrected story. Do you think your partner's sentences are correct?

3 Work in pairs. What is the difference between these words/phrases? V4.2

1   fiction, non-fiction
2   a novel, a biography
3   the characters, the plot
4   a paperback, a hardback
5   browse, flick through

---

4 Choose the correct words. Sometimes both are possible. G4.2

The Kite Runner, ¹*which/where* is set in Kabul, is about the friendship between two boys ²*who/that* grow up together. Amir, ³*who/whose* mother is dead, is brought up by his father and his father's servant, Ali. Hassan, ⁴*who/that* is Ali's son, is Amir's best friend.

One day, ⁵*when/where* the two boys are trying to win a kite race, Hassan is attacked by an older boy and two of his friends. Amir, ⁶*who/that* sees the attack, hides ⁷*where/which* the older boys can't see him. Many years later Amir, ⁸*whose/which* guilt has always haunted him, risks his life to save Hassan's son from the same person ⁹*who/that* had attacked Hassan all those years before.

5 **a)** Complete the sentences so they are true for you. V4.3

1   I like most fruit, apart from ...
2   Even though I ...
3   I couldn't ... last week due to ...
4   Since I can't ... , I have to ...
5   Whereas my best friend ... , I ...

b) Work in pairs. Tell each other your sentences.

Progress Portfolio

a) Tick the things you can do in English.

☐   I can tell a story and give extra detail where necessary.

☐   I can understand summaries describing the characters and plots of novels.

☐   I can talk about books I've read.

☐   I can use connecting words to join sentences and clauses.

☐   I can understand a spoken narrative.

☐   I can express different levels of surprise.

b) What do you need to study again? ⊙ **4A–D**

5 Nature's best

5A Keeping koi

> **Vocabulary** animals
> **Grammar** ways of comparing
> **Review** saying you're surprised or not surprised

QUICK REVIEW ●●●
Think of four interesting or surprising things about you or people you know. Work in pairs. Take turns to tell each other these things and say you're surprised or not surprised. Ask follow-up questions. A *My brother can't ride a bike.* B *You're kidding! Why didn't he learn?*

Vocabulary Animals

1 **a)** Tick the animals you know. Then do the exercise in `V5.1` p123.

> a tiger   an eagle   a crocodile
> a leopard   a bee   a rabbit
> a snake   a butterfly   a spider
> a parrot   a goldfish   a mosquito
> a shark   a bear   a whale

b) Work in pairs. Try to match the animals in **1a)** to these sentences. There is sometimes more than one possible answer.

This animal ...

1 is a fish that can **bite** you.
   a shark
2 is a **mammal** that lives underwater.
3 is a bird with colourful **feathers**.
4 is an **insect** with **wings**.
5 is a **reptile** that might **poison** you.
6 has **stripes** and a long **tail**.
7 has **spots** and sharp **claws**.
8 builds a **nest** to **lay** its eggs in.
9 has **fur** and lives underground.
10 makes honey and can **sting** you.
11 is sometimes **hunted** for its **skin**.
12 makes a **web** out of **silk**.
13 is often kept as a **pet**.

c) Compare answers with another pair. Check new words in **bold** in `V5.1` p123.

Reading and Grammar

2 **a)** Work in groups. Discuss these questions.

1 Which animals do people keep as pets in your country?
2 Has your family ever had any pets? If so, what?
3 Do you think fish make good pets? Why?/Why not?

b) Read the article. Answer these questions.

1 Why are koi such unusual pets?
2 Did the writer buy any koi? Why?/Why not?

c) Read the article again. What does it say about these numbers? Did any of the numbers surprise you?

> 89   £10,000   £250,000   £15,000   £75   5

d) Would you like to own some koi? Why?/Why not?

Help with Grammar Ways of comparing

3 **a)** Look at the phrases in pink in the article. Write them in the table.

a big difference	far more addictive than
a small difference	almost as much as
no difference	as beautiful as

TIP! ● We can also use *much/a lot* with comparatives to talk about a big difference and *a bit/a little* to talk about a small difference.

b) Look at the phrases in the table in **3a)**. Do we use the adjective or its comparative form with: *than*? *as ... as*?

c) Look at the phrases in blue in the article. Answer these questions.

1 Which phrase means the others were half the size?
2 Which two phrases describe something that continuously changes?
3 Which two phrases mean that one thing depends on the other?

d) Check in `G5.1` p124.

4 `R5.1` `P` Listen and practise. Copy the linking and weak forms.

They're₍ᵣ₎ as /əz/ beautiful as /əz/ butterflies.

LIVING JEWELS

John Wilkins goes in search of the world's most expensive and collectable fish.

Before I went to the British Koi Keepers' Annual Show, I didn't understand how people could take fish so seriously. However, the more I learned about koi, the more interested I became. As one expert told me, "Collecting koi is far more addictive than you might think. They're as beautiful as butterflies and very calming to watch." Freddie Mercury, the lead singer of Queen, would have agreed – the pool in his specially-built Japanese garden was home to 89 koi, which cost up to £10,000 each.

At the show I met koi enthusiast Jean Kelly. "Koi are getting more and more expensive," she told me. "One recently sold for £250,000." I was shocked – that's almost as much as I paid for my house. "Well, that was a record," admitted Jean. "The normal price is nowhere near as high as that."

Nevertheless, serious collectors can pay up to £15,000 for a fully-grown koi, which is nearly as expensive as a new BMW, and the bigger they are, the more they cost. The cheapest I could find were £75 each, but they were only about twice as big as my goldfish.

Jean wasn't impressed by some of the koi on sale either. "Actually, these koi aren't any nicer than mine," she commented. "They're slightly bigger than the ones I've got, but I paid considerably less than this." When I asked her why she liked koi so much, she replied, "They're just so amazing to look at. I think of them as living jewels."

Although I wasn't quite as enthusiastic as Jean, I did consider buying one. Then I remembered that all but 5 of Freddie Mercury's koi died when someone accidentally turned off the electricity supply to their pool. Jean assured me that with all the new equipment available the survival rate was getting better and better, and that looking after koi was no harder than taking care of any other pet. However, in the end I decided to stick with my goldfish. They're not nearly as beautiful as koi – but they're a great deal cheaper to replace!

5 **a) Read about cats and dogs. Choose the correct words.**

People often argue about whether cats make better pets ¹*as/than* dogs. While dogs are nowhere ²*far/near* as independent ³*as/than* cats, they tend to be a ⁴*big/great* deal friendlier. Cats can be ⁵*more/as* destructive than dogs and are ⁶*more/much* likely to damage the furniture. It's ⁷*more/far* easier to look after a cat, but dogs are ⁸*considerably/almost* better at protecting your property. Generally the ⁹*small/smaller* the dog, ¹⁰*the/as* easier it is to take care of. In fact, dogs get ¹¹*lazy/lazier* and ¹²*lazy/lazier* as they get older and don't need ¹³*nearly/almost* as much exercise, so an old dog is ¹⁴*no/as* harder to look after than a cat – and they're both ten times easier to look after ¹⁵*as/than* children!

b) Which animals do you think make the best pets? Why?

6 Rewrite these sentences so that they have the same meaning. Use the words in brackets. Sometimes there is more than one possible answer.

1 Koi live much longer than goldfish. (anywhere near)
   Goldfish don't live anywhere near as long as koi.
2 Most butterflies don't live quite as long as bees. (nearly as)
3 Snakes are much less dangerous than people think. (not nearly)
4 A spider's silk is five times stronger than steel. (nowhere near)
5 Lions aren't quite as big as tigers. (slightly)
6 Bears live half as long as elephants. (twice)
7 A blue whale's heart is the same size as a small car. (big)

7 **a) Complete these sentences with your own ideas.**

1 The older you get, ...
2 The harder you study, ...
3 The more you earn, ...
4 The fitter you are, ...
5 The more children you have, ...

b) Work in pairs. Compare sentences. Do you agree with your partner's sentences?

Get ready ... Get it right!

8 **a) Work in pairs. Choose two places, two people or two things that you both know well (cities, actors, actresses, bands, restaurants, etc.).**

b) Work on your own. Write five sentences comparing the places, people or things you and your partner chose in 8a). Use language from 3.

Tokyo isn't any more expensive than London.
I think Reese Witherspoon is a far better actress than Cameron Diaz.

9 **a) Work with your partner. Take turns to say your sentences. If you don't agree with your partner, explain why not.**

b) Tell the class two things you disagreed about.

5B The global garden

Vocabulary plants and gardens
Grammar future verb forms;
Future Continuous
Review ways of comparing

QUICK REVIEW ●●●

Write three true and three false sentences comparing yourself to how you were five years ago. Work in pairs. Take turns to say your sentences. Guess if your partner's sentences are true or false:
A *I'm nowhere near as fit as I was five years ago.* B *I think that's false.*

Vocabulary Plants and gardens

1 **a)** Tick the words you know. Then do the exercise in **V5.2** p123.

> a herb   seeds   a bulb   petals   pollen
> a pot   a vine   a bush   a hedge   a lawn
> a greenhouse   an orchard   a flower bed
> a tree trunk   roots   a branch   leaves   a twig

b) Close your books. Write all the words connected to plants and gardens that you can remember in one minute.

c) Work in pairs. Compare lists. Who has the most words? Take turns to explain the meanings of the words on your lists.

Reading, Listening and Grammar

2 **a)** Work in pairs. Look at the photos of the Eden Project. What kind of place do you think it is? What do you think you can see and do there?

b) Read about the Eden Project. Check your ideas.

c) Read about the Eden Project again. Answer these questions.

1 How many different Biomes are there?
2 What can you see in the Warm Temperate Biome?
3 What do you think the aim of the Eden Project is?

d) Would you like to visit the Eden Project? Why?/Why not?

3 **R5.2** Listen to two friends, Emma and Diane. Tick the topics they talk about.

- Emma's daughter
- Emma's husband's job
- Emma's family's holiday
- the Eden Project
- parking problems
- a TV documentary
- someone's birthday
- travel arrangements

Places to visit: South West England

The Eden Project

The Eden Project in Cornwall is a spectacular global garden that tells the story of mankind's dependence on plants. This unique conservation project has recreated three of the world's climate zones – or 'Biomes' – and filled them with trees, bushes, flowers and other plant life from all over the planet. In the breathtaking Humid Tropics Biome, which is also the world's largest greenhouse, you can experience the sights and smells of the world's tropical rainforests, while the Warm Temperate Biome contains a wide variety of Mediterranean, Californian and South African plant species, including vines, citrus fruit trees and cotton plants.

There's also a 30-acre Outdoor Biome, where you can learn about plants that have changed the world and those that could help us create a better future. There are guided tours, workshops for adults and children, and even live concerts during the summer months.

4 **R5.2** Listen again. Fill in the gaps in these sentences with two words.

1 She's been working *really hard* and I think she**'s going to pass** them all.
2 We**'re staying** in a _____ in Padstow for a week.
3 We**'re going to take** Katy to the _____ .
4 Oh, I'm sure he**'ll have** a _____ .
5 No, don't worry, I**'ll take** a _____ .
6 It's on BBC2 and it **starts** at _____ .
7 Actually, we**'ll be driving** through _____ so we can pick you up on the way.
8 Just think, this time _____ we**'ll be walking** around the Eden Project together!

40

6 [R5.3] [P] Listen and practise. Copy the stress.

We'll be driving through your village.

7 **a)** Read Emma's conversation with her husband, Paul, later that day. Choose the correct verb forms.

EMMA I spoke to Diane. ¹*She's coming*/*She'll come* to the Eden Project with us.

PAUL Oh, that's good. Which day ²*will we go/are we going*?

EMMA Thursday. And there's a programme about it on BBC2 on Saturday at 7.30.

PAUL ³*We'll be having/We'll have* dinner with your parents then.

EMMA Oh yes, I forgot. OK, ⁴*I'll record/I'm going to record* it and ⁵*we'll watch/we're watching* it when we get home.

PAUL Fine. By the way, ⁶*I'm going to buy/I'll buy* a video camera at the weekend. I thought it'd be nice to take one on holiday with us.

EMMA Tina has one she never uses. It's brand new too. Maybe ⁷*she'll let/she's going to let* us borrow it.

PAUL Well, it's worth asking. ⁸*I'll give/I'm giving* her a ring.

EMMA Don't worry, ⁹*I'll be seeing/I see* her at my yoga class tomorrow. ¹⁰*I'll ask/I'm going to ask* her then.

PAUL Good idea. Anyway, where's the babysitter? The film ¹¹*starts/is going to start* in half an hour. ¹²*We're missing/We're going to miss* the beginning.

EMMA Oh, I'm sure ¹³*she'll be/she's being* here soon.

b) Work in pairs. Compare answers. Explain why you have chosen each verb form.

c) [R5.4] Listen and check.

8 **a)** Write sentences about your plans and arrangements for the next few weeks.

I'm meeting my sister for lunch next Monday.
This time tomorrow I'll be playing tennis.

b) Work in pairs. Take turns to tell each other your sentences. Ask follow-up questions if possible.

Help with Grammar
Future verb forms; Future Continuous

5 **FUTURE VERB FORMS**

a) Look at the future verb forms in **bold** in sentences 1–6 in **4**. Match them to these meanings.

1 a personal plan or intention *'re going to take*
2 an arrangement with other people or organisations
3 a decision that is made at the time of speaking
4 a fixed event on a timetable, calendar, etc.
5 a prediction that is based on present evidence (something we know or can see now)
6 a prediction that is not based on present evidence

b) Which verb forms do we use for each meaning in **5a**?

FUTURE CONTINUOUS

c) Look at the verb forms in **bold** in sentences 7 and 8 in **4**. Match them to these meanings.

1 something that will be in progress at a point of time in the future
2 something that will happen in the normal course of events, without any particular plan or intention

d) Fill in the gaps for the Future Continuous with *be*, verb+*ing* or *will*.

subject + _____ or *'ll* + _____ + _____

e) How do we make the negative and question forms of the Future Continuous?

f) Check in [G5.2] p125.

Get ready ... Get it right!

9 Make notes on what life will be like in the year 2050. Use these ideas or your own.

- the environment
- people's lifestyles
- travel and transport
- scientific advances
- families and children
- films, TV and the Internet
- English around the world
- schools and education

10 **a)** Work in groups. Discuss your ideas from **9**. Give reasons for your opinions. Which ideas do you all agree about?

In 2050, I think a lot more people will be living in cities.

Yes, I think you're probably right.

b) Tell the class two things that your group agreed about.

Vocabulary back referencing
Skills Listening: The history of perfume; Reading: The history of flowers
Help with Listening homophones
Review plants and gardens; animals

VOCABULARY AND SKILLS

QUICK REVIEW ●●●
Work in pairs. Student A, write eight words connected to plants and gardens. Student B, write eight words connected to animals. Take turns to define the words on your list. Your partner guesses the words: A *They're part of a tree.* B *Leaves?* A *No, they're underground.* B *Oh, you mean roots.*

Queen Elizabeth I

Listening

1 Work in groups. Discuss these questions.

1 Do you ever wear perfume or aftershave? If so, which one?
2 Have you ever bought perfume or aftershave for anyone else? If so, how did you choose which one to buy?
3 How many different perfumes or aftershaves can you name? Are any of them advertised by celebrities?

Michael Jordan

2 **a)** Check these words with your teacher or in a dictionary.

a tomb   a feast   soak   a glove
a scent   a fragrance   wax

Napoleon Bonaparte

b) Work in pairs. Look at the photos. What do you know about these people?

c) Try to fill in the gaps in these sentences with the names of the people.

1 .... was buried with perfumed oils.
2 .... was given perfumed gloves.
3 .... named a perfume after the fifth sample she was offered.
4 .... used one or two bottles of perfume a day.
5 .... had a perfume named after him.

Tutankhamun

Coco Chanel

3 **a)** R5.5 Listen to a lecture about the history of perfume. Check your answers to **2c)**.

b) Work in pairs. Listen again. Student A, make notes on topics 1–4. Student B, make notes on topics 5–8.

1 Ancient Egyptians
2 the perfume museum in Paris
3 ingredients in perfumes
4 how to choose a perfume

5 Roman feasts
6 becoming a perfumer
7 men and perfumes
8 how to look after perfume

c) Tell your partner about the things you made notes on in **3b)**.

Help with Listening Homophones

● Homophones are words that sound the same, but have different spellings and different meanings (*their/there*, *would/wood*, etc.).

4 **a)** Look at the first sentence from the lecture. Choose the correct homophones.

Although we still don't really ¹*no/know* how our sense of smell works, ²*hour/our* love of perfume goes back a very long ³*weigh/way*.

b) R5.6 Listen to ten sentences from the lecture. Choose the correct words in each sentence.

1 a) flu	b) flew	6 a) new	b) knew
2 a) through	b) threw	7 a) there	b) their
3 a) pear	b) pair	8 a) wear	b) where
4 a) wore	b) war	9 a) weather	b) whether
5 a) sent	b) scent	10 a) buy	b) by

c) Work in pairs. How many more homophones can you think of?

Reading and Vocabulary

5 **a)** Check these words with your teacher or in a dictionary.

> cultivate   a botanist   a botanical garden   confetti   currency

b) Work in pairs. Student A, read about tulips. Student B, read about roses. Answer these questions.

a) Where and when were these flowers first cultivated?
b) When did the flowers reach Western Europe?
c) How was a botanical garden important in the flower's history?
d) When and where were these flowers very valuable?
e) What does the article say about the colours of these flowers?

c) Work with your partner. Take turns to ask and answer the questions in **5b)**.

d) Read about your partner's flower. Are his/her answers correct? Which facts are the most surprising?

Help with Vocabulary Back referencing

- When we speak or write, we often use words like *them*, *where*, *one*, etc. to refer back to people, places or things that we have mentioned earlier.

6 **a)** Look at words/phrases 1–10 in **bold** in the article about tulips. What are they referring to, a) or b)?

1	a) Central Asia	b) tulips
2	a) valleys	b) tulips
3	a) Turkey	b) Central Asia
4	a) the 11th century	b) the time of the Ottoman Empire
5	a) in Holland	b) in Germany
6	a) the thieves	b) the bulbs
7	a) in 1634	b) in 1594
8	a) the bulbs	b) the people
9	a) sold their homes	b) became tulip growers
10	a) tulip	b) colour

b) Look at the article about roses. What do words/phrases 11–20 in **bold** refer to?

c) Work in pairs. Compare answers. Then check in **V5.3** p124.

7 **a)** Work in pairs. You are going to design a new perfume or aftershave. Discuss these ideas.

- for men, women or both
- target age range
- what it will smell like
- the name of the product
- the price
- type of bottle/packaging
- how it will be advertised
- which celebrity you'd like to advertise it

b) Work in groups. Take turns to tell each other about your product. Which do you think is the best?

c) Tell the class about the product your group thought was the best.

The history of flowers

TULIPS

Tulips were originally wild flowers [1]**which** grew in the valleys in Central Asia. [2]**They** were first cultivated in Turkey in the 11th century, [3]**where** they were highly valued for their beauty. They became the symbol of the Ottoman Empire and can be found in many works of art from [4]**that period**.

Tulips were first cultivated in Western Europe in the 16th century by a Dutch botanist called Carolus Clusius. He had been living in Germany for some years, but in 1594 he returned to Holland and became head of a botanical garden [5]**there**. However, he charged so much for the bulbs that thieves broke in and stole [6]**them**. More and more people wanted to buy tulips and in 1634 'Tulipmania' began. [7]**At that time** people would pay a fortune for tulip bulbs – in one instance three of [8]**them** were sold for the equivalent of £75,000 at today's prices. By 1636 ordinary people were selling their homes to become tulip growers. However, the more people [9]**did so**, the less valuable the flowers became. In 1637 Tulipmania ended and most traders lost everything.

Holland now produces three billion tulip bulbs each year in hundreds of different colours, but they still can't grow a truly black tulip. To produce a black [10]**one** is the dream of tulip growers everywhere.

ROSES

According to fossil records, roses are over 35 million years old and [11]**they** were first cultivated in China about 5,000 years ago. A Chinese emperor in the 6th century BC apparently had over 600 books on roses in [12]**his** library, and oil was extracted from [13]**those** grown in his gardens. However, only the highest members of society were allowed to use [14]**it**. If anyone else was found with even a small amount, they were sentenced to death. Roses were also popular with the Romans, [15]**who** used their petals as medicine, a source of perfume and as confetti at weddings.

Cultivated roses were only introduced to Western Europe in the 18th century. Napoleon's wife, Josephine, started a botanical garden near Paris, [16]**where** she collected all the known varieties of rose and encouraged the breeding of new ones. This led to the flowers becoming increasingly popular, and in Britain [17]**at that time** roses became so valuable that [18]**they** were often used as currency in local markets.

All roses in Europe used to be pink or white until the first red [19]**ones** arrived from China 200 years ago. [20]**These** now symbolise love and are the world's most common cut flower.

5D Ecological footprints

Vocabulary adjectives for giving opinions
Real World discussion language (2): opinions
Help with Fluency linking and contractions
Review homophones

QUICK REVIEW ●●●

Write four pairs of homophones (*flu, flew*, etc.). Write sentences for each homophone: *I've got the flu. He flew to Rome.* Work in pairs. Take turns to say your pairs of sentences. Your partner spells the homophone in each sentence.

1 a) Tick the adjectives you know. What are the opposites of the adjectives in B? Check in **V5.4** p124.

A	inevitable damaging disturbing wasteful
B	moral ethical legal sustainable justifiable

b) Choose five of the adjectives from **1a)**. Think of one thing you can describe with each adjective.

c) Work in pairs. Do you agree with your partner's ideas? Why?/Why not?

I think climate change is inevitable.

2 a) What do you think an 'ecological footprint' is?

b) Read the web page. Check your ideas.

c) Work in groups. Make a list of different ways people could reduce their ecological footprints.

walk to work   use renewable energy

3 a) **R5.7** Listen to two friends, Rachel and George, discussing ecological footprints. Which of your ideas from **2c)** do they talk about?

b) Work in pairs. Choose the correct words/phrases.

1 If everyone had a lifestyle like Rachel's, we'd need *3.2/2.3* planets to survive.
2 George *recycles/doesn't recycle* things.
3 Rachel thinks we should buy food *from local supermarkets/grown locally*.
4 An area of land can produce *10/30* times more soya than beef.
5 Rachel thinks *meat/wheat* production is very damaging to the environment.
6 Rachel's arguments have *no/some* effect on George.

c) Listen again. Check your answers to **3b)**.

d) Do you agree with Rachel's ideas? Why?/Why not?

http://www.myecofootprint.org

How big is **your** ecological footprint?

These days we're all becoming more and more concerned about the effect our lifestyle has on the environment. Our ecological footprint tells us how much land and water is needed to support the way we live. It takes into account things like the food we buy, the amount of travelling we do, the amount of rubbish we throw away and how much energy we consume. You can work out your ecological footprint in less than five minutes by clicking <u>here</u>.

Real World Discussion language (2): opinions

4 a) Write these headings in the correct places a)–d).

giving yourself time to think   clarifying your position
giving opinions   giving the opposite opinion

a)	b) ....
It'd be (much) better if (everyone bought ...) I just don't think it's right that ... One argument in favour of (being vegetarian) is that ... I think people should (have the right to) ...	Maybe, but I don't see how (we) can ... Fair enough, but I still think that ... Yes, but then again, ... Well, some people would argue that ...
c)	d) ....
No, that's not what I'm trying to say. What I meant was ... No, that's not what I meant. All I'm saying is that ...	That's an interesting point. I've never really thought about that. Um, let me think. It's hard to say.

b) Check in **RW5.1** p125.

5 **a)** Write more of Rachel and George's conversation using these prompts. Use language from **4a)**.

R / think people / leave their cars at home more often.
I think people should leave their cars at home more often.

G Maybe, but I / not see / you / ask everyone to give up their cars.

R No, that's / what I / try / say. What / mean / people / use public transport if they can.

G Fair / , but / still think a lot of people prefer to drive.

R All / say / that cars are a big environmental problem.

G Yes, but / again, public transport is often more expensive.

R I know, but it / better / we / think / about how much transport costs the planet, not just ourselves.

G That / interesting point. I / never really / think / about / .

b) `R5.8` Listen and check.

Help with Fluency
Linking and contractions

6 **a)** `R5.8` Look at R5.8, p149. Listen again. Notice the linking.

b) Read the conversation again. Find all the contractions.

c) `P` Work in pairs. Practise the conversation in R5.8, p149 until you can remember it. Then close your books and have the conversation again. Try to use natural linking and contractions.

7 **a)** Look at these topics. Think of two things to say about each one.

- public transport
- the fast-food industry
- low-cost airlines
- recycling
- factory farming
- renewable energy

b) Work in groups. Discuss the topics in **7a)**. Use the language in **4a)**.

c) Tell the class which topic was the most controversial and why.

5 Review

1 **a)** Tick the true sentences. Change the animals in the false sentences. `V5.1`

   leopard
1 A ~~tiger~~ has spots and large claws.
2 A parrot is a mammal that lives underwater.
3 A bear is an insect with wings.
4 A rabbit has fur and lives underground.
5 A bee makes honey and can sting you.
6 A shark is often kept as a pet.
7 A snake makes a web out of silk.
8 An eagle builds a nest to lay its eggs in.

b) Work in pairs. Compare answers. Then write definitions for the animals that did not match the definitions in **1a)**.

A tiger has stripes and a long tail.

2 **a)** Fill in the gaps with the correct word. Then tick the sentences that are true for you. `G5.1`

1 I'm not nearly as scared of snakes _____ I used to be.
2 The older I get, _____ less exercise I do.
3 I'm nowhere _____ as extravagant as my best friend.
4 I'm a bit taller _____ my parents.
5 The _____ I practise English, the more confident I get.
6 I eat a far _____ varied diet now than I used to.
7 My life is getting busier and _____ .
8 I'm a _____ deal happier now than when I was a child.

b) Work in pairs. Tell your partner the sentences you ticked. Ask follow-up questions.

3 Fill in the vowels. `V5.2`

1 tr e e tr u nk   7 r _ _ ts
2 p _ t _ ls   8 _ rch _ rd
3 gr _ _ nh _ _ s _ 9 p _ ll _ n
4 l _ _ v _ s   10 s _ _ ds
5 h _ dg _   11 b _ sh
6 v _ n _   12 l _ wn

4 Correct the future verb forms. There is sometimes more than one possible answer. `G5.2`

1 I didn't know Jo was back. I'm giving her a call.
2 I see Jan tomorrow at school. Shall I ask her to call you?
3 I've just seen a fabulous jacket. I think I'll be buying it.
4 I've made an appointment and I see the doctor at 4 p.m. tomorrow.
5 Perhaps I'm seeing Michelle when I'm in Paris next week.
6 See you tomorrow. I'm calling you before I leave.

5 **a)** Replace each underlined word with one back referencing word. `V5.3`

I'm going to Brighton tomorrow to see Jack. I'm very excited about [1]going to Brighton because I've never been [2]to Brighton before. Jack's always wanted a flat in Brighton and the [3]flat he's bought overlooks the sea. So [4]Jack has finally got [5]Jack's dream. As you can imagine, [6]buying his dream flat has made [7]Jack very happy indeed.

b) Work in pairs. Compare answers.

Progress Portfolio

a) Tick the things you can do in English.

☐ I can talk about animals, plants and gardens.

☐ I can compare two or more people or things in different ways.

☐ I can talk in detail about different aspects of the future.

☐ I can understand back referencing in a text.

☐ I can understand the important points of a lecture.

☐ I can take part in a discussion and respond to other people's ideas.

b) What do you need to study again?
● 5A–D

6 Breaking codes

6A Codes of conduct

Vocabulary phrases with *take*
Grammar uses of verb+*ing*
Review discussion language (2): opinions

QUICK REVIEW ● ● ●
Work in groups of three. Choose two of these topics: cosmetic surgery; zoos; being vegetarian; smoking in public places. Take turns to give opinions, clarify your position and give the opposite opinion if appropriate.

Vocabulary Phrases with *take*

1 a) Tick the phrases in **bold** you know. Check new phrases in V6.1 p126.

1 Do you **take a long time** to get ready in the morning?
2 Have you **taken** a lot of **risks** in your life?
3 Do you think you **take** life too **seriously**?
4 Who do you **take advice** from?
5 Do you think anyone you know **takes** you **for granted**?
6 Do you think you **take responsibility for** things you shouldn't?
7 Has anyone ever **taken advantage of** you when you've offered to help them?
8 Do you **take** any **notice of** people who criticise you?
9 Do you **take** your **time** when you're clothes shopping?
10 Do you ever **take sides** in family arguments?

b) Work in pairs. Take turns to ask and answer the questions in **1a)**. Ask follow-up questions if possible.

Reading and Grammar

2 a) Work in groups. Discuss these questions.

1 Do you know any English people? If so, where and how did you meet them? What are they like?
2 Which four adjectives describe English people the best?

b) Read the book review of *Watching the English*. Does Kate Fox think the English are unfriendly? Why?/Why not?

c) Read the review again. Tick the correct sentences. Correct the false ones.

1 English social codes are obvious to everyone.
2 People who commute together often become friends.
3 'Weather-speak' is a common way of starting a conversation with strangers.
4 You should always agree with the person's opinion about the weather.
5 English people don't mind talking about themselves to strangers.
6 It's impolite to ask English people about money.

d) Did anything in the review surprise you? Do people from your country behave in a similar way?

Pick of the week

What every visitor to England needs to know

Henry Hardcastle reviews Kate Fox's new book.

As an Englishman, I was laughing out loud and cringing with embarrassment as I read *Watching the English* by Kate Fox. This highly entertaining book looks at how the English behave and uncovers the hidden social rules that mystify foreign visitors, for example how we behave on public transport. Apart from asking for information – [1]**"Is this train going** to Victoria?" – talking to strangers on trains just isn't done! In fact it's absolutely normal for commuters to spend years travelling on the same train together [2]**without exchanging** a word.

Help with Grammar Uses of verb+*ing*

3 a) Look at phrases in **pink** in the article. Match them to these uses of verb+*ing*.

We use verb+*ing* ...

a) as part of a continuous verb form. *was laughing*
b) after prepositions. *from asking*
c) after certain verbs. *avoid talking*
d) after certain verbs + object. *spend years travelling*

b) Look at the phrases in **blue** in the article. Match them to these uses of verb+*ing*.

We can also use verb+*ing* ...

e) as an adjective. *entertaining*
f) in reduced relative clauses. *standing at bus stop*
g) after *despite* or *in spite of*. *despite not wanting*
h) as the subject (or part of the subject) of a verb. *talking to strangers on train*

c) Check in G6.1 p127.

4 Work in pairs. Look at the review again. Match phrases 1–8 in **bold** to uses of verb+*ing* forms a)–h) in **3**.

However, despite not wanting to engage in conversation with strangers, people standing at a bus stop will often break an uncomfortable silence by talking about the weather. 'Weather-speak' usually starts with a question which invites the other person into a conversation: "Chilly, isn't it?". But the hidden rule is we have to agree – that's taken for granted. ³**Disagreeing could cause** offence and the conversation would stop. The only way of stating our true feelings is after agreeing ("Yes, it is.") we can then take a risk and add "but I quite like this kind of weather".

As Fox points out, foreign visitors ⁴**taking part in any conversation with an English person** may find it tricky at first. There's no use trying to get

personal information out of us because we don't like gossiping about ourselves. We're very uncomfortable when we're being asked questions such as "How old are you?" or "Are you married?". We also avoid talking about money. Indeed, the English ⁵**dislike people asking** them what they earn or what they paid for something – that's very personal information.

Once I'd ⁶**finished reading** *Watching the English*, I did just that – I watched them. It was ⁷**fascinating**. And the more I watched, the more I found myself agreeing with Kate Fox's conclusion. She states that ⁸**in spite of appearing** cold and unfriendly (and often being told that they are) the English are, in fact, just very private people.

5 **a)** Read part of another review of Kate Fox's book. Find and correct ten more mistakes.

b) Work in pairs. Compare answers. Explain why you have made each change.

c) R6.1 Listen and check.

The section of Kate Fox's book ~~explain~~ *explaining* the rules of queuing is fascinating and the English obey these rules without think about it. Jump a queue will certainly annoy those people queue properly. However, despite feel intense anger towards the queue-jumper, the English will often say nothing – stare angrily is more their style.

Then there are the rules for say please and thank you. The English thank bus drivers, taxi drivers, anyone give them a service. In fact the English spend a lot of time say please and thank you, and they hate not be thanked if they think they deserve it. Not say thank you will often cause a person to sarcastically shout out, "You're welcome!".

6 **a)** Use a verb+*ing* form to complete these sentences about you.

1 I can't stand … .
2 … is the best way to relax.
3 I think ..... is really fun.
4 I'm … next week.
5 I think football is … .
6 I really enjoy … .
7 I'm thinking of … next year.
8 I spend a lot of time … .

b) Work in pairs. Take turns to tell each other your sentences. Ask follow-up questions.

Get ready … Get it right!

7 Imagine an English tourist is coming to your country. Write eight tips about the social codes in your country. Use these ideas or your own. Try to use a verb+*ing* form in each tip.

- behaviour on public transport
- queuing
- dress codes
- saying please and thank you
- starting conversations
- talking to strangers
- talking loudly in public
- subjects you shouldn't talk about
- things that might cause offence

People travelling on public transport often chat to each other.

8 **a)** Work in pairs. Take turns to tell each other your tips. If you're from the same country, do you agree? If you're from different countries, are your partner's tips also true for your country?

b) Tell the class the three most important tips for people visiting your country.

Vocabulary compound
adjectives describing character
Grammar modal verbs (1); levels
of certainty about the future
Review phrases with *take*

QUICK REVIEW ● ● ●

Write four phrases with *take*. Work in pairs. Swap papers.
Take turns to make sentences about people you know
with your partner's phrases. Ask follow-up questions:
A *My brother's into dangerous sports and I think he takes
too many risks.* B *What kind of sports does he do?*

Lucy   Don

Vocabulary Compound adjectives describing character

1 **a)** Match the words in A to the
words in B to make compound
adjectives. Which have a positive
meaning (P) and which have a
negative meaning (N)? Check in
V6.2 p126.

A	B
strong-	conscious
self-	minded
laid-	willed P
open-	back

self-	going
narrow-	minded
easy-	centred
big-	headed

bad-	headed
absent-	assured
level-	tempered
self-	minded

b) Work in pairs. Make a list of
other positive and negative
character adjectives that you know.
positive – considerate
negative – stubborn

2 **a)** Write the names of five people
you know. Which adjectives from
1a) and **1b)** can you use to describe
each person?

b) Work in pairs. Take turns to tell
each other about the people you
chose. Which of the people your
partner talked about would you
most like to meet?

Listening and Grammar

3 **a)** Look at the photo. Where are the people? What do you think Lucy and
Don are talking about?

b) **R6.2** Listen to Lucy and Don's conversation. Answer these questions.

1 Why is Bruce difficult to work with?
2 Why is he going to work in the Leeds office?
3 How long is he going for?
4 Is Don going to apply for Bruce's job?
5 Who does Lucy think will get the job?
6 What do Lucy and Don think will happen if Bruce comes back?

c) Listen again. Who said these sentences, Don or Lucy?

1 He's **bound to** upset people.
2 He's **unlikely to** change his personality overnight.
3 **I can't imagine** they'll like him.
4 **I don't suppose** he'll worry about being popular.
5 He's **likely to** be there for at least a year.
6 **I doubt if** Lynn will go for it.
7 But Frieda **may well** apply.
8 But you're **sure to** get the job.
9 **I shouldn't think** they'll employ an outsider.
10 **I dare say** they'll promote him.

Bruce

Help with Grammar Modal verbs (1); levels of certainty about the future

4 MODAL VERBS

a) Look at sentences 1–5 from Lucy and Don's conversation. Which of the <u>underlined</u> modal verbs express future certainty (C)? Which express future possibility (P)?

1 I <u>might</u> go for a bit.
2 I<u>'ll</u> miss him in some ways.
3 I <u>won't</u> be sad to see him go.
4 He <u>could</u> improve things.
5 He <u>may</u> not want to give up his house.

LEVELS OF CERTAINTY ABOUT THE FUTURE

b) Look at the phrases in **bold** in **3c)**. Match sentences 1–10 to these meanings.

a) The speaker thinks this will definitely or probably happen.
b) The speaker thinks this definitely or probably won't happen.

c) Look again at the phrases in **bold** in **3c)**. Which are followed by the infinitive? Which are followed by subject + *will* + infinitive?

d) Check in G6.2 p127.

5 R6.3 P Listen and practise the sentences in **3c)**.

He's bound to upset people.

6 **a)** Rewrite these sentences so that they have the same meaning. Use the words in brackets and change other words if necessary.

1 Maybe I'll do well in my next English test. (might)
   I might do well in my next English test.
2 I probably won't need English for my next job. (unlikely)
3 I'm sure to need English for my work. (bound)
4 I'm fairly sure I'll do an advanced English course at some point. (dare say)
5 I won't be able to visit England next year. (can't imagine)
6 I'll probably spend some time working on the *face2face* CD-ROM this weekend. (may well)
7 I don't think I'll take any more English exams. (doubt)
8 I probably won't be able to watch an English DVD this weekend. (don't suppose)

b) Work in pairs. Compare answers. Are any of the sentences in **6a)** true for both of you?

7 **a)** Write the names of four people you know well. Write sentences about what their lives will be like in a few years' time. Use these ideas or your own.

● get engaged/married
● have children
● be successful in their career or studies
● change jobs
● buy/sell property
● move to a different town/city
● work/go on holiday abroad

b) Work in pairs. Take turns to tell each other about the people you chose. Ask follow-up questions if possible. Whose life do you think will change the most in the next few years?

Get ready ... Get it right!

8 Make notes on at least eight things you will probably do, might do or probably won't do in the next two weeks.

have a day off work

9 **a)** Work in groups. Take turns to tell each other your predictions. Use the language in **3c)** and **4a)**. Ask follow-up questions.

(I may well have a day off work next week.)

(What do you think you'll do?)

b) Tell the class who you think is going to have the busiest, the best or the worst two weeks.

6C Hidden messages

Vocabulary guessing meaning from context
Skills Reading: Codes through the ages;
Listening: Breaking codes
Help with Listening linking (2): /w/, /j/ and /r/ sounds
Review levels of certainty about the future

QUICK REVIEW ● ● ●
Think about your town/city. Predict what you think will/won't change in the next five years: *The traffic is bound to get worse, but they may well ban cars from the centre.* Work in pairs. Compare your predictions. Who is more optimistic?

Reading and Vocabulary

1 a) Work in pairs. Think of three reasons why people might want to send secret messages. Then think of three different ways of sending secret messages.

b) Compare ideas with the class.

2 a) Read this extract about codes from an encyclopaedia. What is the main difference between steganography and cryptology?

b) Work in pairs. Compare answers.

Help with Vocabulary
Guessing meaning from context

3 a) Look at the words in blue in the extract. What parts of speech are they? Do you know a similar word in your language, or another language you know?

b) Choose the correct meaning, a) or b). What information in the extract helped you decide?

1	decipher	a) write sth
		b) work out what sth means
2	wind	a) turn sth repeatedly
		b) push sth
3	make out sth	a) see sth with difficulty
		b) see sth easily
4	reveal	a) remove sth
		b) show sth that was hidden
5	strip	a) a large piece of material
		b) a long, thin piece of material
6	stick	a) a large piece of wood
		b) a long, thin piece of wood
7	straightforward	a) simple
		b) complicated

c) Work in pairs. Look at the words in pink. What parts of speech are they? Can you guess what they mean?

d) Check in `V6.3` p126.

4 Read the extract again. Work in pairs. Student A, describe how pictures 1–3 were used to send secret messages. Student B, describe pictures 4–6.

CODES THROUGH THE AGES

Throughout history, human beings have always needed to communicate secretly and have used countless ingenious ways of sending secret messages. There are two main types of code.

STEGANOGRAPHY

In steganography the message is hidden in some way. One method used by the Romans was to shave a messenger's head, write the message on his scalp and then send him off when his hair had grown back. When he reached his destination, his head was shaved again to show the message. The ancient Chinese wrote messages on silk, which was then scrunched up into a tiny ball, covered with wax and swallowed so the message was hidden in the courier's stomach.

In the sixteenth century an Italian scientist called Giovanni Porta described how to conceal a message within a hard-boiled egg by making an ink from vinegar and alum (a mineral salt). The message is written on the shell, which is porous, and it passes through to the white of the egg. To read the message, the person who received the egg simply had to remove the shell. Invisible ink made from milk or lemon juice is another means of hiding messages. When the 'ink' dries it is invisible, but when heated the message reappears.

However, there was a fundamental weakness with all these methods – if the message was found, it could be read immediately.

Listening

5 **a)** Work in pairs. Look at pictures A–C. How do you think they are connected to codes?

b) `R6.4` Listen to the beginning of a radio programme about breaking codes. Put pictures A–C in order. Were your ideas correct?

c) Work in pairs. Try to match these names to facts 1–7.

> Joe Allen   al-Kindi   Sally Evans   Arthur Conan Doyle

1 … is a professor of mathematics.
2 … worked for the British Secret Service for over 20 years.
3 … was one of the earliest code breakers.
4 … wrote 290 books.
5 … broke codes by working out the frequency of letters in a language.
6 … used stick figures in a coded message.
7 … wrote *The Adventure of the Dancing Men*.

d) Listen again. Check your answers to 5c).

CRYPTOLOGY

In cryptology a code is agreed between the sender and the receiver so that the meaning of the message is hidden. Then if the message is intercepted, it is difficult or impossible to decipher.

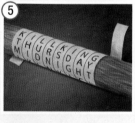

One way of making a coded message is to rearrange the letters. In Ancient Greece, soldiers from Sparta used a system called scytale, in which the person sending the message would wind a piece of leather around a small piece of wood. The secret message was written across the leather so that when the leather was removed from the wood it was impossible to make out what the message said. To reveal the message, the receiver of the strip of leather would simply wind it around a stick of the same size and shape that the sender had used. Alternatively, rather than rearranging the letters of the whole message, a more straightforward way of achieving a similar effect was by rearranging the letters of each word (for example OMSNAR = ROMANS).

Another way to send hidden messages is to replace letters by other letters or symbols. A code invented during the reign of Julius Caesar was based on this principle and was used for centuries. Since then more and more sophisticated codes have been developed, which have led to today's computer-generated digital codes.

(A) *From 'The Adventure of the Dancing Men'*

(B)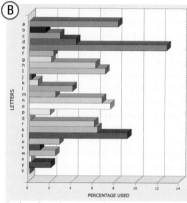
The distribution of letters in English

(C)
Arab mathematician al-Kindi

Help with Listening
Linking (2): /w/, /j/ and /r/ sounds

● When a word ends in a vowel sound and the next word also starts with a vowel sound, we often link these words with a /w/, /j/ or /r/ sound.

6 **a)** `R6.5` Listen to these sentences from the radio programme. Notice the linking sounds.

Well, one of the ⌣/j/ earliest people to ⌣/w/ ever break coded messages was an Arab mathematician called al-Kindi.

Yes, for ⌣/r/ example, let's take the ⌣/j/ English language.

So you look for the most common letter ⌣/r/ and you ⌣/w/ assume that letter represents the letter ⌣/r/ E.

b) Work in pairs. Look at the beginning of the radio programme. Which linking sounds do we hear between the words in **bold**?

Hello ⌣/w/ **and** welcome to the programme. With us **today** ⌣ **in** the **studio** ⌣ **is Joe** ⌣ **Allen**, who's a **professor** ⌣ **of** mathematics, and **Sally** ⌣ **Evans**, **who** ⌣ **actually** worked for the British Secret Service **for** ⌣ **over** twenty years.

c) Look at R6.4, p150. Check your answers.

d) `R6.4` Listen to and read the radio programme again. Notice the extra linking sounds.

7 **a)** Look at part of the code that Julius Caesar used. Work in pairs. Use this code to write a secret message to another pair of students. Use at least ten words.

a = d, b = e, c = f, etc.

b) Swap papers with another pair. Who can decipher their message the fastest?

6D Am I interrupting?

Real World polite interruptions
Help with Listening intonation: being polite
Review compound adjectives describing character

QUICK REVIEW ● ● ●

Write the first part of four compound adjectives to describe character. Work in pairs. Say the first part of your adjective. Your partner says the whole adjective and its meaning: A *laid-* B *laid-back. Laid-back people are very relaxed.*

1

a) What are the advantages and disadvantages of working in an open-plan office?

b) R6.6 Listen to five short conversations. Match people 1–5 to their relationships with Lucy a)–e).

1 Angus   a) a person from the IT department
2 Martin   b) Lucy's PA
3 Clare   c) the company accountant
4 Tina   d) Lucy's husband
5 Julian   e) a junior colleague

c) Listen again. Why does each person want to speak to Lucy?

Real World Polite interruptions

2

ASKING FOR PERMISSION TO INTERRUPT

a) Match the beginnings of sentences 1–6 to the ends of sentences a)–f). Which sentences sound more polite?

1 Sorry to bother you, but have you   a) busy?
2 Is this   b) a word?
3 Sorry to   c) got a minute?
4 I was wondering if   d) disturb you.
5 Are you   e) a good time?
6 Can I have   f) I could see you for a moment.

REFUSING PERMISSION TO INTERRUPT

b) Look at these ways of refusing permission. Fill in the gaps with these words.

> busy   against   tied   time   pushed

1 Sorry, this isn't a good ....
2 I'm really up .... it at the moment.
3 I'm afraid I'm a bit .... up just now.
4 I'm rather .... for time at the moment.
5 I'm really rather .... right now.

TIP! ● If we are refused permission we often say:
Don't worry, *it's not important/it can wait/it's not urgent/ I'll catch you later/some other time.*
When would be *a good time/a better time/more convenient?*

c) What can we say if we want to give someone permission to interrupt?

d) Check in RW6.1 p127.

Lucy

Help with Listening Intonation: being polite

● We know if people are being polite by how much their voices go up and down. If their voices are flat, they often sound rude or impatient.

3 R6.7 Listen to the same sentences said twice. Which sounds polite, a) or b)?

1 (a) b)   3 a) b)   5 a) b)
2 a) b)   4 a) b)   6 a) b)

4 R6.8 P Listen and practise. Copy the sentence stress and polite intonation.

Sorry to bother you, but have you got a minute?

1 a) Fill in the gaps with these words. **V6.1**

> ~~risks~~ seriously time
> responsibility advantage
> sides advice granted

1 I take _risks_.
2 I take my friends' _____ when I'm buying new clothes.
3 I take my health for _____ .
4 I take my _____ when making a big decision.
5 I take my work/studies too _____ .
6 I take _____ of my friends.
7 I take _____ for my mistakes.
8 I take _____ when my friends argue.

b) Tick the sentences in **1a)** that are true for you. Make the other sentences true for you. Use frequency adverbs (*sometimes, hardly ever, never,* etc.).
I hardly ever take risks.

c) Work in pairs. Compare sentences. Ask follow-up questions.

2 a) Choose the correct words. **G6.1**

¹*Be /Being* punctual is extremely important and I hate ²*turn up/ turning up* late for anything. I also really hate people who ³*keep/keeping* me waiting. So yesterday morning was really ⁴*frustrated/frustrating*. I was ⁵*be/being* interviewed for a job, so I decided ⁶*to leave/leaving* home early to avoid ⁷*to get/getting* caught in the rush hour. Despite ⁸*allow/allowing* an extra two hours for the journey, I thought I was going to be late because lots of trains were ⁹*cancelled/cancelling*. But in the end I managed ¹⁰*to get/getting* there on time. However, none of the people ¹¹*interview/interviewing* me did!

b) Work in pairs. Compare answers.

3 a) Complete these compound adjectives. There is sometimes more than one answer. **V6.2**

1 _____-headed   5 _____-minded
2 _____-going   6 _____-centred
3 _____-willed   7 _____-tempered
4 _____-back   8 _____-conscious

b) Work in groups. Which of the adjectives in **3a)** describe you?

4 a) Write true or false sentences about your life in five years' time. **G6.2**

1 I might ...
2 I definitely won't ...
3 I'm bound to ...
4 I may well ...
5 I can't imagine ...
6 I doubt if ...
7 I shouldn't think ...

b) Work in pairs. Guess which of your partner's sentences are true.

5 a) Complete these phrases for interrupting people. **RW6.1**

1 Sorry to bother you, but ... ?
2 Can I have ... ?
3 I was wondering if ... .
4 Sorry to ... .

b) Take turns to say the sentences in **5a)**. Refuse or give your partner permission to interrupt you.

---

5 Fill in the gaps in these conversations. Use words from **2a)** and **2b)**.

1

A ¹*Excuse* me. I was ²_____ if I ³_____ see you for a moment.
B I'm sorry, I'm really up ⁴_____ it at the ⁵_____ .
A When ⁶_____ be a good ⁷_____ ?
B How about 3.30?

2

A Sorry to ⁸_____ you. Can I have a ⁹_____ ?
B Er, I'm ¹⁰_____ I'm a bit ¹¹_____ up right now.
A Don't ¹²_____ . It can ¹³_____ .

3

A Sorry to ¹⁴_____ you, but have you got a ¹⁵_____ ?
B I'm rather ¹⁶_____ for ¹⁷_____ right now.
A OK, I'll ¹⁸_____ you later.

6 Work in groups. Group A → p105. Group B → p108. Follow the instructions.

Progress Portfolio

a) Tick the things you can do in English.

☐ I can describe positive and negative aspects of people's character.

☐ I can express how certain I am about future events.

☐ I can understand a reference text on a subject of general interest.

☐ I can guess the meaning of some words in context.

☐ I can understand a live interview.

☐ I can interrupt people politely.

b) What do you need to study again?
⦿ 6A–D

7 Small world

7A At the airport

Vocabulary state verbs
Grammar simple and continuous aspects; activity and state verbs
Review polite interruptions

QUICK REVIEW ●●●
Think of three ways you can ask to interrupt someone and three ways you can refuse permission to interrupt. Work in pairs. Imagine you are both working in an office. Take turns to interrupt each other. Continue the conversations if possible: A *Can I have a word?* B *Sorry, I'm a bit tied up just now.* A *When would be a good time?*

Vocabulary State verbs

 a) Tick the verbs in **bold** that you know. Check new verbs in V7.1 p128.

1 I **own** _____ that used to **belong** to _____ .
2 I really **respect** people who _____ .
3 I think my friend _____ **deserves** to be successful in life.
4 My job/course **involves** quite a lot of _____ .
5 I **trust** _____ completely.
6 The colour _____ doesn't **suit** me.
7 I **suspect** that I make more mistakes when I _____ than I **realise**.
8 I **envy** people who can _____ .
9 If _____ saw me now, he/she probably wouldn't **recognise** me.
10 I **adore** _____ , but I really **detest** _____ .

b) Complete the sentences in **1a)** for yourself.

c) Work in pairs. Take turns to tell each other your sentences. Ask follow-up questions if possible.

Listening and Grammar

2 Work in groups. Discuss these questions.

1 Do you like flying? Why?/Why not?
2 What was the last flight you took? Where did you go?
3 Have you ever had to wait a long time at an airport? If so, why?

3 **a)** Look at these activities. Tick the ones you've done to pass the time at an airport.

- read
- sleep
- people-watch
- have a coffee
- phone family or friends
- work or study
- text friends
- do some shopping
- have a meal
- talk to other passengers

b) Work in pairs. Compare answers. Which things have you both done?

4 **a)** R7.1 Listen to part of a radio news programme. Tick the things in **3a)** that some people waiting at an airport talk about.

b) Listen again. Fill in the gaps with one word.

1 I usually **buy** a ..*paperback*.. and just go and sit somewhere quiet.
2 Once I got so involved in the book I **was reading** that I _____ my plane.
3 I've **been sitting** here for nearly _____ hours.
4 I've also **called** my _____ to say goodbye.
5 Luckily, I only **live** _____ minutes away.
6 I'm **doing** a part-time _____ management course at the moment.
7 I'm supposed to **be seeing** some _____ as soon as I arrive, but I **see** the flight's been delayed.
8 I **have** three kids and I never get time to shop for _____ , so I'm **having** a great time today.
9 I'm also **thinking** of buying a _____ , but I **think** they might be cheaper online.
10 My youngest **is** usually very good, but he's **being** very _____ today.

6 Read about Fiona. Fill in the gaps with the correct simple or continuous form of the verbs in brackets. Sometimes there is more than one possible answer.

> I ¹ *'ve been working* (work) as a flight attendant for seven years and I ² _____ (love) my job. At the moment I ³ _____ (wait) to fly to Rome, so I ⁴ _____ (phone) some friends to pass the time. I ⁵ _____ (never have) a really scary experience, although once we ⁶ _____ (fly) across the Atlantic and one of the engines ⁷ _____ (stop) working. Luckily it ⁸ _____ (happen) while most people ⁹ _____ (sleep) and we ¹⁰ _____ (manage) to land safely. I ¹¹ _____ (suppose) the best thing about the job is the discounts. Next month I ¹² _____ (fly) to Australia on holiday and the flight only ¹³ _____ (cost) me £95! And the worst thing? I ¹⁴ _____ (hate) security checks – I ¹⁵ _____ (go) through about 20 this week already!

Fiona

7 Fill in the gaps with the correct form of these verbs. Use the same verb for both sentences in each pair.

> be have think see

1 a) What _____ you _____ of this dress?
  b) I _____ of going away next week.
2 a) I _____ lunch with my boss when I got your text.
  b) We _____ this car since 2004.
3 a) _____ you _____ that new Spielberg film yet?
  b) Mr Jones _____ a customer at the moment.
4 a) Rick _____ tall, good-looking and very friendly.
  b) Tricia _____ rather bad-tempered today – she's usually so easy-going.

Help with Grammar Simple and continuous aspects; activity and state verbs

5 **a)** Answer these questions about the sentences in **4b)**.

a) Look at sentences 1 and 2. Which describes something that is: repeated? in progress at a specific point in time?

b) Look at sentences 3 and 4. Which describes something that is: completed? unfinished?

c) Look at sentences 5 and 6. Which describes something that is: permanent? temporary?

b) Look at these verbs. Do they usually describe activities (A) or states (S)? Do we usually use state verbs in continuous verb forms?

> hate *S* play *A* fly know travel listen seem
> run understand work sit dislike need study
> prefer want wait forget mean agree cost

c) Look at sentences 7–10 in **4b)**. What is the difference in meaning between the verb forms in **bold** in each sentence?

d) Check in G7.1 p129.

Get ready ... Get it right!

8 Write these things on a piece of paper. Don't write them in this order.

Something that you …
- have wanted to do for ages
- are worrying about at the moment
- are thinking of doing next weekend
- have forgotten to do this week
- own that really suits you
- are looking forward to

9 **a)** Work in pairs. Swap papers. Take turns to ask your partner about the things he/she has written. Ask follow-up questions if possible.

b) Tell the class two things that you found out about your partner.

Vocabulary business and trade
Grammar Present Perfect Simple and Present Perfect Continuous
Review simple and continuous aspects

QUICK REVIEW ● ● ●
Think of an interesting plane, train or bus journey you've been on. Work in pairs. Take turns to tell your partner about the journey. Use simple and continuous verb forms.

Changing China

Reading and Grammar

1 **a)** Work in pairs. What do you know about China? Discuss these ideas or your own.

- languages
- famous places
- history and culture
- sport and entertainment

b) Work in groups or with the whole class. Compare ideas.

2 **a)** Look at the photo. Which city do you think this is? Would you like to go there? Why?/Why not?

b) Read the article. Find three ways in which Shanghai has changed.

c) Read the article again. Tick the true sentences. Correct the false ones.

1 There weren't any skyscrapers in Pudong 25 years ago.
2 There are more skyscrapers in Shanghai than in the whole of the USA.
3 Liu Zhang doesn't think that the city has changed a lot.
4 China now manufactures more products than any other country.
5 More people in Beijing are cycling to work these days.
6 The writer thinks China will have a big influence on the world in the future.

Our Asia correspondent David Earle reflects on how fast the world's most populated country is changing.

I've visited many amazing cities over the years, but Shanghai is the most spectacular I've ever seen in my life. Today I've been walking around the Pudong area of the city, and I'm both exhausted and exhilarated by the experience. When you see Pudong's incredible collection of space-age skyscrapers up close, it's almost impossible to believe that in 1990 there was nothing there but fishermen's huts.

I've been coming to China for nearly 20 years, and while Beijing is still China's cultural and political centre, Shanghai is now seen as the symbol of the country's new capitalist economy. The city already has more than 2,000 buildings over 150 metres high, more than on the entire west coast of the USA. Even Chinese people I've known for years are amazed at how fast things have changed. Liu Zhang, a property developer who has been working in Shanghai for ten years, says, "My company has been building skyscrapers here since 1993, and business is still booming. This year we've built three new apartment blocks and are planning to build another five. I hardly recognise the city any more." Shanghai has also attracted a lot of foreign investment. There's a huge Armani store on the Bund, the city's main pedestrian street, and you can't walk very far without coming across a McDonald's or a Starbucks.

After 25 years of rapid industrial development, China is now the biggest producer of manufactured goods in the world. However, such rapid economic change has also created environmental problems, and many of China's biggest cities have become more polluted due to increased car ownership. For example, 60% of people in Beijing cycled to work in 1998 – now the figure is less than 20%.

I've just got back to my hotel room, which is 'only' on the fifty-fourth floor. And as I look across the Huangpu River at the millions of lights shining from Pudong's skyscrapers, one thing seems certain – what happens in China in the next ten years will affect us all.

Help with Grammar Present Perfect Simple and Present Perfect Continuous

3 **a)** Look at the verb forms in pink in the article. Which are in the Present Perfect Simple and which are in the Present Perfect Continuous?

b) Match the verb forms in pink in the article to these meanings.

● We often use the **Present Perfect Simple:**

a) for experiences in our lives up to now *'ve visited*
b) for states that started in the past and continue in the present
• c) for completed actions that happened recently, but we don't say exactly when
d) with superlatives
e) to talk about change

● We often use the **Present Perfect Continuous:**

a) for longer actions that started in the past and continue in the present *has been working*
b) for longer actions that have recently finished, but have a result in the present
c) for actions that happened repeatedly in the past and still happen in the present

c) Look at these sentences from the article. Then answer questions a)–c).

1 *My company has been building skyscrapers here since 1993.*
2 *This year we've built three new apartment blocks.*

a) Which sentence talks about how long something has been happening?
b) Which talks about how many things have been completed?
c) How do we make a question with *How long* for sentence 1 and *How many* for sentence 2?

d) Check in G7.2 p130.

4 **a)** Put the verbs in brackets in the Present Perfect Simple or Present Perfect Continuous.

1 a) I _____ Kim and told him where to meet. (call)
   b) I _____ Kim all day, but he never answers his phone. (call)
2 a) David _____ his novel all evening. (write)
   b) David _____ three novels in the last two years. (write)
3 a) I _____ the garage, so we can put the car in there now. (clear out)
   b) I _____ the garage. It's a mess in there! (clear out)
4 a) You _____ down trees all day. You must be tired. (cut)
   b) You _____ your finger. (cut)
5 a) I _____ this book. Do you want to borrow it? (read)
   b) I _____ this book and I'm really enjoying it. (read)

b) Work in pairs. Compare answers. Explain why you chose each verb form.

5 Work in new pairs. Student A → p106. Student B → p109. Follow the instructions.

Vocabulary Business and trade

6 **a)** Look at the words in blue in the article. Are they nouns or adjectives? Do the nouns refer to people or things?

b) Work in pairs. Write the other nouns and adjectives for the words in blue in the article if possible. Check in V7.2 p128.

political → *a politician, politics*

7 **a)** Choose the correct words in these sentences.

1 I've never lived in an *industry/industrial* city.
2 I don't understand *economical/economics*.
3 I like reading about *politics/political*.
4 I think my home town is quite *pollution/ polluted*.
5 My country's always had a *capitalism/ capitalist* system.
6 I think buying a house is a good *investor/ investment*.
7 I like trying new hair *products/production*.
8 I worry about *environment/environmental* issues.

b) Tick the sentences in 7a) that are true for you.

c) Work in groups. Compare sentences. Ask follow-up questions where possible.

Get ready ... Get it right!

8 Write sentences about how things have changed in your country in the last five years. Use these ideas or your own.

● the economy
● public transport
● new buildings
● cost of living
● education
● the price of food/ petrol/property

● unemployment
● pollution
● inflation
● traffic
● industry
● tourism

The economy has been getting stronger recently. The price of petrol has gone up a lot this year. Unemployment's been rising.

9 **a)** Work in groups. Take turns to tell each other your sentences. If you're from the same country, do you agree? If you're from different countries, how many of your sentences are the same?

b) Tell the class two interesting changes that your group discussed.

VOCABULARY AND SKILLS

Vocabulary the Internet; word building (2): prefixes
Skills Reading: Our digital world; Listening: Using the Internet
Help with Listening recognising redundancy
Review business and trade

QUICK REVIEW ●●●
Work in pairs. What are the nouns for the people and the adjectives for these things: *economy; development; industry; pollution; product; politics?* Take turns to make sentences that include one word from each group: *My brother's an economist. It's an economical car.*

Reading and Vocabulary

1 a) Tick the words/phrases connected to the Internet that you know. Check new words/phrases in **V7.3** p128.

> a search engine   a chat room   a forum
> an online encyclopaedia   an online dating agency
> a blog   an online RPG   a webcam   an MP3 file
> a podcast   anti-virus software   wireless/Wi-Fi

b) Work in pairs. Which of the things in **1a)** have you used, visited or downloaded? What else do you use the Internet for?

2 a) Read the article. Match headings a)–e) to paragraphs 1–5.

a) Connecting people
b) How the Internet started
c) We can't live without it
d) It's our Internet
e) Taking the Internet to the people

b) Read the article again. What does it say about these dates, people and things?

> the 1980s   Al Gore   ARPANET   Charles Kline
> 1972   the World Wide Web   1990   news blogs

c) Work in pairs. Compare answers.

Our digital world

1 These days it's almost impossible to imagine a world without the Internet, or to **overestimate** its influence on our daily lives. It's therefore amazing to think that in the 1980s the Internet was only used by a handful of scientists, engineers and **postgraduate** computer experts.

2 Although **ex-vice president** of the USA, Al Gore, famously claimed that he had invented the Internet, it actually began back in the 1960s as part of a US government defence plan. The Internet (then known as ARPANET) first went online in 1969, when four computers at different American universities were connected together. A man called Charles Kline was the first person to try and connect to another computer via the Internet – but the system crashed when he typed in the G in LOGIN!

3 Email first appeared in 1972 and the first discussion groups started in 1979. Back then there were no computers in people's homes or offices, and anyone who wanted to use the Internet had to learn a very complex system. The Internet first became accessible to the **non-scientific** community in 1989, when British scientist Tim Berners-Lee invented the World Wide Web (the system which allows us to move from one website to another). The public were finally allowed access to the Internet in 1990 – and now we use it to do everything from watching a **preview** of a new film to talking to a friend on the other side of the world.

4 Perhaps the most **undervalued** function of the Internet is the way it brings people together. Email and instant messaging services have revolutionised global communication, while chat rooms, forums and blogs allow us to share opinions with people from all over the world. News reporting is no longer only in the hands of **multinational** media companies, as independent news blogs become more popular and influential. And whether you're a **pro-hunting** campaigner or an **anti-nuclear** activist, the Internet will help you find other people that share your views.

5 Of course the Internet can also be **misused**, and policing cyberspace remains a problem. However, the Internet has made us more independent and **self-reliant**, and has **redefined** our relationship with the outside world. And the most wonderful thing about the Internet is that it isn't owned by any government, organisation or corporation – cyberspace belongs to us all.

3 **a)** Look at the words in **bold** in the article. Underline the prefixes. Then complete the table with these meanings and the words in **bold**.

~~for~~ against   do something again   many
after   before   not   do something incorrectly
not enough   too much   of/by yourself   used to be

prefix	meaning	example
pro-	*for*	*pro-hunting*
anti-		
pre-		
post-		
under-		
over-		
multi-		
re-		
mis-		
ex-		
self-		
non-		

b) Work in pairs. Which prefixes can you use with these words? Sometimes there is more than one possible answer.

war   stop   government   cultural
millionaire   colleague   calculate
decorate   build   smoker   wife
understand   qualified   rated
defence   discipline

c) Check in **V7.4** p129.

4 Work in new pairs. Student A → p105. Student B → p108. Follow the instructions.

Listening

5 **a)** Look at pictures A–D. What are the people doing in each one?

b) **R7.2** Listen to four people discussing how they use the Internet. Put pictures A–D in the order they talk about them.

c) Listen again. Answer these questions.

1 Why was Ian surprised when he got to work this morning?
2 Why does Molly like shopping online?
3 Does Clive always pay for the songs he downloads?
4 Why hasn't Ian worked out how to download songs?
5 How many people can play an online RPG at any one time?
6 Why does Olivia use her webcam a lot?

• In spoken English there are often words and phrases that we can ignore, for example fillers (*um, you know*, etc.) and false starts (*It's … It's about the only thing …* , etc.).

6 **a)** Look at these sentences from R7.2. Underline the fillers and false starts.

1 Well, I've only … I'd only been away from the office for like a week.
2 Yeah, I generally, um, I buy a lot of things online too, especially, er, books and CDs and you know things like that.
3 You see, it's … it's just that I've never sort of found the time to work out how to do it.
4 Most of … a lot of my family live in the States, and we kind of, er, use the webcam to keep in touch.

b) **R7.2** Look at R7.2, p151. Listen to the first half of the conversation. Notice the fillers and false starts. Then listen to the second half of the conversation and underline the fillers and false starts.

7 **a)** Work in pairs. Write a survey to find out more about your class's Internet habits. Write at least four questions. Include three possible answers for each question.

1 *How much time do you spend on the Internet every week?*
 a) less than 2 hours
 b) between 2 and 6 hours
 c) more than 6 hours

b) Work on your own. Interview four other students. Make notes on their answers.

c) Work again with your partner from **7a**). Compare notes. Then tell the class about the results of your survey.

7D You're breaking up

Vocabulary on the phone
Real World problems on the phone
Help with Fluency sentence stress and weak forms (2)
Review prefixes

QUICK REVIEW ●●●

Write one word that begins with each of these prefixes: *pro-; anti-; pre-; post-; under-; over-; multi-; re-; mis-; ex-; self-; non-*. Work in pairs. Swap lists. Are your partner's words correct? Take turns to make sentences with four of your partner's words. Are your partner's sentences correct?

1 **a)** Guess the meaning of the words/phrases in **bold** in these questions. Check in **V7.5** p129.

1 Is your mobile **pay-as-you-go** or do you have **a contract**?
2 Which **network** are you with?
3 What's the **reception** like where you live? Do you ever **get cut off**?
4 How do you know when you're going to **run out of credit**?
5 How many different ways can you **top up your phone**?
6 Do you ever change the **ring tone** on your mobile?
7 How often do you check your **voicemail** or **answerphone** messages?
8 When was the last time you used **a payphone**?
9 Is it usually cheaper for you to call a mobile phone or **a landline**?
10 What do you usually say before you **hang up**?

b) Work in pairs. Take turns to ask and answer the questions in **1a)**. Ask follow-up questions if possible.

2 **a)** Work in groups. Discuss these questions.

1 How many different phones do you use in your day-to-day life?
2 Do you spend a lot of time on the phone? Who do you talk to most?
3 What problems can people have when they're on the phone?

b) **R7.3** Listen and match Tony's conversations 1–3 to photos A–C. What is each person doing next Tuesday?

c) Listen again. Answer these questions.

1 Where is Greg calling from?
2 What does Tony offer to do?
3 What time does Greg's flight arrive?
4 Why does Harry call Tony?
5 Where and when is the meeting?
6 Why does Tony call his wife, Jenny?
7 What does Tony suggest doing on Tuesday evening?

Real World Problems on the phone

3 **a)** Fill in the gaps with these words/phrases.

delay	any	breaking up	line	run out	catch
speak up	cut off	credit	losing	reception	

1 There's a bit of a _delay_ on the line.
2 Sorry, you're _____ a bit.
3 I didn't _____ all of that.
4 I'm just about to run out of _____ .
5 Sorry, it's a bad _____ .
6 You'll have to _____ a bit.
7 The _____ isn't very good here.
8 Sorry, I didn't get _____ of that.
9 I keep _____ you.
10 Sorry, we got _____ .
11 I think my battery's about to _____ .

b) Put these words in order to make questions.

1 your / Shall / you / call / landline / back / I / on ?
----
2 phone / like / back / me / you / you / to / Would ?
----
3 you / later / want / ring / Do / to / give / you / me / a ?
----

c) Check in **RW7.1** p130.

Jenny

Tony

Harry

Greg

60

4 a) Work in pairs. Write phone conversations for these prompts.

1

A Why don't we meet outside the cinema at seven?
B Sorry, I / not / get any / that. It's a / line.
A I said let's meet outside the cinema at seven.
B I keep / lose / you. I call you / on / landline?
A Yes, if you don't mind. I think / battery / run out.

2

A The meeting's at 3.30 in Room F.
B Sorry, I / not / catch all / that. You / break up / bit.
A I said, the meeting's at 3.30 in Room F.
B OK … Oh dear, I / about / run out / credit.
A / you like me / phone / back?
B That'd be great, thanks.

b) R7.4 Listen and check.

Help with Fluency Sentence stress and weak forms (2)

5 a) R7.4 Look at R7.4, p152. Listen again and notice the sentence stress and weak forms.

b) P Work in pairs. Practise the conversations in R7.4, p152 until you can remember them. Then close your books and have the conversations again. Try to use natural sentence stress and weak forms.

6 a) Work in new pairs. Plan a conversation that includes some phone problems. Make notes, but don't write the whole conversation.

b) Practise the conversation with your partner.

c) Work with another pair. Role-play your conversations. Which phone problems did you hear?

♫ R7.5 Look at the song *We Are the Champions* on p103. Follow the instructions.

---

1 a) Use these prompts to write true or false sentences about yourself. V7.1

1 I deserve ….
2 I don't own …
3 I adore …
4 … doesn't suit me.
5 I respect people who don't …
6 I don't envy people with …
7 Some of my possessions used to belong to …
8 I don't trust …

b) Work in pairs. Swap sentences. Guess which are true.

2 Choose the correct verb forms. G7.1

1 I *go/'m going* to the same place for my holiday every year.
2 This *is/is being* a great book. I *'ve read/'ve been reading* nearly 100 pages already.
3 Jo *works/'s working* in Rome this month. She *thinks/'s thinking* of moving there permanently.
4 She *'s/'s being* helpful today. That *'s/'s being* very unusual.
5 She *has/'s having* two jobs, but today she *has/'s having* the day off.

3 a) Fill in the gaps with the Present Perfect Simple or Present Perfect Continuous of these verbs. Use the continuous form if possible. G7.2

| go (x 2) know have become |
| study win look work |

1 I .... English for six or seven years.
2 I .... my neighbours since 2004.
3 I .... two holidays so far this year.
4 I .... never .... to Ireland.
5 I don't know anyone who .... the lottery.
6 I .... to bed quite late recently.

7 In the last couple of months I .... interested in politics.
8 I .... for my company since 2003.
9 I .... for a new job, but I haven't found one yet.

b) Choose five sentences from 3a) and make them true for you.

c) Work in pairs. Tell your partner your sentences.

4 Work in pairs. Find eight words related to business and trade. Then write a noun or an adjective for each word. V7.2

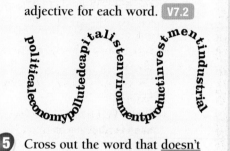

5 Cross out the word that <u>doesn't</u> match the prefix. V7.4

1	**over-**	estimate/rated/cultural
2	**multi-**	decorate/cultural/national
3	**anti-**	smoker/war/government
4	**mis-**	understand/used/hunting
5	**non-**	smoker/scientific/valued
6	**pre-**	understand/war/view
7	**pro-**	hunting/government/stop
8	**self-**	qualified/discipline/reliant

Progress Portfolio

a) Tick the things you can do in English.

☐ I can understand detailed information in a news programme.

☐ I can talk about business and trade.

☐ I can express in detail how things in the past connect to the present.

☐ I can understand a text giving information about technology.

☐ I can recognise fillers and false starts in everyday conversation.

☐ I can deal with problems on the phone.

b) What do you need to study again?
● 7A–D

8 Making ends meet

Vocabulary dealing with money
Grammar wishes (1); *I hope ...*;
It's time ...
Review Present Perfect Simple
and Present Perfect Continuous

QUICK REVIEW ●●●

Work in pairs. Ask questions to find out: something you've been doing longer than your partner; a place you've both been to; something you've both had for a long time; something you've both being doing recently: *How long have you been studying English?* Ask follow-up questions if possible.

Vocabulary Dealing with money

1 **a)** Match the phrases in A to their opposites in B. Check in **V8.1** p131.

A	B
invest money in something	get out of debt
be in credit	pay cash for something
get into debt	be overdrawn
buy/get something on credit	repay a loan
get a loan	spend money on something

have a good credit rating	be short (of money)
get a high interest rate	have a savings account
have a current account	get a low interest rate
be well off	put money into an account
take/get money out of an account	have a bad credit rating

b) Work in pairs. Take turns to test each other on the opposites in **1a)**.

(be in credit)   (be overdrawn)

Listening and Grammar

2 **a)** Work in pairs. What are the advantages and disadvantages of borrowing money from: family members, friends, banks, credit card companies?

b) **R8.1** Look at the photo of Eddy talking to his mother. Listen and choose the correct answers.

1 Eddy wants to borrow *the car/some money*.
2 Eddy's mother wants him to get *a car/a job*.
3 He's *an actor/a student*.
4 He *often gets/doesn't often get* into debt.
5 Eddy's waiting for *a phone call/a friend*.
6 He might get some work *in a bank/as a character in an advert*.
7 His mother needs *a lift/to do some shopping*.

3 **a)** Work in pairs. Who said these sentences, Eddy or his mother?

a) I wish I knew where your father was.
b) I wish you weren't chasing these impossible dreams.
c) I wish I could spare the time.
d) I wish you'd take more care of your things.
e) I hope she calls.
f) It's time you got your own car.
g) It's about time you found yourself a proper job.
h) It's time to go.

b) **R8.1** Listen again and check. Put the sentences in **3a)** in the order you hear them.

Help with Grammar *Wishes (1); I hope ...; It's time ...*

4 **a)** Look at sentences a)–d) in **3a)**. Answer these questions.

1 Do these sentences talk about: a) things that happened in the past? b) imaginary situations in the present?
2 Which verb form follows *I wish ...* in each sentence?

TIP! ● We can say *I wish ...* or *If only ...* : *I wish I could spare the time.* = *If only I could spare the time.*

b) Look again at sentence d) in **3a)**. Answer these questions.

1 What does Eddy's mother want him to do?
2 Does she think Eddy will do this?
3 Is she annoyed?

c) What is the difference in meaning and form between these sentences?

1 I hope she calls.
2 I wish she'd call.

d) Look at sentences f)–h) in **3a)**. Fill in the gaps in these rules with *Past Simple* or *infinitive with to*.

● We often use *It's (about) time* + subject + ... to say that we are annoyed or frustrated that something hasn't happened yet.

● We use *It's time* + ... to say that something should happen now.

e) Check in G8.1 p132.

5 **a)** Fill in the gaps with the correct form of the verbs in brackets.

1 I hope you __get__ (get) the job.
2 I wish you .... (stop) telling me what to do.
3 It's time you and Dad .... (buy) yourselves mobile phones.
4 If only I .... (not have to) work this evening.
5 I wish someone .... (tell) me if I've got the part.
6 It's time I .... (find) a cheaper flat.
7 I wish I .... (can) give up work altogether.
8 I wish it .... (not rain). I have to go out in a minute.

b) Match sentences 1–8 in **5a)** to these sentences.

a) If I could, I'd move tomorrow.
b) This waiting is driving me crazy.
c) Then I could stay at home and finish my book.
d) I could if we didn't owe so much money.
e) I'm going to get very wet.
f) I'm not a child any more.
g) It'd be great to see you on TV. *1*
h) If you did, you could call him.

c) Work in pairs. Compare answers. Who do you think said each pair of sentences, Eddy or his mother?

6 **a)** Write six wishes about your life now.

I wish I could take a year off work.
I wish I didn't have to work next weekend.

b) Work in pairs. Take turns to tell each other your wishes. Give reasons for your wishes. Ask follow-up questions.

I wish I could take a year off work because I really want to go travelling.

Get ready ... Get it right!

7 Think of five things that annoy you. Use these ideas or your own.

● junk mail
● TV adverts
● people's habits
● background music
● mobile phones
● call centres
● other drivers
● rubbish

8 **a)** Work in groups. Take turns to tell each other about the things that annoy you. Do you all get annoyed by the same things?

I wish companies would stop sending me so much junk mail.

Yes, it's really annoying, isn't it?

b) Tell the class about things that annoy everybody in your group.

READ

Every little helps

Vocabulary phrasal verbs (2): money
Grammar wishes (2); *should have*
Help with Listening wishes
Review wishes (1); *I hope ...* ; *It's time ...*

QUICK REVIEW ●●●
Complete these sentences about your country: *I wish ...* ; *I hope ...* ; *It's time ...* .
Work in pairs. Take turns to tell each other your sentences. If you're from the same country, do you agree? If you're from different countries, ask follow-up questions.

Vocabulary Phrasal verbs (2): money

1 **a)** Which words/phrases <u>don't</u> go with the verbs in **bold**? Check new words/phrases in V8.2 p131.

1 I **paid** ~~the account~~/the money/my brother **back**.
2 She **paid off** her mortgage/money/student loan.
3 I **took out** a mortgage/loan/bank account.
4 Mortgage rates/The banks/House prices have **gone down**.
5 The bill/meal/bank account **came to** £35.
6 I've **put down** a deposit/£25,000/a debt on a new house.
7 She **came into** some money/some property/a credit card.
8 The shop **took** £20/15%/100% **off** the price.
9 I'm **saving up for** a new bike/holiday/debt.
10 The hotel/shopkeeper/price **ripped** her **off**.

b) Work in pairs. Test your partner. Use the infinitive form of the verbs.

pay off

pay off a mortgage; pay off a student loan

Reading and Grammar

2 **a)** Work in pairs. Think of at least five things you could do in your country to earn some extra money.

b) Read the article and look at the cartoons. Which do you think is the best way to earn some extra money? Which is the worst?

3 **a)** Try to match these rates of pay in the UK to money-making schemes 1–6 in the article.

a) Between £30 and £100 a session.
b) The usual rate is £7–£10 an hour.
c) Between £70 and £220 a month.
d) Between £10 and £60 a session.
e) Between £8 and £18 an hour.
f) £8–£10 a visit, but could be as high as £100 a day.

b) Work in pairs. Compare answers. Then check on p159. Would you like to do any of these things? Why?/Why not?

How to make some extra cash

Who couldn't do with a little extra money? Maybe you need to pay off a loan or perhaps you just want to save up for a holiday. Whatever your reasons, these simple money-making schemes could make all the difference.

1

Larry

Pose as a live model. You don't have to be young or beautiful to pose for an art class. You just need to be able to sit still for a long time.

2
Invigilate exams. Lots of schools and universities need outside invigilators, mostly in January or during the summer.

Zoë

3

Frank

Join a focus group. If you love expressing your opinions on anything from apple juice to a new TV ad, this might be just the thing for you.

4
Take part in psychological research. It's interesting work because it's all about you, and involves things like simple memory tests or having brain scans while you talk.

Jill

5

Lois

Be a mystery shopper. These are people who are paid to go shopping, eat in restaurants or stay in hotels. All you have to do is write a report on how you were treated as a customer.

6
Let companies advertise on your car. If you travel a lot and you've got a nice car, it could have a starring role in an advertising campaign.

Josh

4 Six people tried these money-making schemes. Match speech bubbles A–F to the people in the cartoons.

> **A** **I wish the ad hadn't been so big.** It was embarrassing.

> **B** **I should have eaten before I went in.** I was starving by the end.

> **C** **I wish I'd learned this stuff about the brain before.** It's fascinating.

> **D** **I wish they hadn't chosen me for the coffee tasting group.** I didn't sleep all night.

> **E** **I should have started doing this years ago.** You're allowed to keep most of what you buy.

> **F** **I shouldn't have moved so often.** But it was so uncomfortable.

Help with Grammar Wishes (2); *should have*

5 **a)** Look at speech bubbles A–F. Are the people talking about the present or the past?

b) Look at the sentences in **bold** in speech bubbles A and B. Then choose the correct words/phrases.

1 The ad on Josh's car *was/wasn't* very big. He *liked/didn't like* it.
2 Zoë *ate/didn't eat* before she went in. She *regrets/doesn't regret* that.

c) Look at the sentences in **bold** in speech bubbles A–F. Answer these questions.

1 Which verb form follows *wish*?
2 Which verb form follows *should/shouldn't have*?

TIP! ● We can also use the third conditional for regrets: *If I'd known about this before, I'd have done it years ago.*

d) Check in **G8.2** p132.

Help with Listening *Wishes*

6 **a)** **R8.2** Listen to these sentences. Notice the difference between the verb forms.

1 I wish I had more time.   I wish I'd had more time.
2 I wish he talked more slowly.   I wish he'd talk more slowly.

b) **R8.3** Listen and write six sentences. You will hear each sentence twice.

7 **R8.4** **P** Listen and practise the sentences in **bold** in the speech bubbles.

I wish the ad hadn't been so big.

8 **a)** Correct the mistakes in these sentences.

1 I wish I didn't agree to do the memory tests. I was useless.
2 I wish they asked me to discuss the new car advert instead.
3 I shouldn't have allow them to paint it yellow. It looked awful.
4 I should insisted on a break after an hour so I could move around.
5 I loved the jewellery I bought. I wish I hadn't have to give it back.
6 I got so bored sitting there for hours. They should allowed me to read a book.

b) Work in pairs. Compare answers. Guess which of the people in the cartoons said each sentence.

9 Rewrite these sentences using the words in brackets.

1 I didn't pay off my student loan last year. (wish)
   I wish I'd paid off my student loan last year.
2 You didn't tell me your brother was on TV last night. (wish)
3 I ate too much at lunch. (If only)
4 I stayed out too late last night. (shouldn't)
5 My sister didn't pay me back the money she owed me. (should)
6 The interest rate didn't go down last month. (wish)
7 You didn't tell me you needed a lift this morning. (should)

Get ready ... Get it right!

10 Make notes on five things that you did or didn't do in the last six months that you now regret.

didn't buy laptop

11 **a)** Work in pairs. Take turns to tell your partner about the things you regret. Ask follow-up questions if possible. What does your partner regret most?

> I wish I'd bought a laptop when they were in the sale.

> How much were they selling them for?

b) Tell the class about the thing that your partner regrets the most.

Vocabulary synonyms
Skills Reading: International tipping etiquette; Listening: UK and US tipping habits
Help with Listening British and American accents
Review dealing with money; phrasal verbs (2): money

VOCABULARY AND SKILLS

QUICK REVIEW ●●●
Write five phrases or phrasal verbs connected to money: *get into debt*; *save up for*, etc. Work in pairs. Take turns to say a phrase or a phrasal verb. Your partner uses it in a sentence. Is the sentence correct?

Reading and Vocabulary

1 Work in groups. Discuss these questions.

1 Who do people usually give tips to in your country?
2 How much do people tip them?
3 Why might people decide not to tip them?

2 a) Read sentences 1–6 about tipping customs. Guess the correct words/phrases.

1 Tipping customs round the world are *fairly similar/quite different*.
2 People from the same country *usually agree/often disagree* about who and how much they should tip.
3 In most countries people *give/don't give* taxi drivers a 10% tip.
4 Most hotel porters in Europe *receive/don't receive* a tip.
5 When the service charge is included in a restaurant bill, people *sometimes/never* leave a tip.
6 People tip waiters and waitresses in *every country/most countries*.

b) Read the article. Check your answers to **2a)**.

c) Read the article again. Answer these questions.

1 If your country is mentioned in the article, do you agree with what it says? Why?/Why not?
2 If your country isn't mentioned, which countries in the article have similar tipping habits to yours?
3 Which information did you find surprising?

d) Work in groups. Compare answers.

International tipping etiquette

When you're abroad, trying to find out who to tip is never **straightforward** and neither is trying to work out the exact amount. To make things even more **complicated**, the rules for tipping **vary** greatly from country to country. Even people from the same country can't agree on how much to tip. However, here are some general guidelines which might help the traveller.

You face your first dilemma as soon as you land at the airport – the taxi ride. Taxi drivers **generally** do expect tips, but rather than there being a precise amount, people round up the fare, or just tell the driver to keep the change.

Your next encounter is with the hotel porter and you know he's expecting a tip, but the problem is trying to figure out how much. It seems that in many European countries €3–€5 would be an appropriate amount.

Then, of course, you have to eat. In some countries **such as** Ireland, Chile, Poland and Portugal, the **customary** tip in restaurants is 10–15% unless a service charge is included, so the first rule of thumb is always check the bill. In other countries such as France, Italy, Germany, Australia and Spain, where a 10–15% service charge is either very common or compulsory, you may want to leave an **additional** tip if you think the service was **particularly** good, but it certainly isn't obligatory. However, in some countries it may seem strange if you do leave a tip. In Iceland, for example, the waitress might be insulted if you tipped her. In Japan, if you left a tip, the restaurant staff wouldn't be offended, but you would probably be pursued down the street by someone trying to return your money. And in New Zealand, although it's unlikely anyone would chase after you, you'd definitely get some **odd** looks if you left a tip.

And your problem with tipping isn't over when you leave the restaurant. Next you discover the tour guide, the hairdresser and the toilet attendant are all expecting a tip, but again, how much? Perhaps the best option in these cases is to ask the local people what is acceptable or **observe** what others do. Of course, you could simply play safe and tip everyone you meet!

Help with Vocabulary **Synonyms**

● We often use synonyms to avoid repeating words or phrases when we are speaking or writing.

 3 **a)** Look at the words/phrases in pink in the article. Check any words you don't know with your teacher or in a dictionary.

b) Look at the words/phrases in blue in the article. Match them to these synonyms. Write the infinitive form of the verbs.

work out	*figure out*	certainly	
exact		insulted	
problem		chase	
appropriate		discover	
compulsory		simply	

c) Look at words a)–j). Match them to the synonyms in **bold** in the article.

a) simple *straightforward*
b) especially
c) usually
d) normal
e) strange

f) watch
g) extra
h) differ
i) difficult
j) for example

d) Check in V8.3 p131.

4 Work in pairs. Take turns to test each other on the synonyms in 3b) and 3c).

> What's the synonym of 'work out'?

> figure out

Listening

 5 **a)** What do you know about tipping in the UK and the USA?

b) R8.5 Listen to Graham, an Englishman, and Ruth, an American, having a conversation in a restaurant. Answer these questions.

1 Which country are Graham and Ruth in?
2 Why do restaurant staff in this country often introduce themselves?
3 Which other people who get tips do they discuss?
4 In which country do people give better tips?

c) Work in pairs. Listen again. Student A, make notes about tipping in the UK. Student B, make notes about tipping in the USA.

d) Work with your partner. Take turns to tell each other the information you heard.

Help with Listening
British and American accents

 6 **a)** R8.6 Listen to five sentences said twice. Which do you hear first, a British accent or an American accent?

b) British and American people usually say the letters in **bold** differently. How do you think they say these words?

1 bigge**r**, late**r**, mo**r**ning
2 wai**t**er, Bri**t**ish, be**tt**er
3 st**a**ff, gl**a**ss, h**a**lf
4 d**o**llar, c**o**ffee, w**a**nt
5 b**ou**ght, f**a**ll, w**a**ter

c) R8.7 Listen and check. You will hear the British person first.

d) R8.5 Look at R8.5, p152. Listen again and notice the difference between the two people's accents.

7 **a)** Work in pairs. Make a list of five groups of people that you think deserve tips (apart from waiters/waitresses and taxi drivers).

b) Compare lists with another pair. Choose the five groups of people who deserve tips the most.

c) Work in groups or with the whole class. Agree on a final list of five groups of people.

8D I didn't realise

Real World apologising
Help with Fluency linking (2)
Review synonyms

QUICK REVIEW ●●●
Write six words/phrases and their synonyms (*observe/watch*, etc.). Work in pairs. Take turns to say one word/phrase from each pair. Your partner says a synonym. Is it the same as yours?

1 a) Work in pairs. Make a list of reasons why you might need to apologise to someone.

turning up late   forgetting someone's birthday

b) Work with a new partner. Compare ideas. Which of the things on your list have you had to apologise for recently?

2 Look at photos A–C. What do you think Eddy is talking to the people about?

A
Eddy and the producer

B
Eddy and his mum

C
Eddy and his agent

3 a) R8.8 Listen to three conversations. Match conversations 1–3 to photos A–C. Why was Eddy surprised at the end of conversation 3?

b) Listen again. Tick the true sentences. Decide why the other sentences are false.

1 Eddy's agent has been really busy all day.
2 Eddy's going to do the Norland Bank advert.
3 Eddy knows how much he'll earn from the cat food advert.
4 Eddy's mother really liked the vase that Eddy broke.
5 Eddy apologised for borrowing money off his mum.
6 Eddy had met the actress before.
7 Eddy's producer hadn't sent him a script.

Real World Apologising

4 a) Match sentences 1–16 to meanings a)–c).

a) apologising
b) giving reasons for your actions or being self-critical
c) responding to an apology

1 I'm **sorry that** I didn't get back to you sooner. *a)*
2 I didn't realise (the time).
3 Don't worry about it.
4 Never mind.
5 I'm really sorry. I'm afraid (I broke your vase).
6 It doesn't matter.
7 I'm **sorry about** (this afternoon).
8 I shouldn't have (said those things to you).
9 I can't believe (I said that).
10 I didn't mean to (upset you).
11 Forget about it.
12 I'm **sorry for** (borrowing money off you all the time).
13 I thought (you knew each other) for some reason.
14 Oh, that's alright.
15 I had no idea (you'd need a script).
16 No need to apologise.

b) Look at the phrases in **bold** in **4a)**. Complete these rules with *a noun*, *a clause* or *verb+ing*.

● After *I'm sorry (that)* we use ....
● After *I'm sorry about* we usually use ....
● After *I'm sorry for* we usually use ....

c) Check in RW8.1 p132.

5 a) Fill in the gaps in these conversations with one word. Use language from **4a).**

1

A I'm sorry ¹ *that* I called you an idiot. I can't ² .... I said that.

B Forget ³ .... it. You're under a lot of pressure.

A I didn't ⁴ .... to upset you.

2

A I'm really sorry ⁵ .... last night. I ⁶ .... have phoned so late.

B No ⁷ .... to apologise. I went straight back to sleep anyway.

A I had no ⁸ .... it was that late. I thought it was much earlier for some reason.

3

A Sorry ⁹ .... losing my temper with you the other day.

B Don't ¹⁰ .... about it.

A I'd only had about two hours' sleep.

B Really, it doesn't ¹¹ .... I could tell you were absolutely exhausted.

b) R8.9 Listen and check.

Help with Fluency Linking (2)

6 a) R8.9 Look at R8.9, p153. Listen again and notice the different types of linking.

b) P Work in pairs. Practise the conversations in R8.9, p153 until you can remember them. Then close your books and have the conversations again. Try to use natural linking and rhythm.

c) Work with another pair. Take turns to role-play two of the conversations. Which pair remembered the conversations best?

7 Work in pairs. Turn to p111. Follow the instructions.

---

8 Review

Language Summary 8, p131

1 a) Write the opposites of these phrases. V8.1

1 put money into an account
2 have a current account
3 be well off
4 get a high interest rate
5 get a loan
6 get out of debt
7 be overdrawn
8 have a bad credit rating

b) Work in pairs. Compare answers.

2 a) Look at these phrases about the present or future. Fill in the gaps with the correct form of the verbs in brackets. Then complete the sentences for you. G8.1

1 I wish I .... (know) how to ...
2 It's time I .... (think) about ...
3 I hope I .... (get) ...
4 I wish I .... (can) speak ...
5 It's time I .... (buy) ...
6 I hope I .... (can) have ...
7 I wish I .... (not have to) ...

b) Work in pairs. Say your sentences. Ask follow-up questions if possible.

3 a) Write five sentences about things you wish were different at school, university, work or home. G8.1

I wish people wouldn't arrive late.

b) Work in pairs. Tell your partner your sentences.

4 a) Complete these phrasal verbs. V8.2

1 pay some money ....
2 come .... some money
3 rip somebody ....
4 pay .... a loan
5 put .... a deposit
6 take 10% .... the price
7 the total comes £200
8 save up .... a new car
9 take .... a mortgage
10 prices are going ....

b) Work in pairs. Compare answers.

5 Fill in the gaps with the correct form of the verbs in brackets. G8.2

1 I should .... my mother on her birthday, but I forgot. (phone)
2 I wish someone .... me there was a meeting. (tell)
3 I wish I .... this coat – it doesn't suit me. (not buy)
4 I shouldn't .... at my boss. She was furious. (shout)
5 I wish I .... more time in the exam. I didn't finish it. (have)
6 I shouldn't .... Mark any money last month. He never paid me back. (lend)

6 a) Replace the underlined words with a synonym. V8.3

In this café tips ¹definitely aren't ²obligatory, so I always try to ³work out who'll give me one. Most people ⁴usually leave an ⁵acceptable amount and they often ask if we actually get the tip or if it ⁶simply goes to the restaurant. When foreign visitors ⁷discover that 10% is the ⁸normal tip, they often leave the ⁹exact amount . However, Americans usually leave an ¹⁰extra 5–10%.

b) Work in pairs. Compare answers.

Progress Portfolio

a) Tick the things you can do in English.

☐ I can talk about my financial situation.

☐ I can express wishes and hopes about the present and the future.

☐ I can express wishes and regrets about the past.

☐ I can understand an article giving general advice.

☐ I can understand standard British and American accents.

☐ I can apologise politely and respond appropriately to apologies.

b) What do you need to study again? 8A–D

9 Out and about

9A The Oscars

Vocabulary the cinema
Grammar the passive
Review apologising

QUICK REVIEW ● ● ●
Write two things that you think people should apologise for. Work in pairs. Swap papers. Imagine you did the things on your partner's paper. Think of reasons why you did them. Take turns to apologise, give reasons and respond to your partner's apology.

Vocabulary The cinema

1 **a)** Tick the words/phrases in **bold** that you know. Check new words/phrases in **V9.1** p133.

1 Do you read film **reviews**? If so, who's your favourite **critic**?
2 Do you prefer films in English to be **subtitled** or **dubbed**?
3 What was the last **remake** or **sequel** you saw?
4 Can you name any films that **are set in** the future or have amazing **special effects**?
5 Have you seen a film that's **based on** a book you've read?
6 Which is more important for a film to be successful – a strong **cast** or a good plot?
7 Which actor gave the best **performance** you've seen this year?
8 Who's your favourite film character? Which actor or actress played this **role**?
9 Have you ever bought the **soundtrack** of a film?
10 What's your favourite **scene** in a movie?

b) Work in pairs. Take turns to ask and answer the questions in 1a). Ask follow-up questions if possible.

Reading and Grammar

2 **a)** Work in groups. Discuss these questions.

1 Have you ever watched the Academy Awards ceremony on TV? Why?/Why not?
2 Can you name any films, actors or actresses that have won an Oscar?
3 Which films, actors or actresses would you nominate for an award? Why?

b) Work in pairs. Predict the correct answers in these sentences about the Academy Awards.

1 The Academy Awards are usually held in *March/May*.
2 They began *before/after* 1940.
3 They have *sometimes/never* been postponed.
4 Newspapers *are/aren't* given the winners' names before the ceremony.
5 One actress was awarded an Oscar after being on the screen for just *8/18* minutes.
6 The Oscars *are/aren't* made of solid gold.

c) Read the article on p71. Check your answers to 2b).

3 Read the article again. What does it say about these numbers and dates?

| 40 million | 1953 | 1981 | 1939 | 55 | 52 | 3 | 400 |

Help with Grammar The passive

4 PASSIVE VERB FORMS

a) Look at the phrases in pink in the article. Then choose the correct words in these rules.

● We usually use the *passive/active* when we are more interested in what happens to somebody or something than in who or what does the action.
● We often use the passive when we *know/ don't know* who or what does the action.
● To make the passive we use: subject + *be/have* + past participle.

b) Match the phrases in pink to these passive verb forms.

1 Present Simple Passive *is held*
2 Present Continuous Passive
3 Past Simple Passive
4 Past Continuous Passive
5 Present Perfect Simple Passive
6 Past Perfect Simple Passive
7 Passive form of *be going to*

OTHER PASSIVE STRUCTURES

c) Look at the phrases in blue in the article. Then complete these rules with *be + past participle*, *to be + past participle* or *being + past participle*.

● After certain verbs (e.g. *enjoy*) we use … *being + past participle*
● After certain verbs (e.g. *want*) we use …
● After prepositions we use …
● After *the first/second/last* (+ noun) we use …
● After *have to* and *used to* we use …
● After modal verbs we use …

d) Check in **G9.1** p134.

And the winner is...

Everyone enjoys being told they are good at what they do and most of us want to be rewarded in some way. But few of us get the same publicity as those working in the film industry, and every actor dreams of being nominated for an Oscar. The Academy Awards ceremony is held in Hollywood once a year, usually in March, and is being shown in more and more countries each year. Over 40 million people in the USA watch the ceremony on TV, all wondering if their favourite stars are going to be awarded an Oscar.

Rachel Weisz (2006)

Take a look at these facts about the Oscars:

The first Academy Awards ceremony was held in 1929 and the first to be televised was in 1953.

Since the Academy Awards began they have only been postponed three times. The ceremony had to be postponed in 1938 because of a flood, in 1968 for Martin Luther King's funeral and again in 1981 after the assassination attempt on President Reagan.

Newspapers used to be given the winners' names in advance of the ceremony, provided that the names wouldn't be published until afterwards. However, in 1939 the Los Angeles Times printed the names before the ceremony so since then they have been kept secret.

Judi Dench was given an Oscar for her role as Queen Elizabeth I in the film Shakespeare in Love. That was the first time anyone had been nominated for a performance that lasted only eight minutes.

A few days before the ceremony in 2000, 55 Oscars mysteriously vanished while they were being driven from Chicago to Los Angeles. 52 of the Oscars were found in some rubbish by a man called Willie Fulgear, who was invited to the Oscar ceremony as a special guest in recognition of his honesty.

It seems that the true origin of the name 'Oscar' has never been confirmed. However, one story claims that Academy librarian, Margaret Herrick, said the statue looked like her uncle Oscar and the name stuck.

The Oscars are made of a metal alloy, which is then gold-plated. Each weighs about 3 kilos and costs around $400 to make.

Roberto Benigni (1999)

---

5 a) Read about the Indian film industry. Choose the correct verb forms.

Bollywood ¹*is/is being* the biggest film industry in the world, and its films ²*watch/are watched* by 15 million people in cinemas across India every day. The films always ³*include/are included* music, spectacular dancing and romance, and usually ⁴*last/are lasted* over three hours. The first Bollywood film ⁵*to be produced/being produced* was in 1908, and by 1930 over 200 films ⁶*were making/were being made* every year. Now studios in Mumbai ⁷*produce/are produced* over 800 films a year, which can ⁸*see/be seen* all over the world. Bollywood ⁹*spends/is spent* far less on production than Hollywood, but now the industry ¹⁰*is forcing/is being forced* to spend more to compete with big-budget American films. So if you enjoy ¹¹*transporting/being transported* to another world, you should ¹²*go/be gone* and see a Bollywood film!

b) [R9.1] Listen and check. Did any of the information surprise you?

6 Rewrite these sentences using a passive verb form. Begin each sentence with the words in brackets.

1 I hate it when people interrupt me.
   (I …) *I hate being interrupted.*
2 You should take the pills with food.
   (The pills …)
3 She doesn't like people telling her what to do. (She doesn't like …)
4 I hope they promote me next year.
   (I hope …)
5 They invited him first. (He was the first …)
6 They had to take her to hospital. (She …)
7 They'll deliver the parcel to me tomorrow. (The parcel …)
8 Someone needs to tell the boss immediately. (The boss …)

Get ready ... Get it right!

7 Work in groups. Group A → p106.
Group B → p109. Follow the instructions.

9B What was it like?

Vocabulary entertainment adjectives
Grammar *as, like, such as, so, such*
Review the cinema

Vocabulary Entertainment adjectives

1 **a)** Tick the adjectives you know. Check new words in **V9.2** p133.

> far-fetched believable predictable moving
> fast-moving slow-moving sentimental
> gripping memorable overrated underrated
> realistic scary weird hilarious

b) Choose six adjectives from **1a)**. Write the name of one film, play or TV drama for each adjective. Don't write the adjectives.

c) Work in pairs. Swap papers. Take turns to ask your partner why he/she chose the films, plays or TV dramas.

Listening and Grammar

2 **a)** **R9.2** Look at the photo. Listen to Richard and Gillie talking to their friend Nick. Answer these questions.

1 What have Richard and Gillie just been to see?
2 Did they enjoy it? Why?/Why not?

b) Listen again. Choose the correct words/phrases in these sentences.

1 *Critics/Actors* **such as** Amis Jones loved it.
2 Well, Jones was *right/wrong*, **like** he usually is.
3 I *don't like/don't mind* Amis Jones **as** a critic.
4 Even though it has *actors/directors* **like** Sy Harris and May Firth?
5 The whole thing was **like** a *wonderful/bad* dream.
6 There were just some black boxes which were used **as** *tables and chairs/beds*.
7 It had **such** a good *cast/plot*.
8 The plot was **so** *believable/far-fetched*.
9 I've no idea why **so many** critics *liked/hated* it.
10 I can't understand why it's getting **so much** *attention/criticism*.

Nick   Richard   Gillie

Help with Grammar *as, like, such as, so, such*

3 *AS, LIKE, SUCH AS*

a) Look at sentences 1–6 in **2b)**. Match the sentences to these rules.

● We use *such as* or *like* to introduce examples. __1__ , _____
● We use *as* + noun to say that somebody has a particular job. _____
● We also use *as* + noun to say what something is used for. _____
● We use *like* + clause to say that things happen in a similar way. _____
● We use *like* + noun (or pronoun) to say that something is similar to something else. _____

SO, SUCH

b) Look at sentences 7–10 in **2b)**. We use *so* and *such* to give nouns, adjectives and adverbs more emphasis. Complete these rules with *so* or *such*.

● We use _____ + adjective
● We use _____ (+ adjective) + noun
● We use _____ + much or many + noun

TIP! ● With *so* and *such* we often use '(*that*) + clause' to say what the consequence is: *The play was so slow (**that**) I actually fell asleep.*

c) Check in **G9.2** p134.

4 **a)** Fill in the gaps with *as*, *like*, *such as*, *so* or *such*. Sometimes there is more than one possible answer.

1

A Sorry I'm ¹ _so_ late. It took ² _____ a long time to get here.

B Don't worry. Brad's late too, ³ _____ he usually is. Anyway, I'm ⁴ _____ pleased we got tickets.

A Me too. It's had ⁵ _____ much good publicity that I didn't think we would.

B Yes, I've read ⁶ _____ many great reviews.

2

A Adela looks gorgeous, ⁷ _____ she usually does. She's got ⁸ _____ beautiful hair.

B Yes, she could easily find work ⁹ _____ a model.

A Apparently she's already had offers from agencies ¹⁰ _____ Now and Model Two.

B And she's ¹¹ _____ tall. I feel ¹² _____ a little kid when I'm standing next to her.

3

A Have you got anything I can use ¹³ _____ a vase for these flowers?

B Oh, they're ¹⁴ _____ lovely. Who are they from?

A My son. It was ¹⁵ _____ a surprise. He's never done anything ¹⁶ _____ that before.

b) Work in pairs. Compare answers. If your answers are different, are they both possible?

5 **a)** Choose the correct words/phrases.

1 Have you ever been to see classic films *such as/as* Gone with the Wind or Casablanca?

2 Do you know anyone who has worked *as/like* an extra in a film?

3 Have you ever been to see a film that was *such/so* bad that you walked out?

4 Do you enjoy watching reality TV programmes *as/like* Big Brother?

5 Have you ever seen a film with *such/so* a sad ending that you cried?

6 Do you ever use TV *as/like* a way of getting to sleep?

7 Has anyone ever said you look *as/like* someone famous?

8 Why do you think *so/such* many people still go to the cinema?

b) Work in pairs. Take turns to ask and answer the questions in **5a)**. Ask follow-up questions if possible.

Get ready ... Get it right!

6 **a)** Work in new pairs. Choose a film, play or a TV drama you've seen recently that your partner hasn't seen.

b) Work on your own. Write five sentences with *as*, *like*, *such as*, *so* or *such* about your film, play or TV drama. Use these ideas or your own.

- the cast
- the main characters
- good/bad performances
- the ending
- the soundtrack
- special effects
- the plot
- your opinion

I thought 'Pirates of the Caribbean' was such an overrated film, even though Johnny Depp was so good as a pirate.

7 **a)** Work with your partner. Take turns to tell him/her about your film, play or TV drama. Include your sentences from **6b)** where appropriate. Ask follow-up questions if possible.

b) Tell the class two things you remember about your partner's film, play or TV drama.

9C Is it art?

Vocabulary homonyms
Skills Listening: Call that art?;
Reading: Michael Landy
Help with Listening missing
words, reduced infinitives
Review *as*, *like*, *such as*, *so*, *such*

QUICK REVIEW ● ● ●
Complete these sentences for yourself: *I love visiting places such as … ; I wouldn't like to work as a … ; I look a bit like my … ; I've got so many … that I … ; I enjoy TV programmes like … .* Work in pairs. Take turns to tell your partner your sentences. Ask follow-up questions.

Listening

1 Work in groups. Discuss these questions.

1 Name one artist whose work you like and one whose work you don't like. Why do/don't you like them?
2 Look at works of art A–D. Do you know any of these works of art? Do you like any of them? Why?/Why not?

Edgar Degas 'Racehorses in Front of the Grandstand' (1866-68)

Tracey Emin 'My Bed' (1999)

The AARON Computer Programme (2006)

Rachel Whiteread 'Embankment' (2005)

2 a) R9.3 Listen to two friends, Gary and Rita, talking about art. Put works of art A–D in the order they talk about them.

b) Listen again. Tick the true sentences. Correct the false ones.

1 Neither Gary nor Rita likes Rachel Whiteread's sculptures.
2 Gary didn't go and see Tracey Emin's *My Bed*.
3 Rita says the bed showed the artist's love of sleeping.
4 Neither Gary nor Rita thought the K Foundation's project was good.
5 Rita thinks computer-generated paintings are art.
6 People have always appreciated Degas's work.

Help with Listening
Missing words, reduced infinitives

● In informal spoken English we often miss out words when the meaning is clear.

3 a) Read the beginning of Gary and Rita's conversation. Notice the missing words. What types of word do we often miss out?

GARY And how's work?
RITA Yeah, (it's) fine.
GARY And your mum? (Is) She any better?
RITA (She's) Much better, thanks.
GARY Did you go and see her last week?
RITA No, I meant to. (I'm) Going (on) Wednesday though. (I) Just couldn't get any time off work last week. I tried to, but we were too busy.

b) Look at the reduced infinitives in blue in 3a). What do they refer back to?

c) R9.3 Look at R9.3, p154. Listen again and notice the missing words. What do the reduced infinitives in **bold** refer back to?

Reading and Vocabulary

4 Work in groups. Discuss these questions.

1 How many possessions do you think you own?
2 Which do you really need?
3 If you were only allowed to keep three of your possessions, which would you choose and why?

5 **a)** Read the article about Michael Landy. Write a title for the article.

b) Work in the same groups as in **4**. Take turns to tell each other your title and why you chose it. Which do you think is the best and why?

c) Read the article again. Choose the correct answers.

1 It took Landy *a few weeks/a long time* to plan the exhibition.
2 He *kept a few things/didn't keep anything*.
3 *Most people hated/There was a mixed reaction to* the exhibition.
4 Landy probably thinks consumerism is a *good/bad* thing.
5 He felt *pleased/upset* at the end of the exhibition.
6 Landy *sold/didn't sell* his destroyed possessions.

d) Would you have gone to see *Break Down* if you'd been in London? Why?/Why not?

Help with Vocabulary Homonyms

- Homonyms are words with the same spelling and pronunciation, but different meanings (*light*, *last*, etc.).

6 **a)** Look at the words in pink in the article. Then fill in the gaps in these pairs of sentences with the same word. The first sentence in each pair shows the meaning of the word as it is used in the article.

1 a) He's in no .... to go to work. He's very ill.
  b) Which US .... is Hollywood in?
2 a) He can .... most problems on his own.
  b) I broke the .... on the window.
3 a) It was a typical .... of food poisoning.
  b) Have you seen my camera .... ?
4 a) That was an interesting .... John made.
  b) At that .... I left the meeting.
5 a) I had to go all .... the town to find a hotel.
  b) I'd like to get a .... table for the kitchen.

b) Work in pairs. Compare answers. Explain the different meanings of each word.

c) Work with your partner. Look at the words in blue in the article. Discuss what these words mean in this context. Then think of another meaning for each word.

d) Check in V9.3 p133.

---

7 Fill in the gaps with the words in blue in the article.

1 Would you .... opening the window, please?
2 This magazine article doesn't make any ....
3 We'll have to .... him. He's always being rude to customers.
4 Have you got .... for a pound?
5 The doctor gave him a complete .... and he was fine.

8 Work in pairs. Turn to p112. Follow the instructions.

Michael Landy *Break Down* (2001)

In 2001, artist Michael Landy destroyed all his possessions in a work he called *Break Down*. The exhibition, which was held in an empty department store in central London, cost £100,000 to put on and lasted for two weeks. Landy had spent three years cataloguing the 7,226 separate items. More than 45,000 people came to watch him and his ten helpers destroy everything he'd ever owned, right down to his last sock, his passport and even his beloved Saab.

Many of those who came to the exhibition applauded and encouraged Landy in his two weeks of destruction, but his mother wasn't one of them. "I had to throw my mum out," said Landy. "She started crying and I couldn't handle those emotions. She had to go."

Many other people were equally upset, especially those in the art world who thought it was unacceptable to destroy famous artists' work. Landy destroyed pieces of art given to him by people such as Tracey Emin and Damien Hirst. But on that point Landy said he felt no guilt. After all, he had destroyed all his own work – a collection that spanned 15 years.

Landy said that *Break Down* was an examination of consumerism* – others said it was a case of madness. In fact, a priest and a psychiatrist believed he was mentally ill and offered him counselling. However, Landy's description of his state of mind at that time was very different. "When I finished I did feel an incredible sense of freedom," he said, "the possibility that I could do anything. But the freedom is eroded by the everyday concerns of life. Life was much simpler when I was on my platform."

The art world eagerly awaited the destroyed remains of his possessions. Indeed, Landy was supposed to give the sacks of crushed metal, plastic and paper to the people who had given him financial backing for the project, and each sack would have been worth £4,000. But he had a change of heart at the last minute and ended up burying it all.

After the exhibition, offers from galleries all round the world poured in. He was even asked to repeat *Break Down* in a Brazilian gallery. However, as Landy points out, *Break Down* was a one-off – it couldn't happen twice.

* consumerism = when too much attention is given to buying and owning things

9D It's up to you

Real World making and responding to suggestions
Help with Fluency natural rhythm
Review homonyms

QUICK REVIEW ● ● ●

Write four homonyms (*state*, etc.). Work in pairs. Swap lists. Take turns to say two sentences for each of your partner's words to show different meanings: *Which state is Miami in? My garden's in a terrible state.* Are your partner's sentences correct?

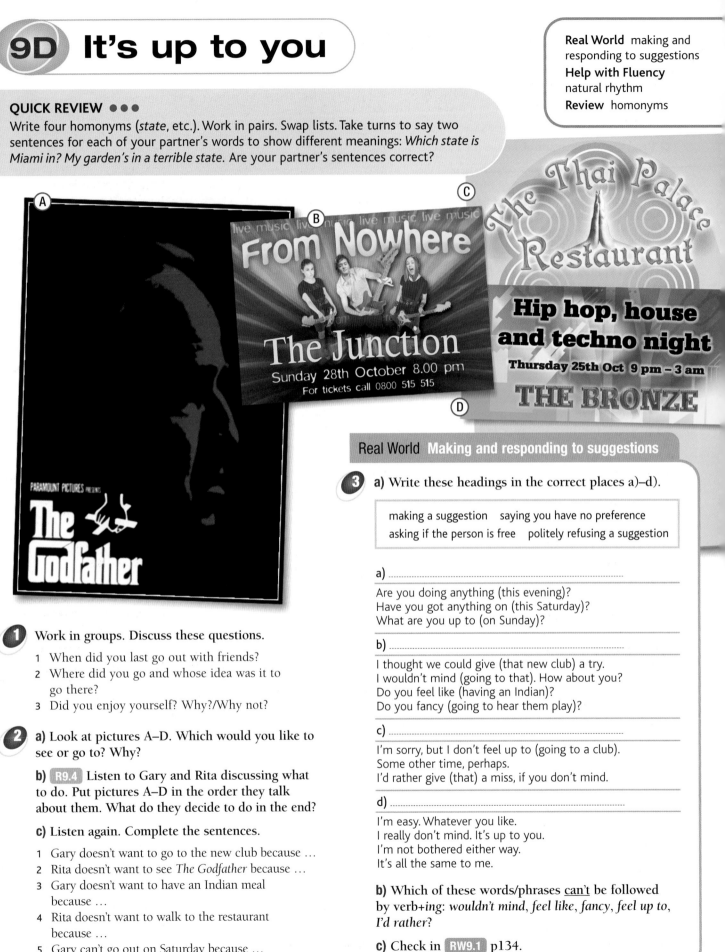

1 Work in groups. Discuss these questions.

1 When did you last go out with friends?
2 Where did you go and whose idea was it to go there?
3 Did you enjoy yourself? Why?/Why not?

2 a) Look at pictures A–D. Which would you like to see or go to? Why?

b) R9.4 Listen to Gary and Rita discussing what to do. Put pictures A–D in the order they talk about them. What do they decide to do in the end?

c) Listen again. Complete the sentences.

1 Gary doesn't want to go to the new club because …
2 Rita doesn't want to see *The Godfather* because …
3 Gary doesn't want to have an Indian meal because …
4 Rita doesn't want to walk to the restaurant because …
5 Gary can't go out on Saturday because …
6 Rita suggests going to The Junction because …

Real World Making and responding to suggestions

3 a) Write these headings in the correct places a)–d).

making a suggestion   saying you have no preference
asking if the person is free   politely refusing a suggestion

a) ....
Are you doing anything (this evening)?
Have you got anything on (this Saturday)?
What are you up to (on Sunday)?

b) ....
I thought we could give (that new club) a try.
I wouldn't mind (going to that). How about you?
Do you feel like (having an Indian)?
Do you fancy (going to hear them play)?

c) ....
I'm sorry, but I don't feel up to (going to a club).
Some other time, perhaps.
I'd rather give (that) a miss, if you don't mind.

d) ....
I'm easy. Whatever you like.
I really don't mind. It's up to you.
I'm not bothered either way.
It's all the same to me.

b) Which of these words/phrases <u>can't</u> be followed by verb+*ing*: *wouldn't mind, feel like, fancy, feel up to, I'd rather*?

c) Check in RW9.1 p134.

4

a) Gary wants to meet up with another friend, Jennifer. Write Gary's half of the conversation from these prompts. Use language from **3a)**.

GARY / you got anything / this Sunday?
Have you got anything on this Sunday?

GARY / you fancy / come / to see Rita's brother's band?

GARY No, don't worry, that's OK. So what / you up / today?

GARY Well, I / not mind / go / see *The Godfather*. How / you?

GARY It's on at 5.00 and 8.20.

GARY I / mind which one we go to. It's / you.

GARY OK. 8.20's fine. / feel like / have / something to eat first?

GARY / easy. / you like.

b) Work in pairs. Write Jennifer's half of the conversation in **4a)**.

c) `R9.5` Listen to Gary and Jennifer's conversation. How similar is it to yours?

Help with Fluency
Natural rhythm

5

a) `R9.5` Look at R9.5, p154. Listen again and notice the sentence stress and weak forms.

b) `P` Work with your partner from **4b)**. Practise the conversation in R9.5, p154. Take turns to be Gary and Jennifer. Try to use natural rhythm.

c) Work with the same partner. Practise the conversation you wrote in **4b)**.

6

a) Make a list of some good places to go and things to do in the town/city you're in now.

b) Work in groups of three. Agree on some things to do and when to do them. Use the language from **3a)** in your conversation.

c) Tell the class what you have decided to do. Would any other students like to join you?

---

9 Review
Language Summary 9, p133

1 Work in pairs. What is the difference between the pairs of words/phrases? V9.1

1 a critic, a review
2 a subtitled film, a dubbed film
3 a remake, a sequel
4 an actor's role, an actor's performance
5 a cast, a scene
6 a soundtrack, special effects

2 **a)** Look at the <u>underlined</u> verb forms. Tick the correct verb forms. Change the incorrect ones. G9.1

As a child I ¹<u>used to describe</u> as shy, so I ²<u>was surprised</u> everyone when I announced I ³<u>had being accepted</u> by a drama school in Bath. The audition ⁴<u>had been</u> awful so I was sure I ⁵<u>wouldn't offer</u> a place, but I was. Of course, ⁶<u>I'd expected to ask</u> to perform a speech from a play, but I had no idea they ⁷<u>had to be convinced</u> that I ⁸<u>could sing</u> as well. Unfortunately I ⁹<u>was the first to being asked</u> to sing. I ¹⁰<u>hate be laughed at</u> and that's exactly what ¹¹<u>happened</u>. But I ¹²<u>didn't run off</u> the stage like others who ¹³<u>were being auditioned</u> – perhaps that's why I ¹⁴<u>accepted</u>.

b) Work in pairs. Compare answers.

3 **a)** Complete these adjectives connected to entertainment. V9.2

1 far-_ _ _ _ _ _ _
2 pred_ _ _ _ _ _ _
3 mov_ _ _
4 sent_ _ _ _ _ _ _
5 under_ _ _ _ _
6 sca_ _
7 memor_ _ _ _
8 grip_ _ _ _
9 bel_ _ _ _ _ _ _
10 over_ _ _ _ _
11 hil_ _ _ _ _
12 real_ _ _ _ _

b) Work in pairs. Use words from **3a)** to talk about the last film you saw.

4 **a)** Choose the correct words/phrases. Then tick the sentences that are true for you. G9.2

1 I always have something healthy *such as/as* fruit and yoghurt for breakfast.
2 I walked here today, *like/such as* I usually do.
3 I've got *so/such* many things to do when I get home tonight.
4 I look *as/like* my mother.
5 I'm usually *so/such* hungry after class.
6 I've never worked *as/like* a shop assistant.
7 I had *so/such* much fun last weekend.
8 I've had *so/such* a busy day today.

b) Work in pairs. Take turns to tell each other your sentences. Ask follow-up questions.

5 **a)** Write two sentences for each of these homonyms to show different meanings. V9.3

case   state   round
change   handle

b) Work in pairs. Compare sentences. Are your partner's sentences correct?

Progress Portfolio

a) Tick the things you can do in English.

☐ I can talk about and express my opinion on different forms of entertainment.

☐ I can say that things are similar.

☐ I can follow a discussion in which the speakers don't agree on a topic.

☐ I can add emphasis.

☐ I can recognise when words are missed out in natural conversation.

☐ I can make and respond appropriately to suggestions.

b) What do you need to study again? ● 9A–D

10 The great divide

10A How practical are you?

QUICK REVIEW ●●●
Work in groups. Imagine you are planning to spend tomorrow evening together. Take turns to make and respond to suggestions. Decide where you're going to eat and what else you're going to do.

> **Vocabulary** household jobs
> **Grammar** *have/get something done, get somebody to do something, do something yourself*
> **Review** making and responding to suggestions

Vocabulary Household jobs

1 a) Which words/phrases <u>don't</u> go with the verbs? Check new words/phrases in p135.

1. change *a plug/a leak/a light bulb*
2. put up *shelves/a lock/a fence*
3. put in *new lighting/a burglar alarm/a duvet*
4. fix *a leak/the roof/a key*
5. check *DIY/the tyres/the oil*
6. decorate *a flat/a room/a bath*
7. replace *a lock/a flat/a window*
8. dry-clean *the floor/a suit/a duvet*
9. cut *the grass/a window/a key*
10. service *a car/clothes/a boiler*

b) Work in pairs. Think of one more word/phrase for each verb in **1a)**.

2 a) Which of the things in **1a)** do the women in your family usually do and which do the men usually do?

b) Work in pairs. Compare ideas. Are any the same?

Listening and Grammar

3 a) Look at the photos. How practical do you think these women are? Try to fill in the gaps with the women's names.

1. .... is very practical.
2. .... is quite practical.
3. .... is not very practical.
4. .... is not at all practical.

b) R10.1 Listen and check.

c) Work in pairs. Who said these sentences, Jan, Donna, Sheena or Penny?

a) I still **get** my car **serviced** at the local garage. *Jan*
b) I **get** my husband **to do** most things round the house.
c) We usually **have** the decorating **done** professionally.
d) I **do** most things round the house **myself**.
e) Now I'm **having** the bathroom **redecorated**.
f) I'd never **had** any kitchen appliances **serviced** before.
g) I've **had** lots of things **done** recently.
h) The roof was leaking so I **got** that **fixed**.
i) I'll **get** the door lock **replaced** as soon as I can.

d) Listen again and check. Put the sentences in **3c)** in the order you hear them.

Jan

Donna

Sheena

Penny

Help with Grammar
have/get something done, get somebody to do something, do something yourself

4 **a)** Look at sentences a)–d) in **3c)**. Match them to meanings 1–3.

1 The speaker pays somebody else to do the job. *a)* , ...

2 The speaker asks somebody they know to do the job. If it's a friend or family member, he/she probably doesn't pay them. ......

3 The speaker does the job without any help from other people. ......

b) Look again at sentences a)–c) in **3c)**. Complete these rules with *past participle* or *infinitive with to*.

- subject + *have* or *get* + something + ...
- subject + *get* + somebody + ... + something

c) Look at the phrases in **bold** in sentences e)–i) in **3c)**. Match the sentences to these verb forms.

1 Present Continuous *e)*
2 Present Perfect Simple
3 Past Simple
4 Past Perfect Simple
5 *will* + infinitive

d) Make negatives and *yes/no* questions for these sentences.

1 Jan has her car serviced regularly.
2 Donna had her hair cut yesterday.
3 Sheena's getting her boiler replaced.

e) What are the reflexive pronouns for *I*, *you* (singular), *he*, *she*, *it*, *our*, *you* (plural) and *them*? *myself*

f) Check in G10.1 p136.

5 R10.2 P Listen and practise the sentences in **3c)**.

I still get my car serviced at the local garage.

6 **a)** Make questions and answers with these words.

1 A your duvet / do / How much / to / dry-cleaned / get / pay / you ?
  B I'm not sure. it / for ages / had / I / haven't / cleaned .

2 A do / yourself / Did / the decorating / you ?
  B Yes, but / me / I / to / my friends / got / help .

3 A yourself / your hair / you / Did / dye ?
  B No, / for / my friend / I / to / got / do / it / me .

4 A some / round the pool / in / had / Have / you / new lights / put ?
  B Actually, / them / myself / I / in / put .

5 A you / get / did / When / serviced / your car / last ?
  B done / haven't / it / I / recently / had .

b) Work in pairs. Compare answers.

7 **a)** Read about Ken, who is married to one of the women in the photos. Fill in the gaps with the correct form of *have* or *get* and the correct form of the verb in brackets. Sometimes there is more than one possible answer.

I can do most DIY myself, but for really big jobs I either ¹ *have* it *done* (do) by professionals or I ² .... a friend .... (help) me. Recently we ³ .... the roof .... (replace) and last month we ⁴ .... a new kitchen .... (put in), which has made cooking much easier. And now I want ⁵ .... the outside of the house .... (paint). When we were first married, my wife ⁶ .... me .... (do) most of the DIY, but because I was often away during the week, she learned to do quite a lot of things around the house herself.

Ken

We don't like gardening so we're going to ⁷ .... someone else .... (do) it for us. But next summer we're going to ⁸ .... the garden .... (redesign) to make it easier to look after.

b) Work in pairs. Compare answers. If your answers are different, are they both possible?

c) Which of the women in the photos do you think Ken is married to? Why?

Get ready ... Get it right!

8 Make three lists: things you have done for you; things you get other people to do for you; things you do yourself. Use these prompts, the phrases in **1a)** and your own ideas.

cut/hair   dye/hair   clean/car   print/photos   do/gardening
clean/windows   do/nails   clean/house   wash/clothes
iron/clothes   deliver/food   alter/clothes   paint/house

9 **a)** Work in groups. Take turns to tell each other about the things on your lists. Ask follow-up questions if possible. Who is the most practical person in the group?

> I have my hair cut about once a month.

> Oh, I get my sister to do mine. She's really good.

b) Tell the class about the most practical person in your group. Who is the most practical person in the class?

10B New man

Vocabulary male, female and neutral words
Grammar quantifiers
Review household jobs

QUICK REVIEW ●●●
Write two nouns that can follow these verbs: *change*; *put up*; *fix*; *replace*; *dry-clean*; *service*. Work in pairs. Take turns to say two nouns. Your partner guesses the verb: A *a plug, a light bulb*. B *change*.

Vocabulary Male, female and neutral words

1 a) Work in pairs. Put these words/phrases into three groups. Some words/phrases can go in more than one group.

> a landlord   a landlady   a chairperson   a soldier
> a widow   a widower   a head teacher
> a flight attendant   a bride   a groom   a firefighter
> an actress   an actor   an author   a spokesperson
> a niece   a nephew   a cousin   a hero   a heroine
> a manager   a salesperson

1 male words   *a landlord*
2 female words   *a landlady*
3 neutral words   *a chairperson*

TIP! ● In modern usage we prefer to use neutral words/phrases which can refer to both men and women.

b) Check in V10.2 p135.

2 Work in pairs. Take turns to test each other on the male, female and neutral words/phrases in **1a)**.

> a landlord

> That's a male word. The female word is 'a landlady'.

Reading and Grammar

3 a) Look at the photo. Why do you think this man might be called a 'new man'? Is there a similar phrase in your language?

b) Read the article. Does the writer think that there are many new men in Britain today? Why?/Why not?

c) Read the article again. Answer these questions.

1 How does the writer think British male behaviour has changed since the 1980s?
2 In what ways does he think his brothers are new men?
3 Why is the writer upset by two articles he has read recently?
4 What point is he making in the last sentence in this article?

d) In what ways do you think the role of men has changed in your country in the last forty years?

Men in the 21st century

John Edmonson defends modern man's role in society.

Back in the 1980s, **everyone** was talking about the 'new man'. **Every** magazine was full of pictures of him holding babies or saucepans, and we were told that no self-respecting modern man would expect his wife to do all the childcare or housework. So we didn't. The division of domestic labour changed and men got in touch with their feminine side. Or at least that's what I thought.

However, read **any of** the articles written today on the subject and **anyone** would think that men haven't changed since the beginning of time. No one seems to think the division of labour has really improved and apparently we're supposed to feel guilty about it. But **all of** my married friends are new men compared to their fathers' generation. They don't expect their wives to do everything for them and they all spend quality time with their kids.

I've got two older brothers and **both of** them do most of the cooking for their families, as well as being the main breadwinners. Neither of them spend hours in the pub with their friends watching football. And I don't think **either of** my brothers want the lifestyle our father's generation had – certainly none of my friends do. However, no newspapers report that. Instead we get surveys such as the one quoted in the *Guardian* saying that on an average day in Britain, men only spend 13 minutes caring for children, 45 minutes cooking and doing housework, but three hours watching TV.

It's hard to find **anything** that shows men in a positive light these days. And **each** time I read about how selfish and unhelpful men are, my blood boils! In fact, I've read two articles on the subject recently, and **each** article suggests that all women are capable of being the breadwinner as well as running the home – apparently men aren't necessary any more! Would a woman tell a man that when she needed a tyre changed or when there was a burglar climbing through her window at four in the morning? I think not!

5 **a) Choose the correct words.**

1 *No/None of* my friends smoke.
2 All of my friends *have/has* computers.
3 Every *room/rooms* in my home gets a lot of light.
4 I've got *none/no* free time this week.
5 I go to the gym *all/every* week.
6 *Both of/Each of* my parents work.
7 In this class *every/all of* the men are over 25.
8 No one *is/are* missing from class today.
9 Almost everyone in this class *own/owns* a mobile phone.

b) Work in pairs. Compare answers. Then decide which of the sentences in 5a) are true for you or your class.

6 **a) Read what Sheena says about her husband, Ken. Fill in the gaps with these words/phrases.**

| ~~all~~ no one every anything none of all of |
| either of neither of everyone no both of |

I think ¹ _all_ men should help in the home, but every woman I know complains that they get ² _____ help from their husbands. For example, ³ _____ their husbands can even cook a meal, but my husband, Ken, can cook ⁴ _____ ! He also puts our two boys to bed ⁵ _____ evening and because ⁶ _____ them are old enough to travel on their own he takes ⁷ _____ them to school in the morning. And if ⁸ _____ them stay at school late, he also goes and picks them up. I tell ⁹ _____ how great he is, but ¹⁰ _____ can quite believe just how much he does – ¹¹ _____ my female friends are extremely jealous.

b) **Listen and check. Do you think Ken is a new man? Why?/Why not?**

Help with Grammar Quantifiers

4 **a) Look at the quantifiers in bold in the article. Answer these questions.**

1 Which quantifiers refer to two things or people?
2 Which refer to more than two things or people?
3 Which quantifier can refer to two or more things or people?

b) Look at the underlined quantifiers in the article, which all refer to a zero quantity. Answer these questions.

1 Which quantifier refers to two things or people?
2 Which refer to more than two things or people?

c) Look at the words/phrases in pink in the article. Then choose the correct words in these rules.

1 *Every* and *each* are followed by a *singular/plural* countable noun.
2 *Both of*, *neither of* and *either of* are followed by *the*, *my*, etc. + a *singular/plural* countable noun, or the pronouns *you*, *us* or *them*.
3 *Any of*, *all of* and *none of* are often followed by *the*, *my*, etc. + a *singular/plural* countable noun.
4 *No* is always followed by a *noun/pronoun*.

d) Look at the verbs in blue in the article. Then choose the correct words in these rules.

● *Everyone*, *every*, *no one*, *each* and *anything* are followed by a *singular/plural* verb form.
● *All of*, *both of*, *neither of*, *either of* and *none of* are followed by a *singular/plural* verb form.

e) Check in G10.2 **p137.**

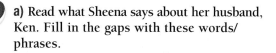 **Get ready … Get it right!**

7 **Write ten sentences about your family. Use words/phrases from 4.**

None of the men in my family can cook very well.
Everyone in my family loves watching sport.

8 **a) Work in pairs. Take turns to tell your partner about your family. Ask follow-up questions if possible.**

b) Tell the class the most interesting thing you found out about your partner's family.

10C The same but different

QUICK REVIEW ●●●
Work in pairs. Use these words/phrases to talk about the people in your class: *all of; none of; every; no one; everyone; anyone; each: All of us were on time today.* Do you agree with each other's sentences?

Vocabulary compound nouns and adjectives
Skills Reading: Women's roles; Listening: *Why Men Lie and Women Cry*
Help with Listening contradicting
Review quantifiers

Reading and Vocabulary

1 Work in pairs. Discuss these questions.

1 Are most of the women you know housewives or do they go out to work?
2 Who do you think are happier – the housewives or the women who go out to work? Why?

2 **a)** Read the article. Which of these titles do you think is the best? Why?

1 Women need to work
2 Families can't live on one salary
3 Desperate to be a housewife

b) Read the article again. Tick the true sentences. Decide why the other sentences are false.

1 The writer of the article always expected to become a housewife.
2 She was greatly influenced by her mother.
3 Darla Shine thinks that being a housewife and mother is as valuable as any other job.
4 The writer has always had a part-time job.
5 The writer says a lot of women are giving up work.
6 The writer has always managed to run her home well.

c) Are the issues raised in the article relevant to your country? Why?/Why not?

When my friends and I were little girls, none of us thought we'd grow up to be housewives. My mother was determined that any daughter of hers would have a career – there would be no stay-at-home mothers among her children. We wouldn't be in the kitchen baking homemade bread, we'd be out there in the workplace showing we were real human beings – just as valuable as any man.

In Susan Faludi's 1993 book, *Backlash*, she predicted that women's liberation would get a bad name. Then in 2005, Darla Shine's book, *Happy Housewives*, told American women that they should be proud to become wives and mothers. "Why wasn't being a mom offered to me as a career?" Shine asks, and she's not alone. Although I haven't given up work completely, I now have a part-time job allowing me more time for my kids and my husband. They now get freshly-prepared food every day, instead of badly-cooked meals that nearly killed them with food poisoning.

These days there are many women like me who are quietly turning away from work and giving up high-powered jobs in law, medicine, banking and the media. As one friend pointed out, when a married couple are both earning good salaries, a great deal of their hard-earned money goes on income tax. So it seems that a lot of people are 'downsizing' and looking for quality of life. Yes, you may have to make cutbacks, but why have it all when you only want a bit?

I think the problem is that women never really thought about what 'work' meant and we never considered all the drawbacks. It's no fun being a woman holding down a job and trying to run a home. Every job in the home is unbelievably time-consuming – if you do it properly, that is. But when I had a full-time job I certainly didn't – the fridge was empty, the house was unloved and the babysitter saw the kids more than I did. At 11 p.m. I'd still be putting their clothes in the washing machine or making them sandwiches because they didn't like the school lunches. I was always exhausted, but I never seemed to achieve anything. And there was a complete breakdown in communication between me and my husband. So tell me Mum, where was the liberation in that?

Help with Vocabulary Compound nouns and adjectives

3 **a)** Look at the compound words in blue and pink in the article. Answer these questions.

1 Which of these compound words do you know?
2 Can you guess the meaning of the other compound words from the context?
3 Which are nouns and which are adjectives?

b) Fill in the gaps in these rules with *adjectives* or *nouns*.

● Compound .... are usually made from noun + noun or verb + preposition.

● Compound .... are usually written as one word or two words.

● Compound .... are usually spelt with hyphens.

c) R10.4 Listen and mark the stress on these compound nouns. Which part of compound nouns is usually stressed?

> housewife   workplace   human being   food poisoning
> income tax   cutback   drawback   babysitter
> washing machine   school lunch   breakdown

TIP! ● The stress on compounds nouns is fixed. However, the stress on compound adjectives can sometimes change, depending on whether they come before a noun or not:
This is homemade bread. This bread is homemade.

d) Check in V10.3 p135.

4 **a)** Write six compound words from the article that are connected to your life in some way.

b) Work in pairs. Take turns to explain why you have chosen these words.

Listening

5 **a)** Work in groups. In what ways do you think women's and men's brains work differently?

b) R10.5 Listen to Naomi, Polly and Matt discussing the roles of men and women. Put these things in the order they first talk about them.

a) couples who both have to work
b) things men and women exaggerate
c) the book *Why Men Lie and Women Cry*
d) whether men or women talk more
e) problem-solving

c) Listen again. Answer these questions.

1 Why doesn't Polly think women should stop working?
2 Who hasn't read *Why Men Lie and Women Cry*?
3 What did Matt think of the book?
4 In what way do men solve problems differently from women?
5 How many more words does a woman use in a day than a man?
6 What sort of things do women say when they exaggerate?
7 What sort of things do men exaggerate?

Help with Listening Contradicting

6 **a)** R10.6 Listen and notice the words that Matt stresses when he contradicts Polly. Then choose the correct words in the rules.

POLLY Most couples these days can't live on one salary.
MATT They **can**.

POLLY I bet you didn't agree with any of it.
MATT You're wrong, I **did** agree with it.

POLLY Men do that all the time.
MATT No, we **don't**.

● When we want to contradict someone, we often stress the *main verb/auxiliary*.

● We *always/sometimes* repeat the main verb.

b) R10.7 Listen to five pairs of sentences from the conversation. Write the auxiliary that the second speaker stresses when he/she contradicts the first speaker.

7 **a)** Work in groups. Discuss these questions.

1 Do you agree that men don't talk about their emotions? Why?/Why not?
2 When women talk about their problems, do you think they want sympathy rather than solutions?
3 In what other ways do you think men and women behave differently?
4 Are these differences true for the men and women you know?
5 What should the roles of men and women be in the future?

b) Tell the class about two of the things your group disagreed about.

10D I did tell you!

Real World adding emphasis
Help with Fluency contradicting
Review compound nouns and adjectives

QUICK REVIEW ●●●

Work in pairs. Student A, write the first word of five compound adjectives. Student B, write the first word of five compound nouns. Swap papers. Take turns to say what you think your partner's compound words are: *break → breakdown*.

1 Work in groups. Discuss these questions.

1 Do you like having people round for a meal? Why?/Why not?
2 When was the last time people came to your home for a meal? Who came? What did you cook/eat?

2 a) R10.8 Listen to Polly and Matt talking at home. Tick the true sentences. Correct the false ones.

1 Polly wants Matt to tidy up the living room.
2 Polly's parents, Val and Tom, are coming for lunch.
3 Matt forgot to buy the bread.
4 Matt doesn't want to go to the shops.
5 Matt's parents got lost on the way.
6 Polly and Matt think the living room is a bit small.

b) Listen again. Fill in the gaps with one or two words.

1 The thing I don't like about this flat is _the kitchen_.
2 One thing I love about you is you always laugh at ....
3 The thing that amazes me about your mother is she still can't read ....
4 One thing that annoys me about you is you never give me time to .... a map.
5 What I like about the flat is it's ....
6 What worries me about the size of the kitchen is I can't help Polly with the ....

c) Work in pairs. Compare answers. Who said the sentences in **2b**): Polly, Matt, Val or Tom?

Real World Adding emphasis

● We can use introductory phrases at the beginning of a sentence to emphasise what we are going to say next.

3 a) Look at these two patterns for introductory phrases that add emphasis. Do sentences 1–6 in **2b**) match pattern A or B?

A

The thing One thing What	I	(don't) like love hate admire	about ...	is ...

B

The thing that One thing that What	amazes annoys worries upsets	me about ...	is ...

b) Check in RW10.1 p137.

4 R10.9 P Listen and practise the sentences in **2b**).

is the kitchen → The thing I don't like about this flat is the kitchen.

5 a) Rewrite these sentences using the introductory phrases in **3a**). Begin the sentences with the words in brackets.

1 I admire Val's patience. (What)
   What I admire about Val is her patience.
2 I like the food Polly cooks because it's really healthy. (The thing)
3 Polly amazes me because she never gets angry. (One thing)
4 I worry about Tom because he drives so fast. (The thing)
5 I love Matt's sense of humour. (One thing)
6 I don't like the way Tom interrupts me. (What)
7 Matt never remembers my birthday. That annoys me. (What)

b) Work in pairs. Compare answers.

6 **a)** Look at this conversation between Val and Tom. Make introductory phrases with the words in **bold**. Then fill in the gaps with a positive or negative form of *be*, *have* or *do*.

v **What / like / Sundays is**
   I ¹ 've got time to read the paper. Where ² _____ it?

T I ³ _____ seen it.

v Yes, you ⁴ _____ . You ⁵ _____ reading it an hour ago.

T I ⁶ _____ . I ⁷ _____ reading the TV guide.

v OK. No need to get angry.

T **One thing / upset / me / you is** you always contradict me!

v No, I ⁸ _____ .

T You ⁹ _____ . You ¹⁰ _____ doing it now!

v No, I ¹¹ _____ not. **And the thing / annoy / me / you is** you always have to be right.

T That's because I ¹² _____ !

b) R10.10 Listen and check.

Help with Fluency Contradicting

7 **a)** R10.10 Look at R10.10, p156. Listen again and notice the sentence stress. Which of the stressed words are used to contradict the other person?

b) P Work in pairs. Practise the conversation in R10.10, p156. Take turns to be Val and Tom. Remember to stress the auxiliaries when you are contradicting each other.

8 **a)** Write five sentences about people you know. Use introductory phrases from **3a)**.

What worries me about my mum is she works too hard.

b) Work in pairs. Compare sentences. Ask follow-up questions.

♪ R10.11 Look at the song *Wonderwall* on p103. Follow the instructions.

---

1 **a)** Find ten nouns connected to houses, cars or gardens. V10.1

```
S O G R O O F M I
H S B O I L E R N
E Q R C L B A J T
L I G H T B U L B
V M R F E N C E F
E D U V E T K A O
S R E L L O C K I
T Y R E S G H I B
```

b) Work in pairs. Write a verb for each noun in **1a)**. Sometimes there is more than one possible answer.

fix the roof

2 **a)** Put the verbs into the correct form. G10.1

1 I _____ (never have) my hair _____ (dye) in my life.

2 I _____ (get) a friend _____ (help) me decorate last weekend.

3 I _____ (get) Lorna _____ (alter) these trousers. They fit perfectly now.

4 John _____ (have) a new kitchen _____ (put in) next week.

5 I _____ (get) my brother _____ (check) my tyres. They were fine.

6 _____ Sue _____ (have) her roof _____ (fix) yet?

7 How often _____ you _____ (get) your boiler _____ (service)?

b) Work in pairs. Compare answers.

3 **a)** Which of these words can we use for both men and women? V10.2

landlord   chairperson   hero
widower   flight attendant
firefighter   headmaster   actor
nephew   manager   cousin
spokesman   groom   soldier

b) Work in pairs. Look at the words in **3a)** that are not neutral. Write the female word.

landlord   landlady

---

4 **a)** Correct the mistakes in these sentences. G10.2

1 None us work in education.
2 Every adult have a car.
3 Each person speak more than one language.
4 None of my cousins is married.
5 No one wear glasses.
6 Neither my parents have blue eyes.
7 All us studied English at school.

b) Work in pairs. Compare answers. Are any of the sentences in **4a)** true for your family?

5 **a)** Match a word in A to a word in B to make compound nouns or adjectives. V10.3

A	B
home	poisoning
high	back
cut	tax
human	consuming
break	down
baby	powered
food	made
time	being
income	sitter

b) Work in pairs. Compare answers. Are the compound words adjectives or nouns? Are they written as one word, two words or with a hyphen?

Progress Portfolio

a) Tick the things you can do in English.

☐ I can talk about household jobs.

☐ I can talk about things other people do for me and things I do myself.

☐ I can understand neutral words and use them appropriately.

☐ I can talk about the quantity of things.

☐ I can contradict people.

☐ I can emphasise things when giving my opinions.

b) What do you need to study again? 10A–D

11 Making a living

11A Meeting up

Vocabulary work collocations
Grammar describing future events; Future Perfect
Help with Listening Future Perfect and Future Continuous
Review adding emphasis; Future Continuous

QUICK REVIEW ● ● ●
Complete these sentences for yourself: *What I like about ... is ...* ;
One thing I admire about ... is ... ; *The thing that worries me about ... is ...* ; *One thing that amazes me about ... is ...* . Work in pairs. Take turns to say your sentences. Ask follow-up questions.

Vocabulary Work collocations

a) Look at the words/phrases in **bold**. Then choose the correct verbs. Check in V11.1 p138.

1 What do you think is the easiest way to *do*/make **a living**?
2 What does your best friend *do/make* **for a living**?
3 Do you know anyone who *works/has* **freelance**?
4 Has anyone you know ever **been** *made/done* **redundant**?
5 Do you know anyone who *is/has* **out of work** at the moment?
6 Do you *get/have* **a lot of work on** at the moment?
7 Are you the kind of person who *is/has* **on the go** all the time?
8 Do you find it difficult to *run/get* **down to work**?
9 Are you *working/studying* **on an interesting project** at the moment?
10 Have you ever *made/given* **a talk** to more than 30 people?

b) Work in pairs. Take turns to ask each other the questions in 1a). Ask follow-up questions if possible.

Listening and Grammar

a) R11.1 Look at the photos. Rob is talking to his friend Mike, an advertising executive. Listen to their conversation and answer these questions.

1 Do you think Mike is happy in his job? Why?/Why not?
2 Why is Rob calling him?
3 Why is Mike going to Southampton on Wednesday?
4 When do Mike and Rob arrange to meet up?

b) Listen again. Correct one word in each of these sentences.

                                                boss
1 **I'm having** lunch with my ~~colleague~~ tomorrow.
2 Sorry, **I'll be interviewing** people for our management trainee programme then.
3 No, sorry, **I'll be in the middle of** a conference at four.
4 No, **I'll be on my way to** Southampton at ten.
5 Well, **I'll have arrived** by mid-afternoon.
6 **I'll have finished** giving the talk by five thirty.

Rob

Help with Grammar
Describing future events; Future Perfect

DESCRIBING FUTURE EVENTS

a) Look at the verb forms in **bold** in sentences 1 and 2 in 2b). Answer these questions.

a) Which sentence talks about an arrangement in the future?
b) Which sentence talks about something that will be in progress at a point of time in the future?
c) How do we make these two verb forms?

b) Look at the phrases in **bold** in sentences 3 and 4 in 2b). Match them to these meanings.

a) The person will be travelling at this time.
b) The action will be in progress at this time.

FUTURE PERFECT

c) Look at the verb forms in **bold** in sentences 5 and 6 in 2b). Choose the correct word in this rule.

● We use the Future Perfect to talk about something that will be completed *before/after* a certain time in the future.

d) Fill in the gaps for the Future Perfect with *past participle*, *have* or *will*. How do we make the negative and question forms of the Future Perfect?

● subject + _____ or 'll + _____ + _____

e) Check in G11.1 p139.

86

Mike

June 8th

9.00–11.00
meeting freelance designer

11.00–1.00
interviews x 4 (new PA)

1.00–2.00
lunch with Max

2.00–3.00
phone meeting Jack Wells

3.15
go to Redhouse plc (taxi)

4.00–5.30
Redhouse presentation new ad

7 **a)** Look at Mike's appointments for Thursday. Fill in the gaps with the correct form of these verbs. Use the Future Perfect or Future Continuous.

> ~~have~~ travel leave give
> have talk finish interview

1 At 10.00 Mike *will be having* a meeting.
2 The meeting .... by 11.15.
3 By lunchtime he .... four people for a job.
4 He .... to Jack Wells on the phone at 2.30.
5 He .... his office by 3.20.
6 At half past three he .... to Redhouse plc.
7 At 4.30 he .... a presentation.
8 By the end of the day he .... two meetings.

b) Work in pairs. Compare answers. In which sentences could we also use *in the middle of* or *on the way to*?

Help with Listening Future Perfect and Future Continuous

4 **a)** [R11.2] Listen to these sentences. Notice the contractions (*I'll*, etc.) and the weak form of *have*.

1 I'll have /əv/ gone home by then.
2 We'll be waiting outside the cinema at seven.

b) [R11.3] Listen and write six sentences. You will hear each sentence twice.

5 [R11.4] [P] Listen and practise. Copy the stress, the contractions and the weak form of *have*.

She'll have /əv/ moved out by the end of the week.

6 **a)** Look at these pairs of sentences. Do they have the same meaning or different meanings?

1 a) I'll have done my homework by nine o'clock.
  b) I'll be doing my homework at nine o'clock.
2 a) This time next week she'll be travelling to Spain.
  b) This time next week she'll be on her way to Spain.
3 a) I'll still be writing the report at seven.
  b) I won't have finished the report by seven.
4 a) Jake's seeing the doctor on Thursday.
  b) Jake will have seen the doctor by Thursday.
5 a) At ten o'clock I'll be doing an exam.
  b) At ten o'clock I'll be in the middle of an exam.

b) Work in pairs. Compare answers.

Get ready … Get it right!

8 Complete these sentences for you. Use the Future Perfect or Future Continuous.

- By this time next week …
- This time tomorrow …
- By the time I'm (age) …
- At midnight on New Year's Eve …
- By the end of this course …
- In a month's time …
- At eight o'clock tomorrow evening …
- By the end of the year …

9 **a)** Work in pairs. Take turns to tell your partner your sentences. Ask follow-up questions if possible.

b) Tell the class the most interesting thing you found out about your partner.

Vocabulary business collocations
Grammar reported speech
Review Future Perfect; Future Continuous

QUICK REVIEW ● ● ●
Write three things you'll have done by the end of the week and three things you'll be doing at the weekend: *I'll have finished the book I'm reading*. Work in groups. Take turns to tell each other your sentences. Are any the same?

Vocabulary Business collocations

1 Match the verbs in A to the words/phrases in B. Check in **V11.2** p138.

A	B
close	business
take over	a company
go out of	a branch
make	the business
expand	business with somebody
go into	a profit or a loss
do	a new company
set up	business with somebody
go	bankrupt
import	products to another country
export	a chain of restaurants
run	products from another country

2 a) Fill in the gaps with words/phrases from **1**. Use the correct form of the verbs. There is sometimes more than one possible answer.

1 Do you know anyone who _runs_ their own business?
2 Would you ever _____ into business with someone in your family?
3 Would you like to run a _____ of restaurants? Why?/Why not?
4 Where's the nearest _____ of your bank?
5 Can you think of three things that your country _____ ?
6 Do you think oil companies make too much _____ ?
7 Do you know of any shops or companies that have _____ business recently?
8 If you could _____ a new company, what kind of company would it be?

b) Work in pairs. Take turns to ask and answer the questions in **2a)**. Ask follow-up questions if possible.

Listening and Grammar

3 a) **R11.5** Listen to Mike talking to his wife, Daisy. Answer these questions.

1 What is Mike's friend Rob planning to do?
2 What does Rob want Mike to do?
3 How much would they each have to invest?
4 How does Daisy feel about the idea?

b) Listen again. Fill in the gaps with two words.

1 You said that you had _something interesting_ to tell me.
2 Rob told me that he was planning to set up his _____ .
3 He said he'd been looking for a good location _____ .
4 Rob asked me if I wanted to go _____ with him.
5 He wanted to know whether I could come up with the _____ .
6 I asked how long it would take for the business to make _____ .
7 He asked me to meet him in Brighton _____ .
8 Rob told me not to talk to _____ about it – except you, of course.

Help with Grammar Reported speech

4 **a)** Work in pairs. Look at reported sentences 1–3 in **3b)**. Answer these questions.

a) What did Mike and Rob say in their original conversation?

b) What usually happens to verb forms when we report what people say?

b) Look at the reported questions 4–6 in **3b)**. Answer these questions.

a) What did Mike and Rob say in their original conversation?

b) How is the word order in the reported questions different from the original questions?

c) When do we use *if* or *whether* in reported questions?

d) Do we use the auxiliaries *do*, *does* and *did* in reported questions?

c) Look at sentences 7 and 8 in **3b)**. Answer these questions.

a) Which sentence is reporting an imperative?

b) Which sentence is reporting a request?

c) Which verb form follows *told me …* and *asked me …* ?

d) Check in G11.2 p139.

5 **a)** It's Saturday afternoon. Mike is phoning Daisy to tell her about his meeting with Rob. Put what Rob and Mike said into reported speech. Use the words in brackets.

Rob said to Mike …

1 Say hello to Daisy. (tell)
   He told me to say hello to you.
2 What do you think of my business plan? (ask)
3 The plan has already been approved by the bank. (tell)
4 I've been talking to an interior designer. (say)
5 Will you help with the advertising? (want to know)

Mike said to Rob …

6 I can't say yes or no until I talk to Daisy. (tell)
7 I'll be talking to the bank on Tuesday. (say)
8 When do you need a decision by? (ask)
9 Are you talking to any other investors? (ask)
10 You must name the coffee shop after Daisy! (tell)

b) Work in pairs. Compare answers.

c) R11.6 Listen to Mike and Daisy's phone conversation. Tick the reported sentences when your hear them. What do Mike and Daisy decide to do?

6 **a)** Tick the correct sentences. Change the incorrect ones. There is sometimes more than one possible answer.

1 She told ∕ that he'd call later today. *me*
2 I told her I hadn't been there before. ✓
3 He asked me what was my last job.
4 She asked if I did have any children.
5 He asked me to not tell anyone.
6 She said me that she wasn't coming.
7 I said that I couldn't go on Friday.
8 He asked his brother he could phone back later.
9 He told his cousin not be late.
10 I asked her to come to the theatre.

b) Work in pairs. Compare answers.

Get ready ... Get it right!

7 **a)** Write one interesting question that you can ask all the students in the class.

What do you really dislike doing?

b) Take turns to ask and answer the questions. Talk to as many students as you can. Try to remember all the questions you are asked. You can write one word to help you remember each question.

8 **a)** Work in pairs. Take turns to tell each other what each student asked you. Then tell your partner what your answer was.

> Hasan asked me what I really disliked doing. I told him I hated getting up early.

> I said that I couldn't stand people talking in cinemas.

b) Tell the class two things that you told other students.

Vocabulary verb patterns (2): reporting verbs
Skills Reading: A problem at Daisy's; Listening: Decision time
Help with Listening back referencing
Review work and business collocations; reported speech

QUICK REVIEW ● ● ●
Write three work and three business collocations: *work freelance*; *make a profit*. Work in pairs. Compare lists. Then take turns to make sentences about people you know with the collocations on both lists: *My friend Wayne wants to set up his own business.*

Reading and Vocabulary

1 **Work in groups. Discuss these questions.**

1 Where is your favourite coffee shop or café? Why do you like it?
2 When did you last go there? What did you have?
3 What do you think are the three most important things for a good coffee shop to have?

2 **a)** Look at the photo. Rob and Mike's coffee shop has been open for a year. How well do you think it is doing?

b) Read Mike's email to his wife, Daisy. What decision do they have to make?

c) Read the email again. Tick the true sentences. Correct the false ones.

1 The coffee shop isn't making money at the moment.
2 Rob doesn't want to work there any more.
3 Rob has been talking to another company without telling Mike.
4 Rob's bank thinks selling the coffee shop is a bad idea.
5 If they sold the coffee shop, Rob and Mike would make £50,000 profit between them.
6 Mike and Daisy have been invited to Rob's place this weekend.

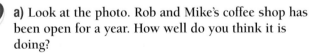

| | search |

from: mf_jackson@hotmail.com save address?
to: daisy371@burketandtomas.co.uk
cc:
subject: coffee shop

Hi Daisy

Hope your day's going well. I've just phoned Rob and reminded him to sort out the staff wages, and I'm afraid something's come up.

The good news is that the coffee shop is still doing very well – Rob mentioned that the profits were up 20% last month. However, the bad news is that he wants to give up running the business. He explained that he found the work really exhausting and then he blamed me for not letting him hire enough staff. As you know, he agreed to run the shop on his own for the first year, and I pointed out that we'd already taken on two extra waitresses to help him. Then he told me that Café Pronto – the big coffee shop chain – has offered to buy the business! I got really angry and accused him of talking to people behind my back – after all, we are partners. At first he denied doing anything wrong, but eventually he admitted that Café Pronto had contacted him a few weeks ago. He apologised for not telling me sooner and promised to be completely honest and open with me from now on. Apparently Rob's already talked to his bank, and they've advised us to accept the offer immediately. They also recommended starting the paperwork as soon as possible. Rob claimed that we'd both make £25,000 profit from the deal – then he threatened to close the shop if I didn't accept the offer. At that point I was so angry I refused to discuss it any further and hung up.

After I'd calmed down, I called Rob back and persuaded him not to talk to Café Pronto again without me being there. I've also insisted on seeing all the correspondence between him and Café Pronto, and warned him not to try and hide anything from me again. He suggested meeting up this weekend, and invited me to go round to his place on Saturday to try and sort this mess out.

So you and I need to decide what to do – have a think about it and we'll talk when I get home.

Love
Mike

Help with Vocabulary
Verb patterns (2): reporting verbs

 a) Look at the reporting verbs in blue in the email. Tick the verbs you know. Check the other verbs with your teacher or in a dictionary.

b) Look again at the reporting verbs in blue and <u>underline</u> the verb form that follows them. Then write the infinitive form of the verbs in blue in the table.

mention	+ *that* + clause
agree	+ (*not*) + infinitive with *to*
remind	+ object + (*not*) + infinitive with *to*
deny	+ verb+*ing*
apologise	+ preposition + (*not*) + verb+*ing*
blame	+ object + preposition + (*not*) + verb+*ing*

c) Check in V11.3 p138.

4 Look at what Mike and Rob said to each other on the phone. Put these sentences into reported speech. Use the phrases in brackets.

1 You've been keeping secrets from me. (Mike accused …)
 Mike accused Rob of keeping secrets from him.
2 I'm sorry I went behind your back. (Rob apologised …)
3 I won't do it again. (Rob promised …)
4 The coffee shop was my idea. (Rob pointed out …)
5 You're only interested in the money. (Mike claimed …)
6 I'll take you to court if you close the shop. (Mike threatened …)
7 I'll work until the end of the month. (Rob agreed …)
8 I want to be paid for every hour I've worked. (Rob insisted …)
9 You should sell your half of the business. (Rob advised …)
10 Don't talk to the people at Café Pronto again. (Mike warned …)
11 We should see a lawyer. (Mike suggested …)
12 Don't forget to bring your copy of the contract. (Rob reminded …)

Listening

5 **a)** Work in pairs. Discuss these questions.

1 What does Rob want Mike and Daisy to agree to?
2 What options do Mike and Daisy have?
3 What do you think they should do? Why?

b) Compare ideas with the class.

6 **a)** R11.7 Listen to Mike and Daisy's conversation later that day. Which of the options you discussed in **5** do they talk about? What do they decide to do?

b) Listen again. Answer these questions.

1 How did Daisy feel when she got Mike's email?
2 Why doesn't Mike like option one?
3 What's the problem with option two?
4 Why does Daisy think Mike hates his job?
5 How does Daisy suggest getting the money for option three?
6 What do they think might happen in a few years?

c) Do you think Mike and Daisy made the right decision? What would you have done in their situation?

Help with Listening **Back referencing**

7 **a)** Work in pairs. Look at this part of Mike and Daisy's conversation. What do the words/phrases in **bold** refer to?

MIKE I just don't want our coffee shop to become another ⓐ<u>branch of Café Pronto</u>. They're all the same, aren't ⓐ**they**?

DAISY ⓑ**That**'s true. I'm not keen on the idea either. You're very fond of ⓒ**the place**, aren't you?

MIKE Of course. I know we don't go ⓓ**there** very often, but think of all that work we did getting ⓔ**it** ready.

DAISY How could I forget ⓕ**it**?

b) R11.7 Look at R11.7, p157. Listen again and notice what the words/phrases in **bold** refer to.

8 **a)** Work in pairs. Imagine you are going to open a coffee shop, café or restaurant together. Decide on these things.

- name
- location
- theme
- the menu
- interior decoration
- opening hours
- entertainment/music
- your own ideas

b) Work in groups. Take turns to tell each other about your new business. Which is the best, do you think?

c) Tell the class about the best new business in your group.

11D Advertising works

Vocabulary advertising
Real World discussion language (3)
Help with Fluency review
Review verb patterns (2): reporting verbs

QUICK REVIEW ●●●

Write five reporting verbs (*offer, deny*, etc.). Think of sentences about people you know using these verbs. Your sentences can be true or false. Work in pairs. Take turns to say your sentences: *My parents offered to buy me a car.* Your partner guesses if they are true or false.

1 **a)** Tick the words/phrases you know. Check new words/phrases in **V11.4** p138.

1 advertising, publicity
2 a slogan, a logo
3 an advertising campaign, an advertising budget
4 the press, the media
5 a leaflet, a free sample
6 design a new product, launch a new product

b) Work in pairs. Take turns to explain the difference between the pairs of words/phrases in **1a)**.

2 Work in groups. Discuss these questions.

1 Which famous brands have slogans that you remember?
2 Which advertising campaigns do you like at the moment? Why?
3 How many different ways to advertise a product can you think of?

3 **a)** **R11.8** Look at the photo of a meeting at Target Advertising. Listen to the people discussing the launch of a new product called *Go!*. What type of product is it?

b) Listen again. Answer these questions.

1 Which different types of advertising do they talk about?
2 What do they say are the disadvantages of using celebrities in ads?
3 Why do they discuss increasing the advertising budget?
4 Why is giving away a free sample of *Go!* a good idea?

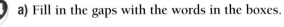

Real World Discussion language (3)

4 **a)** Fill in the gaps with the words in the boxes.

putting forward new ideas

> ~~could~~ about wonder know

One thing we [1] _could_ do is (use ...)
I [2] .... if it'd be a good idea (to have ...)
I [3] .... ! Why don't we (give ...)?
I've got an idea. How [4] .... (giving ...)?

reacting positively to ideas

> work try makes like

That sounds [5] .... a good idea.
Well, it's worth a [6] ....
Yes, that [7] .... sense.
Yes, that could [8] ....

reacting negatively to ideas

> avoid such rather problem

Personally, I'd [9] .... we didn't (use a celebrity).
OK, maybe we should [10] .... (using celebrities).
The main [11] .... with (TV ads) is that ...
I'm not sure that's [12] .... a good idea.

summarising and recapping

> right over what saying

So [13] .... you're saying is that ...
Am I [14] .... in thinking that ... ?
Are you [15] .... that ... ?
Can we just go [16] .... this again?

b) Check in **RW11.1** p140.

Roger   Judy   Amanda   Colin

5 **a)** Write Amanda and Colin's conversation using these prompts.

A / know! Why / we use cartoon characters?
I know! Why don't we use cartoon characters?

C I / not sure / such / idea. I think we need some real people.

A Yes, maybe you're right.

C / thing we / do / show someone drinking the product.

A Yes, / make / sense. / about / use / some attractive models?

C Personally / rather we / not use / models. They always look so false.

A So / you / say / is / you want ordinary-looking people.

C Yes, exactly. The kind of people who might actually go out and buy *Go!*.

A Well, it / worth / try.

C / wonder / be / good idea / show how much fruit is in it?

A Yes, that / work. OK, / we / go / this again?

b) `R11.9` Listen and check.

Help with Fluency Review

6 **a)** `R11.9` Look at R11.9, p158. Listen again and notice the sentence stress and linking.

b) `P` Work in pairs. Practise the conversation in R11.9, p158. Take turns to be Amanda and Colin. Try to use natural sentence stress and linking.

7 **a)** Work in groups. You are going to design a campaign for a new product. Choose a product and discuss these things. Use language from 4a) and make notes on your decisions.

- a name for the product
- a logo or a slogan
- who the product is aimed at
- what is different about it
- how you're going to advertise it

b) Work with students from other groups. Take turns to present your campaign. Which is the best?

11 Review
Language Summary 11, p138

1 Fill in the gaps with the correct form of these verbs. `V11.1`

> do make work (x 2)
> give have be

1 Lee's never _____ out of work in his life.
2 What do you _____ for a living?
3 He'd like to _____ freelance.
4 Sue _____ a lot of work on now.
5 He _____ a talk on J S Bach last Friday.
6 I _____ on a new project at the moment.
7 I was _____ redundant last week.

2 Choose the correct verb forms. `G11.1`

1 By this time next week I *'ll arrive/ 'll have arrived* in Cardiff.
2 At this time tomorrow I *'m/'ll be* in the middle of giving my talk.
3 I *won't have/'m not* finished before 2 p.m.
4 I'm sure I'll *do/be doing* the same job in five years' time.
5 If you need me later, I'll *stay/ be staying* at the Hilton.
6 On Saturday I'll *have been/be* married for two years.

3 **a)** Fill in the gaps with the correct form of these verbs. `V11.2`

> expand run make set up
> take over export import go

In 1980 Meg [1] _____ a new clothing company. It was so successful that she [2] _____ the business by [3] _____ her clothes to other countries. Soon she [4] _____ a chain of clothes shops all over Europe. Unfortunately she nearly [5] _____ bankrupt last year, but she began [6] _____ clothes from India and soon her business [7] _____ a profit again. Meg wants her son to [8] _____ the business from her when she retires.

b) Work in pairs. Take turns to say a sentence from 3a). Are your partner's sentences correct?

4 Put these sentences into direct speech. `G11.2`

1 She said she'd be working late.
2 He told me I couldn't use his car.
3 I asked him what he thought.
4 She told me not to wait for her.
5 He asked me if I wanted to stay.
6 She wanted to know what my next job was going to be.
7 He asked me where I'd been staying.
8 She told me I had to leave.

5 **a)** Correct the mistakes. `V11.3`

1 Where would you recommend to go for a holiday in your country?
2 Have you ever been blamed doing something you hadn't done?
3 When was the last time somebody warned you not do something?
4 Have you ever promised do something that you didn't do?
5 Has anyone ever accused you of do something you hadn't done?
6 When was the last time you agreed helping someone, then regretted it?
7 Has anyone ever persuaded you do something you didn't want to?

b) Work in pairs. Ask each other the questions.

Progress Portfolio

a) Tick the things you can do in English.

☐ I can talk about work and business.

☐ I can talk about things I'll be doing and will have done in the future.

☐ I can report what other people have said or asked in different ways.

☐ I can follow a discussion where the speakers are trying to reach a decision.

☐ I can talk about advertising.

☐ I can put forward and react to ideas in a discussion.

b) What do you need to study again?
`11A–D`

12 That's weird!

12A Where's my mobile?

Vocabulary colloquial words/phrases
Grammar modal verbs (2): deduction in the present and the past
Help with Listening modal verbs in the past
Review discussion language (3)

QUICK REVIEW ●●●
Work in groups. Imagine that you are trying to raise money for charity. Take turns to put forward ideas about how you can do this. React positively or negatively to your partners' ideas: A *I know! Why don't we organise a concert?* B *That sounds like a good idea.* Which is the best idea?

Vocabulary Colloquial words/phrases

1 **a)** Guess the meanings of the words/phrases in **bold**. Check in V12.1 p141.

1 **What's up?** You look really **stressed out**.
2 It really **bugs** me when people talk loudly in restaurants.
3 Cycling at night without lights is a **crazy** thing to do.
4 That old lamp doesn't work. Let's **chuck** it **out**.
5 **Hang on a sec**. I'm just going to **pop into** the newsagent's.
6 I really **messed up** that interview. I'll never get the job now.
7 On Friday evenings I usually just **chill out** in front of the **telly**.
8 Can you lend me a few **quid**? I'm completely broke.
9 The **loo** is up the stairs and on your right.
10 Last night I went to a **trendy** bar with some **mates**. It was **pretty** expensive, actually.
11 I really **fancy** that **guy** sitting over there. He's very good-looking.
12 It's such a **hassle** getting there – you have to take three different buses.

b) Write six sentences about your life. Use words/phrases from **1a)**.

I chucked out my old computer last week.
I messed up my first driving test.

c) Work in pairs. Take turns to say your sentences. Ask follow-up questions if possible.

Listening and Grammar

2 **a)** Work in new pairs. Discuss these questions.

1 What do you always carry with you?
2 Do you often lose things? If so, what?
3 Do you usually find them again? If so, where?

b) R12.1 Listen to Louise and Angie talking about what they did last night. Put photos A–D in the order they did them. What does Louise think happened to her mobile phone?

A

B

C

D

3 R12.1 Listen again. Fill in the gaps in these sentences with one word.

1 It **might be** in the _bathroom_ .
2 Yeah, of course, but it **must be** switched ....
3 Or someone **could have taken** it from your ....
4 But someone **might be using** it to phone .... !
5 Then we popped into that trendy new café for a ....
6 OK, so you didn't leave it in the ....
7 So you **may have left** it on the ....
8 You **can't have left** it at the ....
9 He **might have been waiting** for a chance to .... my phone.
10 That guy in the .... **must have stolen** it.

Help with Grammar Modal verbs (2): deduction in the present and the past

 4 **a)** Look at the sentences in **3**. Answer these questions.

1 In which sentences is the speaker making a deduction about: a) the present? b) the past?
2 In which two sentences does the speaker know that something is definitely true or definitely not true?

b) Fill in the gaps in these rules with *could*, *can't*, *must*, *might* or *may*.

● When we believe something is true, we use ....

● When we think something is possibly true, we use .... , ... or ....

● When we believe something isn't true, we use ....

c) Look at verb forms in **bold** in the sentences in **3**. Match the sentences to these rules.

To make deductions about …

● a state in the present we use: modal verb + infinitive. ...1... , ...

● something happening now we use: modal verb + be + verb+*ing*. ....

● a state or a completed action in the past we use: modal verb + *have* + past participle. .... , ... , ... , ...

● a longer action in the past we use: modal verb + *have* + *been* + verb+*ing*. ....

TIP! ● We can also use *couldn't* to make deductions in the past: *You couldn't have left it at the restaurant.*

d) Check in G12.1 p142.

Help with Listening Modal verbs in the past

 5 **a)** R12.2 Listen to these sentences. Notice the weak forms of *have* and *been*. Which words are stressed?

1 Someone could have /əv/ taken it from your bag.
2 He might have /əv/ been /bɪn/ waiting for a chance to steal my phone.

b) R12.3 Listen and write six sentences. You will hear each sentence twice.

6 R12.4 Listen and practise. Copy the stress and weak forms.

I think I must have /əv/ left it at home.

 7 **a)** Read the next part of Louise and Angie's conversation. Choose the correct modal verbs and fill in the gaps with the correct form of the verbs in brackets.

LOUISE Now, what number do I call?

ANGIE Try the Internet. The phone company ¹can't/(might) _have_ (have) a number on their website.

LOUISE Good idea. Any interesting post?

ANGIE Yes, a postcard from my cousin. He's travelling around South America for a year.

LOUISE He ²*must/can't* .... (have) a good time.

ANGIE Yes, he is. Hey, look at this envelope. There's no name or address on it.

LOUISE Let me see. That's weird. Someone ³*might/must* .... (deliver) it by hand.

ANGIE Who do you think it ⁴*could/can't* .... (be) from?

LOUISE Well, it ⁵*can't/might* .... (be) from my parents, they're in France … . Wow, look, it's my mobile! It ⁶*must/couldn't* .... (lie) on the floor all this time!

ANGIE Great! I guess someone ⁷*must/can't* .... (find) it. Have a look inside the envelope. Whoever found it ⁸*might/couldn't* .... (write) a note or something.

LOUISE Oh, yes. Oh, there is a note. It says …

b) Work in pairs. Compare answers. Who do you think the note is from?

c) R12.5 Listen and check.

8 Look at these sentences. Write deductions about the present or the past. There is more than one possible answer.

1 The boys are covered in mud.
   They might have been playing football.
2 Brian fell asleep on the train home from work.
3 Sylvia is going to a shop that sells wedding dresses.
4 Mo didn't send her brother a birthday card.
5 Kate's got four voicemail messages from Dylan.

Get ready … Get it right!

9 Work in pairs. Look at p111. Follow the instructions.

Vocabulary news collocations
Grammar past forms of modal and related verbs
Review colloquial words/phrases

Vocabulary News collocations

1 **a)** Look at these sentences. Which words/
phrases do <u>not</u> go with the verbs in **bold**?
Check new words/phrases in V12.2 p141.

1 The government **sent** *troops/soldiers/~~news~~*
   into the north of the country.
2 *The virus/Buildings/The news* **spread** rapidly
   throughout the country.
3 Thousands of people have been forced
   to **flee** *their homes/their lives/the city*
   because of the hurricane.
4 The company tried to **sue** the newspaper
   for *millions of pounds/the article/damages*.
5 The government's decision **caused**
   a political crisis/troops/a public outcry.
6 The man claimed that he **was attacked**
   by *muggers/the police/a gun*.
7 The terrorists said they would **release**
   a poisonous gas/the building/the hostages.
8 *The country/The island/A crisis* **was invaded**
   two years ago.

b) Work in pairs. Make sentences about
what's happening in the news at the
moment. Use the language from **1a)** if
possible. Have you heard about your
partner's news stories?

Reading and Grammar

2 **a)** Work in groups. Discuss these questions.

1 Have you ever read or seen *The War of the
   Worlds*? If so, what is it about?
2 Which other books, TV programmes or
   films about aliens have you read or seen?

b) Check these words/phrases with your
teacher or in a dictionary.

> Martians   a news bulletin   a meteorite
> an adaptation   broadcast   fictitious

c) Work in pairs. Look at A–C on p97.
What do you think the article is about?

d) Read the article and check your ideas.

The Martians are coming!

On August 30th 1938, millions of radio listeners in the USA were
convinced that their country was being invaded by Martians. An
evening music programme was interrupted by a series of news
bulletins, which reported that a meteorite had landed on a farm in
New Jersey. Apparently aliens "as large as bears, with black eyes
and V-shaped mouths" had emerged from inside the meteorite and
were releasing poisonous gas into the atmosphere. Further
bulletins told of more Martian landings in other parts of the USA.
As the news spread, thousands of people fled their homes to
avoid the alien attack. Some people even phoned local radio
stations to say they could see a cloud of poisonous gas
approaching New York.

Of course, they needn't have worried. What they were listening to
was an adaptation of H G Wells's novel *The War of the Worlds*, first
published in 1898. The director of the radio programme, Orson
Welles, **could broadcast any play he wanted**, so he had asked a
young playwright, Howard Koch, to rewrite H G Wells's novel as a
series of realistic news bulletins using real place names.

Once people realised that the broadcast wasn't reporting real
events, there was a public outcry. Orson Welles was accused of
deliberately causing the panic, and people tried to sue his
company and the radio station for millions of dollars. Fortunately,
Welles **was able to avoid a lengthy court case** because he had
told listeners that the broadcast was fictitious at the beginning of
the programme.

Today, most people's reaction is that the citizens of America
should have realised they were listening to a play. Of course they
could have listened to other radio stations to see if the story was
real, instead of fleeing their homes. However, this type of realistic
radio drama had never been broadcast before and it's hard to say
whether you or I would have reacted differently.

Amazingly, the same thing happened when the play was broadcast
in Chile in 1944. On that occasion the governor of Santiago even
sent troops into the streets. Fortunately, the troops didn't need to
fight an army of Martian invaders!

3 Read the article again. Find the answers to these questions.

1 Where did the radio play say that the first Martians had landed?
2 According to the radio play, how did the aliens arrive on Earth?
3 Why did some people phone local radio stations?
4 How was *The War of the Worlds* different from other radio plays?
5 How did people react when they realised it was a radio play?
6 Why didn't Orson Welles have to go to court?
7 What happened when the play was broadcast in Chile in 1944?

RADIO PLAY CREATES PANIC ACROSS USA

Orson Welles

Help with Grammar Past forms of modal and related verbs

4 *WOULD HAVE, COULD HAVE, SHOULD HAVE*

a) Look at the phrases in blue in the article. Fill in the gaps in these rules with *would have*, *could have* or *should have*. How do we make these verb forms negative?

● We use ___would have___ + past participle to imagine something in the past that didn't happen.

● We use _____ + past participle to criticise people's behaviour in the past.

● We use _____ + past participle to say something was possible in the past, but didn't happen.

NEEDN'T HAVE, DIDN'T NEED TO

b) Look at the sentences in pink in the article. Answer these questions.

1 In the first sentence, did the people worry?
2 In the second sentence, did the troops fight?
3 How do we make the verb form in each sentence?

COULD, WAS/WERE ABLE TO

c) Look at the words/phrases in **bold** in the article. Fill in the gaps in these rules with *could* or *was/were able to*.

● We usually use _____ to talk about a general ability in the past.

● We usually use _____ to talk about ability at one specific time in the past.

TIP! ● We usually use *could* with verbs of the senses (*see, hear,* etc.): *They could see a cloud of poisonous gas approaching New York.*

d) Check in G12.2 p142.

5 R12.6 P Listen and practise. Copy the stress and the weak form of *have*.

They needn't have /əv/ worried.

6 Choose the correct words/phrases.

1 In your position I *would have/needn't have* done the same thing.
2 It's your fault. You *should have/would have* told him we were going to be late.
3 I *could have/needn't have* stayed longer, but I *would have/should have* missed the last bus.
4 We *should have/would have* gone to see that play instead of going to the cinema.
5 I *didn't need to go/needn't have gone* to work today, so I stayed in bed.
6 We *needn't have/couldn't have* bought all this milk. Look, we've got lots in the fridge.
7 I lost my house keys last night, but I *could/was able to* get in through a window.
8 He *shouldn't have/couldn't have* told her because now she's really upset.

Get ready ... Get it right!

7 Write six of these things on a piece of paper. Don't write them in this order.

Something that you …

● should have done last week
● did recently that you needn't have done
● would have done last weekend if you'd had time
● could do well when you were a child
● would have done last year if you'd had the money
● could have done yesterday, but didn't
● didn't need to do this morning
● bought recently that you shouldn't have

8 **a)** Work in pairs. Swap papers. Take turns to ask your partner about the things he/she has written. Ask follow-up questions if possible.

> Why have you written 'pay the phone bill'?

> Because I should have paid it last week!

b) Tell the class two things you found out about your partner.

12C Spooky!

Vocabulary idioms
Skills Reading: Look behind you!
Help with Listening natural rhythm: review
Review past forms of modal verbs: deduction in the present and the past

QUICK REVIEW ●●●
Complete these sentences for you:
I needn't have ... ; I could ... by the time I was ... ; I should have ... ; If I'd known about ... ; I could have ... ; I probably shouldn't have ... .
Work in pairs. Take turns to say your sentences. Ask follow-up questions.

Reading and Vocabulary

 Work in groups. Discuss these questions.

1 Have you seen any films or plays, or read any books with ghosts in them? If so, which ones? Did you enjoy them?
2 Do you believe in ghosts? Have you, or has anyone you know, seen a ghost?

2 a) Check these words with your teacher or in a dictionary.

> sceptical   haunted   spooky
> werewolves   vanish   proof

b) Read the article. Match headings a)–e) to paragraphs 1–5.

a) A weekend invitation
b) A spooky experience
c) A nation of believers
d) Still a sceptic
e) Our first evening

c) Read the article again. Tick the true sentences. Correct the false ones.

1 More than half the population of the UK say they have seen a ghost.
2 The writer didn't expect to see a ghost at Brockfield Castle.
3 The writer thought most of the other ghost-hunters were strange.
4 The ghosts who haunt the castle are Ashley's brothers.
5 There had been a fire in the room where the writer saw the old man.
6 The writer has changed her mind about the existence of ghosts.

d) Work in pairs. Discuss these questions.

1 What do you think really happened at Brockfield Castle that weekend?
2 Would you like to go on a ghost-hunting weekend? Why?/Why not?

Look behind you!

Kathy Blake investigates the growing popularity of ghost-hunting weekends

1 A recent survey revealed that 68% of people in the UK believe in ghosts, and 1 in 10 people claim that they've actually seen a ghost. Being naturally sceptical, I always **take** these kinds of survey **with a pinch of salt**, but it does seem that nowadays everyone wants to meet a real-life ghost.

2 So when my sister-in-law Pat suggested going on a ghost-hunting weekend, I didn't need to be asked twice. Pat was hoping to see her first ghost, while I just wanted a few days off to **recharge my batteries**. We were soon heading off to Brockfield Castle in Somerset, one of Britain's most haunted houses, to spend the weekend looking for ghosts – I thought it was going to **be a piece of cake**.

Help with Vocabulary Idioms

● An idiom is an expression (usually informal) which has a meaning that is different from the meanings of the individual words. The words are in a fixed order.

3 a) Look at the idioms in **bold** in the article. Match them to meanings 1–12. Write the infinitive forms of the verbs.

1 be completely different from something
  be a far cry from something
2 watch for somebody or something to appear
3 not believe something to be accurate or true
4 tell somebody something that isn't true as a joke
5 be very easy to do
6 do something to get new energy and enthusiasm
7 a long way from any towns, villages or other houses
8 completely unexpectedly
9 make you think seriously about a topic
10 make people more relaxed in a new situation
11 make somebody extremely happy
12 sleep very well without waking

b) Check in V12.3 p141.

 Work in pairs. Student A → p106. Student B → p109. Follow the instructions.

3 Brockfield Castle, a spooky old building **in the middle of nowhere**, certainly **was a far cry from** my modern London flat. There were eight other guests and we all had dinner together on the first evening to **break the ice**. Our fellow ghost-hunters seemed normal enough – apart from one strange old lady who kept telling us to **keep an eye out for** werewolves (she must have booked the wrong weekend break). After dinner Ashley, our guide, gave us a talk on the history of the castle, which is apparently haunted by two brothers who died in a fire over 200 years ago. Then we were taken on a tour of the castle's 37 rooms. Sadly the brothers were nowhere to be seen – perhaps they'd gone away for the weekend too.

4 That night I **slept like a log**, but on the second evening things started to get weird. Pat and I were walking in the gardens after dinner when **out of the blue** she shouted, "Look, there's a ghost!" I thought she **was pulling my leg**, but she pointed to one of the windows. An old man was standing there, arms outstretched. We watched him for about a minute and then he suddenly vanished. When we told Ashley what we'd seen, he said we'd been looking up at the room where the brothers had died.

5 Of course, Pat's first ghostly encounter really **made her day**, and I have to admit that the experience **gave me food for thought**. However, as someone once said, for the believer, no proof is required – but for the sceptic, no proof is sufficient.

Listening

5 **a)** R12.7 Listen to a conversation between three friends, Laura, Chris and Mark. What problem does Laura have? What do Chris and Mark think about her problem?

b) Listen again. Make notes on the reasons why Laura thinks she has this problem.

c) Work in pairs. Compare notes. What do you think Laura should do?

Help with Listening Natural rhythm: review

● Sentence stress, weak forms, linking and extra sounds all combine to give spoken English its natural rhythm.

6 **a)** Look at this part of the conversation. Work in pairs. Student A, mark the stressed words and circle the weak forms. Student B, mark the linking and extra sounds (/w/, /j/, /r/).

LAURA   Well, first all, my /j/ old cat refuses to go into my bedroom. In my last flat she slept on the end of my bed every night, so I thought that was rather odd.

MARK   Well, the previous owners' cat might have slept in that room. Or they could have had a dog.

LAURA   They didn't have a cat or a dog.

b) Work with your partner. Compare answers.

c) Look at R12.7, p159. Check your answers to 6a).

d) R12.7 Listen to the conversation again. Notice how the sentence stress, weak forms, linking and extra sounds give spoken English its natural rhythm.

7 **a)** Do you believe in any of these things? Why?/ Why not? Put a question mark if you're not sure.

● telepathy   ● fate
● UFOs   ● fortune-telling
● life on other planets ● astrology and horoscopes

b) Work in groups. Discuss your opinions on the things in 7a). Give reasons for your opinions.

c) Tell the class about anything that your group all believe in or don't believe in.

1 a) **Fill in the gaps with these words/phrases.** V12.1

> stressed out   chuck out
> bugs   chill out   telly
> trendy   mate   hassle

1 Is it ever a _____ travelling to school?
2 Do you get _____ about work?
3 When did you last _____ something you didn't want?
4 Do you watch a lot of _____ ?
5 How do you _____ on holiday?
6 Do you ever go to _____ bars and clubs?
7 Who's your best _____ ?
8 What really _____ you about day-to-day life?

b) **Work in pairs. Ask each other the questions in 1a).**

2 a) **Look at these sentences. Make deductions about the present or the past.** G12.1

1 I left a message for Jan, but she hasn't called me back. *She might have gone away.*
2 Tim's not answering the door.
3 I had the key when I left home, but I can't find it now.
4 I've never seen Kelly eat meat.
5 Pat is buying a tent.
6 Pete always flies first class.

b) **Work in pairs. Compare answers. Are any of your deductions the same?**

3 **Match the verbs in A to the words/phrases in B.** V12.2

A	B
cause	your home
flee	a hostage
sue	an outcry
release	somebody for damages
invade	a poisonous gas
send	a country
release	a political crisis
cause	troops into a place

4 a) **Fill in the gaps with the correct form of these pairs of verbs.** G12.2

> ~~need/pay~~   need/buy   need/change
> should/stay   could/drive   would/call

1 I knew the band so I *didn't need to pay* for a ticket.
2 I _____ out so late last night. I overslept this morning.
3 I _____ this coffee. We've got lots in the cupboard.
4 I _____ you to the station. Why didn't you ask me?
5 I _____ you, but I didn't have your work number with me.
6 Fortunately, I _____ trains. There was one that was direct.

b) **Work in pairs. Compare answers.**

5 **Choose the correct words in these idioms.** V12.3

1 Take what he says with a pinch of *sugar/salt*.
2 It's a piece of *bread/cake*.
3 Keep an *arm/eye* out for Jane.
4 Are you pulling my *leg/hand*?
5 I always sleep like a *log/plant*.
6 The news came out of the *sky/blue*.
7 He lives in the *centre/middle* of nowhere.
8 That really made my *hour/day*.

Progress Portfolio

a) **Tick the things you can do in English.**

☐ I can understand some colloquial words and phrases.

☐ I can make deductions about the present and the past.

☐ I can criticise people's past behaviour.

☐ I can talk about general and specific ability in the past.

☐ I can understand some idioms.

☐ I can follow a conversation between three people on a subject familiar to me.

b) **What do you need to study again?**
🔊 12A–C

Work in groups of four. Read the rules. Then play the game!

Rules

You need: One counter for each student; one dice for each group.

How to play: Put your counters on *START HERE*. Take turns to throw the dice, move your counter and follow the instructions on the square. The first student to get to *FINISH* is the winner.

Grammar and **Vocabulary** squares: The first student to land on a Grammar or Vocabulary square answers question 1. The second student to land on the same square answers question 2. If the other students think your answer is correct, you can stay on the square. If the answer is wrong, move back to the last square you were on. You can check your answers with your teacher. If a third or fourth student lands on the same square, he/she can stay on the square without answering a question.

Keep Talking squares: If you land on a Keep Talking square, talk about the topic for 40 seconds. Another student can check the time. If you can't talk for 40 seconds, move back to the last square you were on. If a second or third student lands on the same square, he/she also talks about the same topic for 40 seconds.

End of Course Review

7 Talk about and compare two interesting places you have visited.

8 Which prepositions do we use with these adjectives?
1 shocked, sick, sure, excited
2 fascinated, famous, fond, disappointed

23 Choose the correct words.
1 I'm *so/such* close to Jo, she's *as/like* a sister.
2 I made *so/such* a lot of money working *as/like* a waiter.

24 Talk about your plans for the future.

FINISH

6 Say eight words/phrases connected to:
1 the Internet
2 phones

9 Talk about things you used to do when you were a child.

22 What are the crimes and criminals for these verbs?
1 steal, burgle, shoplift, rob
2 mug, smuggle, murder, vandalise

25 HAVE A REST

38 Choose the correct verb form in this sentence.
1 This time tomorrow we'll *drive/be driving* home.
2 I'll *be writing/have written* it by the end of May.

5 MOVE FORWARD TWO SQUARES

10 Put this question into reported speech.
1 What do you think of my new dress?
2 Can you let me know by Sunday?

21 Talk about your past and present wishes for work, studies or home life.

26 Put this sentence into the passive.
1 Someone's interviewing Lee at the moment.
2 They might fix the computer tomorrow.

37 Which verb pattern comes after these reporting verbs?
1 claim, warn, blame, agree
2 accuse, point out, deny, advise

4 Correct the mistake in this sentence.
1 If he'd have a car, he'd drive to work.
2 I'd go out last night if I hadn't been so tired.

11 MOVE BACK TWO SQUARES

20 Explain the meaning of these prefixes and give an example for each one.
1 pro-, multi-, re-, under-
2 anti-, pre-, mis-, ex-

27 Talk about the last time you went to the cinema, the theatre or an art gallery.

36 Correct the mistake in this sentence.
1 He warned me not walking across the park.
2 They accused him for stealing the diamond.

3 Talk about the best or worst day you've had this year.

12 Choose the correct verb form in this sentence.
1 Tim *'s written/'s been writing* dozens of articles.
2 They *played/I've been playing* golf since 1.30.

19 MOVE FORWARD TWO SQUARES

28 Say nine words/phrases connected to:
1 books and reading
2 plants and gardens

35 Talk about a book or film that you enjoyed.

2 Which two prepositions can we use with these verbs?
1 apply, talk, depend
2 complain, shout, apologise

13 HAVE A REST

18 Correct two mistakes in this sentence.
1 It's twice as big than my car, but not any hard to drive.
2 The more old they are, more they cost.

29 Talk about things in life that annoy you.

34 HAVE A REST

1 Are both verb forms possible in this sentence?
1 When I was 10, I *used to have/'d have* a pet rabbit.
2 He *'s always losing/always loses* his keys.

14 What are the nouns and adjectives for these verbs?
1 decide, originate, convince, criticise
2 weaken, prefer, improve, recognise

17 Talk about your schooldays.

30 MOVE BACK THREE SQUARES

33 Explain the meaning of these words/phrases.
1 a deposit, a mortgage, property, rip sb off
2 a hassle, mess sth up, chill out, chuck sth out

START HERE

15 What's the difference between these sentences?
1 I've fixed my car. I've had my car fixed.
2 I could have gone. I should have gone.

16 Which verb pattern comes after these verbs?
1 persuade, refuse, let, regret
2 end up, manage, force, had better

31 Talk about tipping and other social rules in your country.

32 MOVE FORWARD THREE SQUARES

Complicated 2D p21

 1 Match the words/phrases in **bold** in the song in **2a)** to these synonyms.

1 fashionable   4 pretending
2 relax   5 shouting
3 an idiot   6 behaving

2 **a)** [R2.8] Listen to the song. Match 1–22 to a)–v).

Uh huh, life's like this
Uh huh, uh huh, that's the way it is (x 2)

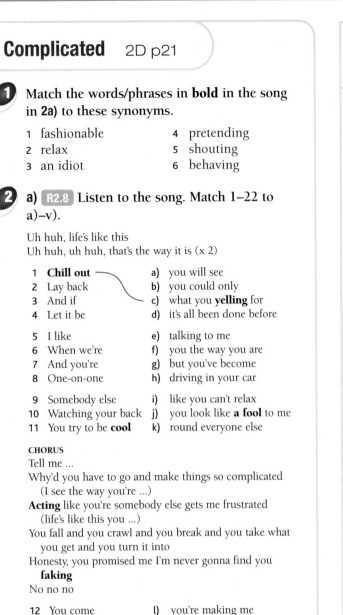

1 **Chill out**   a) you will see
2 Lay back   b) you could only
3 And if   c) what you **yelling** for
4 Let it be   d) it's all been done before

5 I like   e) talking to me
6 When we're   f) you the way you are
7 And you're   g) but you've become
8 One-on-one   h) driving in your car

9 Somebody else   i) like you can't relax
10 Watching your back   j) you look like **a fool** to me
11 You try to be **cool**   k) round everyone else

CHORUS
Tell me ...
Why'd you have to go and make things so complicated
   (I see the way you're ...)
Acting like you're somebody else gets me frustrated
   (life's like this you ...)
You fall and you crawl and you break and you take what
   you get and you turn it into
Honesty, you promised me I'm never gonna find you
   faking
No no no

12 You come   l) you're making me
13 Dressed up   m) aren't where it's at
14 Well you   n) over unannounced
15 You see   o) like you're something else

16 Laugh out   p) you're not fooling
17 Take off   q) when you strike your pose
18 You know   r) when you become
19 Anyone   s) all your preppy clothes

20 Somebody else   t) like you can't relax
21 Watching your back   u) you look like a fool to me
22 You try to be cool   v) round everyone else

CHORUS

REPEAT LINES 1–4 AND 9–11

CHORUS (x 2)

b) Work in pairs. Compare answers.

3 **a)** Read the song again. What does the singer want her boyfriend to change about himself?

b) Work in pairs. Compare ideas.

I Heard it Through the Grapevine 4D p37

 1 **a)** Match these words/phrases from the song. Check the meaning of new phrases with your teacher or in a dictionary.

1 make somebody   a) your mind
2 take somebody   b) somebody go
3 hear something   c) (feel) blue
4 lose   d) by surprise
5 let   e) through the grapevine

b) Work in pairs. Look at the phrases in **1a)** again. What do you think the song is about?

2 **a)** [R4.8] Listen to the song. Choose the correct words/phrases.

Ooh, I bet you're wondering how I ¹*knew*/*heard*
About your ²*plans*/*dreams* to make me blue
With some other guy you ³*met*/*knew* before
Between ⁴*both*/*the two* of us guys
You know I ⁵*love*/*want* you more
It took me by surprise I ⁶*must*/*have to* say
When I found out ⁷*the other day*/*yesterday*
Don't you know that ...

CHORUS
I heard it through the grapevine
Not much longer would you be mine
Oh, I heard it through the grapevine
Oh, I'm just about to lose my mind
Honey, honey, yeah (I heard it through the grapevine not
   much longer would you be mine, baby)

I know a man ain't ⁸*supposed*/*allowed* to cry
But these ⁹*fears*/*tears* I can't hold inside
¹⁰*Losing*/*Choosing* you would end my life you see
'Cause you mean ¹¹*that*/*this* much to me
You ¹²*could*/*should* have told me yourself
That you ¹³*love*/*have* someone else
Instead ...

CHORUS
People say believe ¹⁴*all*/*half* of what you see
Son, and none of what you ¹⁵*read*/*hear*
But I can't help but be ¹⁶*confused*/*amused*
If it's ¹⁷*you*/*true*, please tell me dear
Do you ¹⁸*plan*/*have* to let me go
For the other guy you ¹⁹*knew*/*loved* before
Don't you know ...

CHORUS
Honey, honey, I know that you let me go
Said I heard it through the grapevine ...

b) Work in pairs. Compare answers.

3 **a)** Read the song again. Were your predictions in **1b)** correct? What advice would you give the singer?

b) Work in pairs. Compare ideas.

We Are the Champions 7D p61

1 Work in groups. Discuss these questions.

1 Has your country ever produced any famous world champions? If so, who?

2 Do you support a team that has won a championship or another competition? If so, what did they win?

3 Have you, or has anyone you know, ever been successful in sport, music or other activities?

2 **a)** R7.5 Listen to the song. Fill in the gaps.

I've ¹ _paid_ my dues, time after ² _____
I've done my ³ _____ , but committed no ⁴ _____
And bad ⁵ _____ , I've made a ⁶ _____
I've had my share of sand kicked in my ⁷ _____
But I've come through (and I need to go on and on and on and on)

CHORUS
We are the champions, my ⁸ _____
And we'll keep on ⁹ _____ till the ¹⁰ _____
We are the champions, we are the champions
No ¹¹ _____ for ¹² _____
'Cause we are the champions of the ¹³ _____

I've ¹⁴ _____ my bow, my curtain call
You've brought me ¹⁵ _____ and fortune
And everything that goes with it, I ¹⁶ _____ you all
But it's been no bed of ¹⁷ _____
No pleasure ¹⁸ _____
I consider it a challenge before the ¹⁹ _____ human race
And I never lose (and I need to go on and on and on and on)

CHORUS (x 2)

b) Work in pairs. Compare answers.

3 **a)** Read the song again. <u>Underline</u> all the examples of the Present Perfect Simple you can find.

b) Find words/phrases in the song for these meanings. Write the infinitive form of the verbs.

1 earn respect through hard work and experience
pay your dues

2 something that you find on beaches

3 hit somebody or something with your foot

4 when you bend your head and body forward to show respect or thanks

5 something that needs a lot of effort and determination to do successfully

6 all people as a single group

c) Work in pairs. Compare answers.

Wonderwall 10D p85

1 **a)** Write the names of your favourite: band, male singer, female singer, musician, album.

b) Work in groups. Compare ideas. Does anyone share your taste in music?

2 **a)** R10.11 Listen to the song. Cross out the extra word in each line (1–28).

¹ Today is gonna be the ~~first~~ day
² That they're gonna throw it all back to you
³ By now you really should've somehow
⁴ Realised exactly what you got to do
⁵ Although I don't believe that anybody
⁶ Feels the way I do about you right now

⁷ Backbeat the word is heard on the street
⁸ That the fire burning in your heart is out
⁹ I'm quite sure you've heard it all before
¹⁰ But you have never really had a doubt
¹¹ I just don't believe that anybody
¹² Feels the way that I do about you now

¹³ And all the worlds we have to walk today are winding
¹⁴ And all the bright lights that lead us there are blinding
¹⁵ There are many important things that I
¹⁶ Would like to say to you now, but I don't know how

CHORUS
¹⁷ Because maybe, you're gonna be the only one that saves me
¹⁸ And after all this, you're my wonderwall

¹⁹ Today was maybe gonna be the day
²⁰ But they'll never throw it back again to you
²¹ By now you probably should've somehow
²² Realised what you're not supposed to do
²³ I don't believe that anybody here
²⁴ Actually feels the way I do about you now

²⁵ And all the long roads that lead you there were winding
²⁶ And all the lights that light the way home are blinding
²⁷ There are so many things that I
²⁸ Would like to say to you, but I just don't know how

I said maybe (I said maybe), you're gonna be the one who saves me
And after all, you're my wonderwall (x 2)
I said maybe (I said maybe), you're gonna be the one that saves me (saves me) ...

b) Work in pairs. Compare answers.

3 **a)** Think of three people you know who you can rely on.

b) Work in new pairs. Take turns to tell each other about the people you chose. Ask follow-up questions.

Pair and Group Work: Student/Group A

1C ④ p11

a) Work on your own. Fill in the gaps with the correct form of the verbs in brackets.

1 Have you ever tried _taking_ natural medicines to cure an illness? (take)
2 Do you think all children should .... sports at school? (do)
3 Which songs do you remember .... when you were at primary school? (sing)
4 When you were a child, did your parents ever let you .... up late? (stay)
5 Has anyone ever forced you .... something that you didn't want to? (study)
6 Have you ever pretended .... ill to avoid .... to school or work? (be; go)
7 Did anyone help you .... your homework when you were a child? (do)
8 If you saw someone hitchhiking, would you stop .... them a lift? (give)

b) Work with your partner. Take turns to ask and answer your questions. Ask follow-up questions if possible.

4B ⑧ p33

a) Work with a student from group A. Add extra information to this story by replacing each number with a non-defining relative clause. Then finish the story in your own words.

Wendy worked in a bookshop called Bookworld, ①. One Monday morning her car broke down while she was driving to work. Her manager, Brian, sacked her because she was 15 minutes late. Wendy, ②, decided to become a novelist. Her first novel, ③, took her nearly three years to write. She managed to find a publisher, and soon the book became so successful that Wendy was asked to go on a book-signing tour. One day she went back to Bookworld, ④, and there were hundreds of people queuing up to buy her book. When she saw Brian, ⑤, she smiled at him and …

b) Work with a student from group B. Take turns to read out your stories. Which do you think is the best?

4A ⑨ p31

a) Work on your own. Read this urban legend. Then write ten words/phrases from the urban legend on a piece of paper to help you remember the story.

A woman in Miami, USA, was getting ready for a dinner party. She'd been preparing the food for hours and was just about to serve the first course, which was salmon. She'd already put the fish onto ten separate plates, but while she wasn't looking her cat came into the kitchen and ate one portion of the salmon. The woman put the cat outside, hurriedly divided the remaining nine portions into ten, and then served the fish to her guests. At the end of the meal there was a knock at the door. It was her neighbour, who had come to tell her that he'd found her cat lying dead in his front garden. Horrified, the woman went back and told the guests that the salmon was poisonous. Everyone at the dinner party was taken to hospital, where they spent an uncomfortable and sleepless night. When the woman got home the next morning, she found a different neighbour waiting for her. He'd come to apologise for running over her cat the previous evening.

b) Close your book. Work with your partner. Take turns to tell each other your urban legends in your own words. Use the words/phrases you wrote in a) to help you.

c) Do you know any other urban legends? Tell the class.

3A ⑥ p23

a) Work in pairs with a student from group A. Fill in the gaps with the correct form of the verbs in brackets.

1 If you _____ (hit) a parked car at 3 a.m., _____ you _____ (leave) a note with your phone number?
2 Imagine you _____ (find) an expensive camera on a park bench, _____ you _____ (hand) it in to the police?
3 Suppose your company _____ (pay) you twice for last month's work, _____ you _____ (keep) the money?
4 If you _____ (get) home from the supermarket and _____ (realise) that they hadn't charged you for something, _____ you _____ (take) it back?
5 Imagine you _____ (borrow) a friend's laptop and _____ (drop) it on the way home, _____ you _____ (tell) your friend what happened?

b) Work with a student from group B. Take turns to ask and answer the questions. Make brief notes to help you remember your partner's answers.

> If you hit a parked car at 3 a.m., would you leave a note with your phone number?

> Yes, I would, assuming I'd damaged the car.

c) Work with your partner from group A. Discuss how your partners from group B answered each question. Were their answers similar? Which student from group B do you think is more honest?

6D ⑥ p53

a) Work with a student from group A. Look at the speakers in conversations 1 and 2. Decide if each conversation should be polite or neutral. Then rewrite the conversations to make them sound more natural. Invent your own endings.

1 **Two friends**
  A Busy?
  B Tied up. Important?
  A No. When?
  B …

2 **A teacher and a student**
  A See you?
  B Not a good time.
  A Quick question.
  B …

b) Practise the conversations with your partner.

c) Work in groups of four with a pair from group B. Take turns to role-play your conversations. Guess who the people are in the other pair's conversations. Use these ideas (there is one extra idea).

- A doctor and his/her receptionist
- A son/daughter phoning a parent at work
- Two work colleagues

7C ④ p59

a) Work on your own. Complete the words in **bold** with a prefix. Sometimes there is more than one possible answer.

1 What do people in your country do that you think is _____**social**?
2 Do you have a lot of _____**discipline**?
3 Do you know anyone who has done or is doing a _____**graduate** degree?
4 Are most people in your country _____**hunting**?
5 How many people in your family are _____**smokers**?
6 Which films or TV programmes do you think are _____**rated**?
7 If you were a _____**millionaire**, what would you spend your money on?
8 When you were a child, did you _____**behave** a lot?

b) Work with your partner. Take turns to ask and answer the questions. Ask follow-up questions if possible.

3C ⑧ p27

a) Work on your own. Read about a crime that happened in the UK. Then write five words/ phrases to help you remember the crime.

A 34-year-old London postman was the mastermind behind a £20 million cheque book fraud. The man stole cheque books from post office sorting offices and then used them to withdraw money from people's bank accounts.

b) Work with the other people in your group. Take turns to tell each other about the crime in **a)**. Use your own words if possible. After each crime, decide what punishment you would have given the criminal if you'd been the judge.

c) Turn to p159. Read what happened to the criminals. Do you agree with the sentences that the judges gave them? Why?/Why not?

9A 7 p71

a) Work with a student from group A. Write questions with these words. Use the correct passive form of the verbs.

Oscars quiz

1 In which year / the ceremony first / broadcast / in colour?
   In which year was the ceremony first broadcast in colour?
   a) 1956   b) **1966**   c) 1976
2 How many Oscars / refuse / so far?
   a) none   b) 3   c) **6**
3 Which of these films / not award / an Oscar for best movie?
   a) *The Godfather*   b) ***Jurassic Park***
   c) *Gone with the Wind*
4 Approximately how many Oscars / award / each year?
   a) **50**   b) 75   c) 100
5 How many Oscars / award / since the Academy Awards began?
   a) over 7,500   b) over 5,000   c) **over 2,500**
6 At what time of day in the USA / the nominations / announce ?
   a) **5.30 a.m.**   b) 9 a.m.   c) midday

b) Work with a pair from group B. Take turns to ask and answer your questions. Say the three possible answers when you ask your questions. (The correct answers are in **bold**.)

c) Which pair got most answers right?

7B 5 p57

a) Work on your own. Make questions with *you* with these words. Use *How long …?* or *How much/many …?* and the Present Perfect Simple or Present Perfect Continuous. Use the continuous form if possible.

1 / countries / visit ?
   How many countries have you visited?
2 / live / in your house or flat?
3 / phone calls / make / today?
4 / study / English?
5 / know / your oldest friend?
6 / spend / on food today?

b) Work with your partner. Take turns to ask and answer the questions. Ask follow-up questions.

3D 7 p29

a) Work on your own. Read about your situation. Make a list of at least five things you need to do. Which of these things can you do yourself? Which do you need help with?

You're organising a 21st birthday party for your cousin Sam tomorrow. The party will be at your home and you've invited 25 people (four are coming by train and two by plane). Your house is a mess and you haven't started preparing for the party.

b) Read about your partner's situation. Make a list of at least five things you can offer to do to help him/her.

He/She is going on holiday to New York on Sunday for two weeks. He/She has got a plane ticket and a visa, but hasn't done anything else to prepare for the holiday. He/She is worried about being burgled while he/she is away and he/she also has two cats.

c) Work with your partner. Take turns to discuss your situations. Use your lists from **a)** and **b)** to help you make, accept or refuse offers.

12C 4 p98

a) Work on your own. Complete the idioms in these sentences.

1 In an old farmhouse in the middle of _____ .
2 I'm taking a few days off to _____ my batteries.
3 No, I was just pulling your _____ .
4 Yes, but it's a far _____ from the small village where I grew up.
5 No, I always sleep like a _____ .
6 Congratulations! That must have made your _____ .

b) Work with your partner. Say sentences a)–f) to him/her. Listen to his/her responses. Do you think they're correct?

a) Have you done the homework yet?
b) Have you seen my dictionary anywhere?
c) I'm worried about making a speech in front of so many people.
d) I had no idea that William was moving to the USA.
e) The clients are going to read our report tomorrow.
f) Our teacher says I'm the best student he/she's ever had.

c) Listen to your partner's sentences. Respond with the correct sentence from **a)**.

Pair and Group Work: Student/Group B

1C ❹ p11

a) Work on your own. Fill in the gaps with the correct form of the verbs in brackets.

a) Have you ever tried _to learn_ another foreign language? (learn)

b) Where do you think you'll end up .... when you retire? (live)

c) What would you encourage your children .... at university? (study)

d) Have you stopped .... to the music you liked when you were 16? (listen)

e) When you were a child, did your parents make you .... jobs around the house? (do)

f) Did you remember .... your best friend a card on their last birthday? (send)

g) Would you allow your children .... what they studied at school? (choose)

h) What kind of mistakes in English do you keep ....? (make)

b) Work with your partner. Take turns to ask and answer your questions. Ask follow-up questions if possible.

4B ❽ p33

a) Work with a student from group B. Add extra information to this story by replacing each number with a non-defining relative clause. Then finish the story in your own words.

> Olivia's favourite novel was called *Second Chance*. She'd read the book, ①, over a dozen times. One day she went into town to meet her boyfriend, Graham, ②. When she got there she realised that she'd left the book on the bus. Olivia, ③, was really upset because the book had been signed by the author. The next day Graham wrote to the author, ④, and explained what had happened. Three weeks later it was Olivia's birthday. Graham gave Olivia her present, ⑤. It was a hardback copy of *Second Chance*. When she opened the book …

b) Work with a student from group A. Take turns to read out your stories. Which do you think is the best?

4A ❾ p31

a) Work on your own. Read this urban legend. Then write ten words/phrases from the urban legend on a piece of paper to help you remember the story.

A young couple from Bristol, UK, were having terrible problems with their marriage. They'd been having arguments almost every day for the last six months, mainly caused by the husband's terrible moods. One morning, just before he set off on a three-week business trip, he told his wife that he couldn't stand living with her any more and the marriage was over. He also told her that she should get out of *his* house by the time he got back. When he arrived home three weeks later his wife had gone, but she'd left the house in a terrible mess. While he was clearing up, he noticed that the phone was off the hook. He put it back and thought no more about it. A few weeks later the phone bill arrived. It was enormous – over £3,000! He immediately called the telephone company to complain, but was told that the bill was correct and that the phone had been connected to the speaking clock in Australia for a three-week period.

b) Close your book. Work with your partner. Take turns to tell each other your urban legends in your own words. Use the words/phrases you wrote in **a)** to help you.

c) Do you know any other urban legends? Tell the class.

3A 6 p23

a) Work in pairs with a student from group B. Fill in the gaps with the correct form of the verbs in brackets.

a) If you _____ (want) to go to a club but it was full, _____ you _____ (try) to bribe the doorman?
b) Imagine a female friend _____ (ask) for your opinion about her new hairstyle and you _____ (think) it looked terrible, _____ you _____ (tell) her the truth?
c) Supposing you _____ (find) a copy of the end-of-course exam paper, _____ you _____ (give) it back to your teacher without looking at it?
d) If a shop assistant _____ (give) you too much change, _____ you _____ (give) it back?
e) Suppose a friend _____ (ask) you to look after his tropical fish and one of them died, _____ you _____ (tell) your friend what happened?

b) Work with a student from group A. Take turns to ask and answer your questions. Make brief notes to help you remember your partner's answers.

> If you wanted to go to a club but it was full, would you try to bribe the doorman?

> Yes, I would, as long as I didn't have to give him too much.

c) Work with your partner from group B. Discuss how your partners from group A answered each question. Were their answers similar? Which student from group A do you think is more honest?

7C 4 p59

a) Work on your own. Complete the words in **bold** with a prefix. Sometimes there is more than one possible answer.

a) Do you live in a _____**cultural** area?
b) How many _____**presidents** of the USA can you name?
c) Do any of the rooms of your house or flat need _____**decorating**?
d) Have you ever been _____**charged** in a restaurant or a shop?
e) Do you ever _____**understand** people when they speak English?
f) Which professions do you think are _____**paid**?
g) Would you like to work for a _____**national** company?
h) What's the longest _____**stop** flight you've been on?

b) Work with your partner. Take turns to ask and answer the questions. Ask follow-up questions if possible.

6D 6 p53

a) Work with a student from group B. Look at the speakers in conversations 1 and 2. Decide if each conversation should be polite or neutral. Then rewrite the conversations to make them sound more natural. Invent your own endings.

1 Two work colleagues
A Got a minute?
B Sorry. Pushed for time.
A When?
B …

2 A son/daughter phoning a parent at work
A Good time?
B Busy. Urgent?
A Yes. Lost keys.
B …

b) Practise the conversations with your partner.

c) Work in groups of four with a pair from group A. Take turns to role-play your conversations. Guess who the people are in the other pair's conversations. Use these ideas (there is one extra idea).

- A teacher and a student
- An employee and his/her manager
- Two friends

3C 8 p27

a) Work on your own. Read about a crime that happened in the UK. Then write five words/phrases to help you remember the crime.

A 35-year-old secretary stole £4.3 million from the company she worked for over a period of several years. She was caught a few weeks before she was planning to leave her job and start a new life in a £750,000 villa in Cyprus.

b) Work with the other people in your group. Take turns to tell each other about the crime in a). Use your own words if possible. After each crime, decide what punishment you would have given the criminal if you'd been the judge.

c) Turn to p159. Read what happened to the criminals. Do you agree with the sentences that the judges gave them? Why?/Why not?

9A 7 p71

a) Work with a student from group B. Write questions with these words. Use the correct passive form of the verbs.

Oscars quiz

1 On which day / the Academy Awards ceremony now / hold ?
On which day is the Academy Awards ceremony now held?
a) Friday b) Saturday c) **Sunday**

2 In which year / the first Oscar / award / for special effects?
a) **1939** b) 1959 c) 1979

3 How many Oscars / the film *Titanic* / nominate / for in 1997?
a) 8 b) 11 c) **14**

4 How many people / tell / the results before the ceremony?
a) 1 b) **2** c) 7

5 Which country / award / the most Oscars for best foreign film?
a) Japan b) France c) **Italy**

6 In approximately how many countries can the Oscars / see / live on TV?
a) 50 b) **100** c) 150

b) Work with a pair from group A. Take turns to ask and answer your questions. Say the three possible answers when you ask your questions. (The correct answers are in **bold**.)

c) Which pair got most answers right?

7B 5 p57

a) Work on your own. Make questions with *you* with these words. Use *How long …?* or *How much/many …?* and the Present Perfect Simple or Present Perfect Continuous. Use the continuous form if possible.

a) / time / spend / watching TV this week?
How much time have you spent watching TV this week?

b) / live / in this town or city?

c) / novels / read / in English?

d) / have / your mobile?

e) / come / to this class?

f) / times / go / to the cinema this month?

b) Work with your partner. Take turns to ask and answer the questions. Ask follow-up questions.

3D 7 p29

a) Work on your own. Read about your situation. Make a list of at least five things you need to do. Which of these things can you do yourself? Which do you need help with?

You're going on holiday to New York on Sunday for two weeks. You've got a plane ticket and a visa, but you haven't done anything else to prepare for the holiday. You're worried about being burgled while you are away, and you also have two cats.

b) Read about your partner's situation. Make a list of at least five things you can offer to do to help him/her.

He/She is organising a 21st birthday party for his/her cousin Sam tomorrow. The party will be at his/her home and he/she has invited 25 people (four are coming by train and two by plane). His/Her house is a mess and he/she hasn't started preparing for the party.

c) Work with your partner. Take turns to discuss your situations. Use your lists from **a)** and **b)** to help you make, accept or refuse offers.

12C 4 p98

a) Work on your own. Complete the idioms in these sentences.

1 Yes, it was a piece of _____ .

2 Good. That should give them _____ for thought.

3 Nor did I. The news came completely out of the _____ .

4 No, but I'll keep an _____ out for it, if you like.

5 I'd take that with a pinch of _____ if I were you!

6 Why not tell a joke first to break the _____ ?

b) Work with your partner. Listen to his/her sentences. Respond with the correct sentence from **a)**.

c) Say sentences a)–f) to your partner. Listen to his/her responses. Do you think they're correct?

a) What are you doing next week?

b) Do you tend to wake up a lot in the night?

c) Whereabouts does your uncle live?

d) Hey, guess what? I've just won £100!

e) Do you like living in the city?

f) Are we really doing an exam tomorrow?

Pair and Group Work: Other activities

1A 7 p7

a) Work on your own. Make notes on these things.

English learner profile

1	length of time I've been studying English	
2	things I remember about my first English classes	
3	exams I've taken in English	
4	why I'm studying English now	
5	English-speaking countries I'd like to go to	
6	how I feel about my level of English now	
7	things I do to improve my English outside class	
8	things I want to do (or do better) in English	
9	things I don't like about the English language	
10	things I like about the English language	

b) Make questions with *you* about the things in a).

1 *How long have you been studying English?*

2 *What do you remember about your first English classes?*

c) Work in pairs. Take turns to ask and answer your questions. How many things do you have in common?

> How long have you been studying English?

> For about six years. What about you?

d) Tell the class two things that you and your partner have in common.

4C 8 p35

a) Work on your own. You are going to tell other students a story. It can be about you or someone you know. Choose from these ideas or your own. Then make notes on the main events of your story.

- a practical joke
- a story from school, college or university
- a holiday experience
- a wonderful or terrible night out
- an interesting or unusual journey
- the most enjoyable or frightening day of your life

b) Look at your notes from a) again. Decide where you can use some of these words/phrases.

> Actually   Anyway   Apparently   According to
> Meanwhile   Luckily   By the way   In the end

c) Work in groups. Take turns to tell your story. Which is the most interesting or the funniest?

d) Tell the class the most interesting or the funniest story in your group.

3C 8 p27

a) Work on your own. Read about a crime that happened in the UK. Then write five words/phrases to help you remember the crime.

A man was arrested for illegally copying and selling DVDs. He was caught with 1,000 DVDs in his car, and the police also found another 18,000 DVDs in his house and in a warehouse in Cambridge. It was the second time the police had arrested him for this crime.

b) Work with the other people in your group. Take turns to tell each other about the crime in a). Use your own words if possible. After each crime, decide what punishment you would have given the criminal if you'd been the judge.

c) Turn to p159. Read what happened to the criminals. Do you agree with the sentences that the judges gave them? Why?/Why not?

2C ⑧ p19

a) Work on your own. Tick the sentences that are true for you. Think of reasons why you chose these sentences.

- I often put things off.
- I'm quite organised.
- I'm a perfectionist.
- I'm rather forgetful.
- I'm good at multitasking.
- I'm always making lists.
- I'm very punctual.
- I'm a control freak.
- I plan everything in advance.
- I tend to do things spontaneously.

b) Work in pairs. Take turns to tell each other which sentences you ticked in **a)**. Give reasons why you chose these sentences. How many similarities are there between you and your partner?

c) Tell the class two things that you and your partner have in common.

12A ⑨ p95

a) Work with your partner. Look at the pictures of some other people who were in Patrick's taxi yesterday. Make at least two deductions about the present or the past for each picture.

> The people in picture 1 could have been to the theatre.

> Yes, or they might have been out to dinner.

b) Work in groups of four with another pair. Take turns to tell the other pair your deductions about the people in each picture. Are your ideas the same?

c) Tell the class some of your deductions.

3C ⑧ p27

a) Work on your own. Read about a crime that happened in the UK. Then write five words/phrases to help you remember the crime.

> Two burglars broke into a farmhouse at night. The farmer heard the burglars and came downstairs carrying a shotgun. While the burglars were running away, the farmer shot one of them in the back and killed him. He also shot and seriously injured the other burglar. The farmer was charged with murder.

b) Work with the other people in your group. Take turns to tell each other about the crime in **a)**. Use your own words if possible. After each crime, decide what punishment you would have given the criminal if you'd been the judge.

c) Turn to p159. Read what happened to the criminals. Do you agree with the sentences that the judges gave them? Why?/Why not?

8D ⑦ p69

a) Work with your partner. Choose situation 1 or 2. Then write a conversation between the people.

Situation 1
Chris and Pat were playing doubles in a tennis tournament yesterday. They lost the match. Chris was extremely angry afterwards and said it was Pat's fault that they lost. Now Chris is phoning Pat to apologise and to try and arrange another match.

Situation 2
Sam and Alex went to the cinema last night. Sam loved the film, but Alex hated it. They had a big argument about it, then Alex got very upset and went home. Now Sam is phoning Alex to apologise and to suggest going to another film together.

b) Swap papers with another pair. Read their conversation and correct any mistakes you find.

c) Practise the conversation with your partner until you can remember it.

d) Work in groups of four. Take turns to role-play the conversation for the students who wrote it.

Pair and Group Work: Other activities

9C **8** p75

a) Work with your partner. Look at photos 1–12. Which do you think are real works of art? Which do you think are not?

b) Work with another pair. Discuss your ideas. Do you agree which are real works of art? Give reasons for your choices.

c) Check on p159. How many real works of art did you identify correctly?

Vocabulary

V1.1 Language ability (1A ❶ p6)

(my) first language (is) …
be bilingual* in …
be fluent* in …
be reasonably* good at …
can get by* in …
know a few words of …

can't speak a word of …
can have a conversation in …
speak some … , but it's a bit rusty*
pick up* a bit of … on holiday

TIP! • In the Language Summaries we only show the main stress (•) in words and phrases.

*bilingual /baɪˈlɪŋgwəl/ able to speak two languages, usually because you learned them as a child
*fluent able to speak a language easily, quickly and well
*reasonably /ˈriːzənəbli/ to quite a good level
*get by (in a language) know just enough of a language for simple communication
*rusty not as good at a language as you used to be because you haven't used it for a long time
*pick up (a language) learn a language by practising it, rather than by learning it in a class

V1.2 Education (1B ❶ p8)

a college /ˈkɒlɪdʒ/ any place where people study for qualifications after leaving school
a campus the land and buildings of a university or college
an undergraduate somebody who is studying for their first degree at university or college
a graduate /ˈgrædʒuət/ somebody who has a first degree from a university or college
a postgraduate somebody who has a first degree and is now studying for a higher degree
a Master's (degree) an advanced university or college degree
a PhD /piːeɪtʃˈdiː/ the highest university or college degree
a tutor a teacher who works with one student or a small group of students
a lecturer somebody who teaches at a university or college
a professor a teacher of the highest level in a university department
a tutorial a period of study with a tutor
a seminar a class in which a small group of students discuss a particular subject
a lecture a talk on a particular subject, especially at university or college
fees the amount of money you pay to go to a private school, university, etc.
a student loan the money that a student borrows from a bank while at university or college
a scholarship /ˈskɒləʃɪp/ an amount of money paid by a school, university, etc. to a student who has a lot of ability, but not much money
a career /kəˈrɪə/ the job, or series of jobs, that you do during your working life

TIPS! • A state school (UK) = a public school (US). In British English, a public school is an expensive type of private school.
• university (UK) = college (US)
• We often use abbreviations to talk about university degrees: a BSc = Bachelor of Science; an MA = a Master of Arts, etc.: He's got a BSc in chemistry.
• Graduate can be a noun or a verb. Notice the different pronunciation: Tim's a graduate /ˈgrædʒuət/. I graduate /ˈgrædʒueɪt/ next year.

V1.3 Verb patterns (1) (1C ❸ p11)

• When we use two verbs together, the form of the second verb usually depends on the first verb.

avoid end up* regret* **begin prefer** keep **start** don't mind **continue** finish **love like hate** miss enjoy			+ verb+ing (doing)
refuse **begin** need hope pretend manage **prefer start** seem **continue** forget **love like hate** plan decide			+ infinitive with to (to do)
make **help** let			+ object + infinitive (sb/sth do)
allow force* encourage* expect persuade* ask teach **help** pay convince*			+ object + infinitive with to (sb/sth to do)
might can will could would rather should had better			+ infinitive (do)

TIPS! • The verbs in blue in the table show the form of the verbs in blue in the article 'Under examination' on p10.
• The verbs in **bold** in the table have more than one verb pattern. Both verb patterns have the same meaning:
I began **reading**. = I began **to read**.
He helped me **get** a job. = He helped me **to get** a job.
• **sb** = somebody; **sth** = something

*end up finally be in a particular situation or place: I never thought I'd end up being a teacher.
*regret feel sadness about something you have done: I regret leaving school at 16.
*force make somebody do something they don't want to do: He forced me to tell him everything I knew.
*encourage /ɪnˈkʌrɪdʒ/ talk or behave in a way that gives somebody confidence in something: My uncle encouraged me to become a musician.
*persuade /pəˈsweɪd/ make somebody decide to do something by giving them reasons why they should do it: I persuaded Steve to buy a new car.
*convince make somebody feel certain that something is true: I hope this will convince you to change your mind.

TIPS! • Continuous verb forms of begin, start and continue are always followed by the infinitive with to: I'm starting to worry about my health. not I'm starting worrying about my health.
• We can also say teach somebody how to do sth: My brother taught me how to drive.

Language Summary 1

- In British English, the verbs *love, like, dislike* and *hate* are usually followed by verb+*ing*: *I love playing tennis.* In American English, these verbs are usually followed by the infinitive with *to*: *I love to play tennis.*
- We can also say *love/like/dislike/hate somebody doing something*: *I love people calling me on my birthday.*

VERBS WITH DIFFERENT MEANINGS

- *remember* + verb+*ing* = remember something that you did before: *I remember **staying up** all night before my maths exam.*
- *remember* + infinitive with *to* = make a mental note to do something in the future: *I always remember **to wish** my daughters luck.*
- *stop* + verb+*ing* = stop something that you were doing: *Maybe it's time to stop **testing** how much children remember.*
- *stop* + infinitive with *to* = stop doing one thing in order to do something else: *They usually study for half an hour and then stop **to call** their friends or watch TV.*
- *try* + verb+*ing* = do something in order to solve a problem: *If you need to add up a few numbers, try **using** a calculator.*
- *try* + infinitive with *to* = make an effort to do something difficult: *I was trying **to learn** dozens of equations by heart.*
- Look at these pictures. Notice the difference in meaning between the verb forms in **bold**.

She remembered **to post** the letter.   She remembered **posting** the letter.

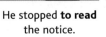

He stopped **to read** the notice.   He stopped **reading** the notice (to talk to his friend).

He's trying **to lose** 10 kilos.   "I've got a terrible headache." "Try **taking** some painkillers."

G1.1   The English verb system   (1A **4** p7)

- The English verb system has three aspects: simple, continuous and perfect. These aspects refer to how the speaker sees the event or situation.

THE SIMPLE ASPECT

- We usually use **simple** verb forms to talk about things that are repeated, permanent or completed.
  Present Simple: *We always **tell** students they need two things to succeed.* (repeated); *More people **speak** English than any other language.* (permanent)
  Past Simple: *We **visited** one acting class.* (completed)

THE CONTINUOUS ASPECT

- We usually use **continuous** verb forms to talk about things that are in progress, temporary or unfinished.
  Past Continuous: *A student **was pretending** to be the film star Orlando Bloom.* (in progress)
  Present Continuous: *The way people study English **is** also **changing**.* (temporary)
  Present Perfect Continuous: *The government **has been building** English immersion schools all over the country.* (unfinished)

THE PERFECT ASPECT

- We usually use **perfect** verb forms to talk about things that connect two different time periods (the past and the present, etc.).
  Present Perfect Simple: *Other multinational companies **have started** moving towards an English-only email policy.*
  Past Perfect Simple: *By the end of last year, the number of adult English speakers in Asia **had reached** 350 million.*

THE PASSIVE

- We usually use **passive** verb forms when we are more interested in what happens to somebody or something than in who or what does the action.
  Present Simple Passive: *80% of the world's electronic information **is stored** in English.*
  Past Simple Passive: *English **was chosen** as the working language of the Japanese, French and Czech staff.*

ACTIVITY AND STATE VERBS

- Activity verbs talk about activities and actions (*learn, change, run, play, hit, lose,* etc.): *These new English speakers **aren't** just **learning** the language – they're **changing** it.*
- State verbs talk about states, feelings and opinions (*need, seem, know, remember, love, want,* etc.): *We always tell students they **need** two things to succeed.*
- We don't usually use state verbs in continuous verb forms: *And they **seem** to enjoy the experience.* not ~~And they're seeming to enjoy the experience.~~
- Other common state verbs are: *have got, hear, believe, agree, forget, mean, understand, like, hate, prefer, belong, own* and *cost.*

G1.2 Uses of auxiliaries (1): auxiliaries in verb forms `1B 4 p9`

- We make all continuous verb forms with *be* + verb+*ing*: *I **was walking** around for ages.* (Past Continuous) *What **are** you **studying**?* (Present Continuous)

- We make all perfect verb forms with *have* + past participle: *My brother's (= **has**) **done** that course.* (Present Perfect Simple)

- We make all passive verb forms with *be* + past participle: *I **was told** it was really expensive.* (Past Simple Passive)

- In the Present Simple and Past Simple we use a form of *do* to make questions and negatives: *Anyway, **do** you **live** here on campus? I **didn't understand** very much.*

TIP! • We don't use auxiliaries in the positive forms of the Present Simple and Past Simple: *Most people **think** economics is really boring. Well, at least you **found** it in the end.*

MODAL VERBS

- We also use modal verbs as auxiliaries. The modal verbs are: *will, would, can, could, may, might, shall, should, ought to, must* and *have to*.

- Modal verbs are different from the auxiliaries *be, do* and *have* because they have their own meanings. Most modal verbs also have more than one meaning:
  *I'**ll** see you at six.* (a promise)
  *I think we'**ll** win.* (a prediction)
  ***Can** you pick me up?* (a request)
  *He **can** play the piano.* (ability)
  *You **must** be here at nine.* (obligation)
  *You **must** see that film.* (strong recommendation)

G1.3 Uses of auxiliaries (2): other uses of auxiliaries `1B 5 p9`

- We also use auxiliaries in the following ways:
a) in question tags: *You went to Professor Lee's geography lecture yesterday, **didn't you**?*
b) in echo questions to show interest:
   TIM *He graduated last July.*   MIA ***Did he**?*
c) to agree with somebody with *so* or *neither*:
   TIM *I keep getting lost!*   MIA *Yes, **so do I**.*
d) to avoid repeating a verb or phrase:
   *Most people think economics is really boring, but I **don't**.*
e) in short answers to *yes/no* questions:
   TIM *Do you live here on campus?*   MIA ***No, I don't**.*
f) to add emphasis:
   TIM *Maybe you should get a map.*   MIA *I **did have** a map!*

TIPS! • To add emphasis to a verb in the positive form of the Present Simple or Past Simple, we use the auxiliaries *do, does* or *did*. We stress these auxiliaries: *I **do** understand! He **does** have a job. We **did** enjoy ourselves.*
• To add emphasis to other verb forms, we stress the uncontracted form of the auxiliary: *I **am** going to do it.*

RW1.1 Keeping a conversation going `1D 3 p12`

- We often use short questions to keep a conversation going and to show interest.
  How's (it) going? (= Are you enjoying it or being successful at it?)
  Why's that? (= What's the reason?)
  Like what, exactly? (= Can you give me an example?)
  How do you mean? (= Can you explain this more clearly?)
  What's (the teacher) like? (= Can you describe him/her?)
  What else are you doing? (= Can you tell me about something different?)
  Such as? (= Can you give me an example?)
  How come? (= Why?/What's the reason?)
  In what way? (= Can you explain this more clearly?)
  What sort of (dancing)? (= Can you be more specific?)

TIPS! • In informal English, we also use *How's it going?* as a greeting: *Hi, Andy. How's it going?* (= How are you?)
• We can also say *Who else ... ?* and *Where else ... ?*: *Who else are you going with? Where else are you going?*
• We can say *What sort of ... ?, What kind of ... ?* and *What type of ... ?*: *What sort/kind/type of course?*

QUESTIONS WITH PREPOSITIONS

- We often make short questions with 'question word + preposition':
  KIM *I go every week.*
  SUE *Really? **Who with**?*

  SUE *I'm off to the USA on Sunday.*
  KIM *Are you? **How long for**?*

TIPS! • In these types of short questions, both the question word and the prepositions are stressed.
• The most common question words for these types of questions are *Who, Where* and *What*:
A *I'm going away.*   B *Where to?*
A *I talked to Vicky.*   B *What about?*
• We often use *What for?* as an alternative to *Why?*:
A *I'm going into town.*   B *What for?*
• We also use echo questions (KIM *It's really difficult, actually.* SUE *Is it?*) and questions with question tags (*It's been ages, **hasn't it**?*) to keep a conversation going.

I've just started an English course.

Really? How's it going?

I'm really enjoying it, actually.

What's the school like?

Language Summary 2

V2.1 Expressing frequency (2A 6 p15)

lower frequency	higher frequency
rarely /ˈreəli/	frequently
occasionally /əˈkeɪʒənəli/	more often than not
seldom	most weeks
every so often	most of the time
once in a while	
every now and again	

TIP! • We can also say *most mornings/days/weekends*, etc.:
I go running most mornings.

WORD ORDER

● *Rarely, seldom* and *frequently* usually come before the main verb: *I rarely drink coffee now. I seldom pay attention to government reports about food. I frequently go to the gym.*

● *Occasionally* can come at the beginning of the sentence, before the main verb or at the end of the sentence: *Occasionally I eat vegetables. = I occasionally eat vegetables. = I eat vegetables occasionally.*

● All adverbs of frequency come after the verb *be*: *He's rarely home before eight.*

● *Every so often, once in a while, every now and again, more often than not, most weeks* and *most of the time* can come at the beginning or the end of the sentence: *Most of the time I eat healthy food. = I eat healthy food most of the time.*

V2.2 Feelings and opinions (2B 1 p16)

● We often use prepositions with adjectives. The most common prepositions for these adjectives are in **bold**. Other prepositions that we can also use for these adjectives are in brackets.

terrified **of** (by)	impressed **by*** (with, at)
fascinated **by** (with)	aware **of***
excited **about** (by, at)	famous **for**
satisfied **with** (by)	fond **of***
shocked **by*** (at)	sure **about** (of)
disappointed **in** (by, with)	sick **of***

> ***shocked** /ʃɒkt/ **by/at sth** feeling surprised and upset by something very unexpected or unpleasant
> ***impressed by/with/at sb/sth** admire somebody or something because you notice how good, successful, clever, etc. they are
> ***aware of sth** knowing that something exists, or having knowledge or experience of a particular thing
> ***fond of sb/sth** like somebody or something very much
> ***sick of sth** very annoyed at or fed up with something

TIPS! • We must use the prepositions with *fond of* and *sick of* for these meanings. The other adjectives can be used without a preposition: *I was absolutely terrified.*
• After prepositions we use a noun, a pronoun or verb+*ing*.

V2.3 Word building (1): suffixes (2C 3 p19)

verb	noun	adjective	adverb
prefer	preference	preferable	preferably
decide	decision	decisive	decisively
originate	originality origin	original	originally
–	realism reality	realistic real	realistically really
convince	conviction	convinced convincing	convincingly
–	responsibility	responsible	responsibly
weaken	weakness	weak	weakly
improve	improvement	improved	–
criticise	criticism	critical	critically
recognise	recognition	recognisable	recognisably

● We can make **verbs** by adding these suffixes to nouns or adjectives: *-ate, -en, -ise.*

● We can make **nouns** by adding these suffixes to verbs or adjectives: *-ence, -ion, -ity, -ism, -ility, -ness, -ment.*

● We can make **adjectives** by adding these suffixes to verbs or nouns: *-able, -ive, -al, -ic, -ed, -ing, -ible.*

● We usually make **adverbs** by adding *-ly* or *-ally* to adjectives.

TIPS! • Sometimes the verb and the noun are the same, for example, *plan, test, need, run,* etc.: *I **plan** to go to college next year. That's a good **plan**.*
• If an adjective ends in *-e*, we usually replace *-e* with *-ly* to make the adverb: *responsible → responsibly.* If an adjective ends in *-ic*, we add *-ally* to make the adverb: *realistic → realistically.*

G2.1 Present and past habits, repeated actions and states (2A 3 p15)

PRESENT HABITS, REPEATED ACTIONS AND STATES

● We use the **Present Simple** to talk about present habits, repeated actions and states: *I **know** what I like and I **eat** what I like.*

● We often use the **Present Continuous** with *always* to talk about present habits and repeated actions that annoy us or happen more than usual: *My mom's **always telling** me what I should and shouldn't eat.*

● We can use *will* + **infinitive** to talk about repeated and typical behaviour in the present: *Every day when I get home from work, I'll have a coffee and half a packet of chocolate cookies.* We don't usually use this verb form with state verbs for this meaning.

● Compare these sentences:

Sometimes I'll eat things I know are unhealthy. (repeated and typical behaviour)

Tonight I'll probably **have** *a burger.* (a future action)

TIP! ● To show criticism, we stress the uncontracted form of *will: He* **will** *leave the door open all the time!*

PAST HABITS, REPEATED ACTIONS AND STATES

● We use the **Past Simple** and **used to + infinitive** to talk about past habits, repeated actions and states: *And then I* **read** *a lot of books about health and nutrition, and I* **knew** *I had to change. I* **used to be** *addicted to chocolate chip cookies – my mom* **used to hide** *them from me.*

● We can use **would + infinitive** to talk about past habits and repeated actions: *But when I was a teenager I'* **d get up** *in the morning and go straight to the cookie jar.* We don't usually use this verb form with state verbs.

● We make **negative** sentences with *used to* with: subject + *didn't* + *use to* + infinitive.

I **didn't use to like** vegetables.

● We make **questions** with *used to* with: (question word) *did* + subject + *use to* + infinitive.

Where **did** you **use to live**?

TIPS! ● We can also make negative sentences with *never used to: My brother never used to help with the washing-up.*

● We don't use *used to* + infinitive or *would* + infinitive for something that only happened once: *In 2003 I gave up smoking.* not *In 2003 I used to/would give up smoking.*

● We often use *used to* when we begin describing past habits, then continue with *would* + infinitive: *I used to sleep until midday, then I'd get up and have breakfast in the garden. After that I'd get the bus to work.*

G2.2 *be used to, get used to* 2B ❹ p17

● We use *be used to* to talk about things that are familiar and no longer strange or difficult for us: *I'm used to getting up at 5 a.m. every day.*

● We use *get used to* to talk about things that become familiar, less strange or less difficult over a period of time: *And as for driving, well, I'm slowly getting used to it.*

When Peter first arrived in Mexico City, he wasn't used to getting up at 5 a.m. every day.

Peter has been in Mexico City for some time. Now he's used to getting up at 5 a.m. every day.

● After *be used to* and *get used to* we use verb+*ing*: *I still haven't got used to* **being** *a pedestrian here. I'll never get used to* **doing** *that!*

● After *be used to* and *get used to* we can use a noun or a pronoun: *I wasn't used to* **people** *driving so close to me. It just takes a while for a foreigner to get used to* **them**.

● We can use *be used to* and *get used to* in any verb form, for example:

Present Simple: *I'** m used to** getting up at 5 a.m. every day.*
Present Continuous: *I'm slowly* **getting used to** *it.*
Present Perfect Simple: *I still* **haven't got used to** *being a pedestrian here.*
Past Simple: *I* **wasn't used to** *people driving so close to me.*
will + infinitive: *I'll never* **get used to** *doing that!*
infinitive with *to*: *It just takes a while for a foreigner* **to get used to** *them.*

TIP! ● The form of *used to* in *be/get used to* doesn't change in questions and negatives: *She isn't used to it.* not ~~She isn't use to it~~.

USED TO OR BE/GET USED TO?

● Compare these sentences:

I **used to live** *in Mexico City.*
The speaker lived in Mexico City in the past, but he/she doesn't live there now.

*I'** m used to living** in Mexico City.*
The speaker lives in Mexico City now and has probably lived there for some time. When he/she started living there, life was probably strange or difficult, but now it isn't.

RW2.1 **Discussion language (1): agreeing and disagreeing politely** 2D ❸ p20

agreeing

I see what you mean.
I see your point.
I suppose that's true, actually.
You might be right there.
That's a good point.
Well, I can't argue with that.
I suppose you've got a point there.

disagreeing

I don't know about that.
I can't really see the point of (forcing kids to eat).
Oh, do you think so?
Oh, I wouldn't say that.
Well, I'm still not convinced.

TIP! ● We often follow an agreement phrase with *but* to challenge the other person's opinion: *I see what you mean,* **but** *I think it's much better to let them eat when they want.*

Language Summary 3

V3.1 Types of crime (3A 1a p22)

robbery stealing from people and banks

theft stealing money and things

burglary /ˈbɜːgləri/ stealing from houses and flats

mugging using violence to steal from somebody in a public place (a street, a park, etc.)

shoplifting stealing things from a shop while it is open

smuggling taking things illegally from one country to another

kidnapping taking a person by using violence, often in order to get money for returning them

fraud /frɔːd/ obtaining money illegally, usually by using clever and complicated methods

bribery /ˈbraɪbəri/ trying to make somebody do something you want by giving them money, presents, etc.

murder /ˈmɜːdə/ killing somebody intentionally

arson starting a fire in a building in order to damage or destroy it

vandalism intentionally damaging public property, or property belonging to other people

looting stealing from shops or homes that have been damaged in a war, natural disaster, etc.

terrorism the use of violence such as bombing, shooting, etc. for political purposes

V3.2 Criminals and crime verbs (3A 1b p22)

crime	criminal	verb	crime	criminal	verb
robbery	robber	rob	fraud	fraudster	–
theft	thief	steal	bribery	–	bribe
burglary	burglar	burgle	murder	murderer	murder
mugging	mugger	mug	arson	arsonist	–
shoplifting	shoplifter	shoplift	vandalism	vandal	vandalise
smuggling	smuggler	smuggle	looting	looter	loot
kidnapping	kidnapper	kidnap	terrorism	terrorist	–

TIPS! • The plural of *thief* is *thieves* /θiːvz/.

• We can say *commit fraud*, *commit arson* and *commit an act of terrorism*.

• We usually use *shoplift* in its verb+*ing* form: *I saw some boys shoplifting. My neighbour was caught shoplifting.*

They're **robbing** a bank and **stealing** all the money.

He's just **burgled** a house and **stolen** a DVD player.

V3.3 Crime and punishment (3B 1 p24)

commit a crime

arrest somebody for a crime

charge* somebody with a crime

take somebody to court*

give evidence*

find somebody (not) guilty*

acquit*/convict* somebody of a crime

send somebody to prison (for 10 years)

sentence* somebody to (10 years) in prison

fine* somebody (£500)

*charge sb with a crime when the police charge somebody with a crime, they formally accuse them of committing that crime: *Three men were charged with shoplifting.*

*take sb to court take legal action against somebody: *My landlord is taking me to court for not paying my rent.*

*give evidence tell a court of law what you know about a crime: *Three witnesses of the mugging gave evidence in court today.*

*guilty /ˈgɪlti/ responsible for committing a crime: *The jury had to decide if he was innocent or guilty.*

*acquit /əˈkwɪt/ decide in a court that somebody is not guilty of a crime: *They were acquitted of all charges.* (opposite: **convict**)

*sentence when a judge decides what a person's punishment should be after they have been convicted of a crime: *The two men were sentenced to six months in prison.*

*fine make somebody pay money as a punishment for a crime they have committed: *He was fined £1,000.*

TIPS! • *Arrest, charge, sentence* and *fine* are also nouns.

• A *court* is a large room where lawyers formally present all the evidence about a crime: *He's appearing in court today.*

V3.4 Verbs and prepositions (3C 4 p26)

spend sth **on** sb/sth

insist **on** sth*

explain sth **to** sb

worry **about** sb/sth

cope **with** sb/sth*

provide sb **with** sth*

apply **to** sb/sth **for** sth

complain **to** sb **about** sb/sth

talk **to** sb **about** sb/sth

shout **at** sb **for** sth

apologise **to** sb **for** sth

depend **on** sb/sth **for** sth

*insist on sth say strongly and forcefully that you want to do something

*cope with sb/sth deal with a difficult person, problem or situation

*provide sb with sth give somebody something that they want or need

TIP! • We can say *depend on sb/sth for sth* or *rely on sb/sth for sth*: *I depend/rely on my parents for financial support.*

Grammar

G3.1 Second conditional; alternatives for *if*

3A **3** p23

SECOND CONDITIONAL

- We use the second conditional to talk about imaginary situations in the present or the future: *I'd take the books back if I didn't have to pay a fine.* (I don't have to take any books back.)
- We make the second conditional with:
if + subject + Past Simple, subject + *'d (= would)/wouldn't* + infinitive

if clause	main clause
If they **clamped** my car,	**I'd be** stuck there all day.
If he **didn't stay up** so late,	he **wouldn't feel** tired all the time.

- We can use *could* or *might* in the main clause instead of *would* to mean 'would perhaps': *If the bank found out, I could say I didn't count the money. If I really needed it, I might keep it.*

TIPS! • *Even if* = it doesn't matter whether the situation in the *if* clause exists or not: *I'd take the books back, even if I had to pay a fine.*
• In second conditionals we can say *If I/he/she/it was* … or *If I/he/she/it were* … : *If I was/were rich, I'd buy a Ferrari.*

ALTERNATIVES FOR *IF*

- We often use *provided, as long as, assuming, imagine* and *suppose* instead of *if* in conditionals.
- *Provided* and *as long as* mean 'only if (this happens)': **Provided** *no one was looking, I'd take as much paper as I needed. I'd tell a security guard* **as long as** *he/she agreed not to call the police.*
- *Assuming* means 'accepting that something is true': **Assuming** *no one else saw the boy, I'd just tell him to return the things he'd stolen.*
- *Imagine* and *suppose* have the same meaning (= form a picture in your mind about what something could be like).
- We can use *imagine* and *suppose* as an alternative for *if* in questions: *Imagine/Suppose you found some library books that were due back eight months ago, would you return them?*

TIPS! • We can also use *provided, as long as, assuming, imagine* and *suppose* in other types of conditionals to talk about real situations: *We'll see you tonight, provided Alex doesn't have to work late. We'll hire a car, as long as it's not too expensive. Let's go to that nice Japanese restaurant, assuming it's still open.*
• We can say *provided* or *providing* and *suppose* or *supposing*.
• We can also use *unless* in conditionals to mean *if not*: *I wouldn't hit somebody unless I had to.* (= if I didn't have to).

G3.2 Third conditional 3B **5** p24

- We use the third conditional to talk about imaginary situations in the past. They are often the opposite of what really happened: *If the woman had shot the men, she'd have been in serious trouble.* (The woman didn't shoot the men, so she didn't get in serious trouble.)

POSITIVE AND NEGATIVE

- We make the third conditional with:
if + subject + Past Perfect, subject + *'d (= would)/wouldn't* + *have* + past participle.
  If **I'd seen** him, **I'd have said** hello.
  If we **hadn't got** lost, we **wouldn't have been** late.
- We can also use *could* and *might* in the main clause to mean 'would perhaps': *If the men hadn't run away, she* **could** *have killed them. If it had been me, I* **might** *have left a note on the car.*
- The *if* clause can be first or second in the sentence.

QUESTIONS

- We make questions in the third conditional with:
(question word) + *would* + subject + *have* + past participle … + *if* + subject + Past Perfect.
  What **would** the owner of the car **have done** if he **'d seen** him?

TIPS! • We don't usually use *would* in the *if* clause: *If I'd known, I'd have helped.* not ~~If I would have known, I'd have helped~~.
• We can also use *imagine* and *suppose* instead of *if* in third conditional questions: *Imagine/Suppose he'd seen you, what would you have done?*

Real World

RW3.1 Making, refusing and accepting offers

3D **3** p28

making offers

Would you like me to (come round)?
Let me (give them a ring for you).
Would it help if I (sorted it out for you)?
Why don't I (look after the kids)?
I'll (make a bed up for you), if you like.
What if I (picked the kids up from school)?

refusing offers

No, it's OK, but thanks for offering.
No, thanks. I'd better (phone them myself).
No, don't worry. It'd be easier if (I brought the kids back here).
No, that's OK. I can manage.

accepting offers

Are you sure you wouldn't mind?
Thanks. That'd be a great help.
Well, it'd be wonderful if you could.
As long as you don't mind.

- *Let me* … , *Why don't I* … and *I'd better* … are followed by the **infinitive**.
- *Would it help if I* … , *What if I* … and *It'd be easier if I* … are followed by the **Past Simple**.
- *Thanks for* … is often followed by **verb+ing**.

TIP! • We can also say: *It'd be great/nice/helpful/fantastic*, etc. *if you could.*

Language Summary 4

V4.1 Phrasal verbs (1) (4A ❶ p30)

pass sth on (to sb) or **pass on sth (to sb)** tell somebody a piece of information that another person has told you: *Could you pass this message on to your classmates?*

make sth up or **make up sth** invent an excuse, explanation, a story, etc.: *I was late for work so I made up an excuse.*

turn out happen in a particular way or have a particular result, which is often unexpected: *I wasn't looking forward to the evening, but it turned out to be a lot of fun.*

run sb/sth over or **run over sb/sth** hit somebody or something while you are driving and knock them to the ground: *I accidentally ran over a cat last night.*

go off when a bomb goes off, it explodes: *The bomb went off at exactly 6.37 p.m.*

run away leave a place quickly because you are frightened or don't want to get caught: *The thief took my bag and ran away.*

work sth out or **work out sth** understand or find the answer to something by thinking about it: *It took me ages to work out the answer to question 3.*

take off leave the ground and begin to fly: *The plane took off over an hour late.*

knock sb out or **knock out sb** hit somebody hard so that they become unconscious: *The mugger hit the man so hard that he knocked him out.*

come round become conscious again after being knocked out: *When he came round, he couldn't remember anything.*

TIPS! • *Turn out* is often followed by the infinitive with *to* or '(that) + clause': *The trip turned out **to be** rather exciting. It turns out **(that) we went to the same school**.*

• *Work out* is often followed by a question word: *I couldn't work out **what** was happening.*

V4.2 Books and reading (4B ❶ p32)

fiction /ˈfɪkʃən/ books and stories about imaginary people and events (opposite: **non-fiction**)

a copy a single book, newspaper, CD, etc.

a character /ˈkærɪktə/ a person in a book, film, etc.

a plot the story of a book, film, play, etc.

a novelist a person who writes novels

a biography /baɪˈɒgrəfi/ a book about a person's life, written by somebody else

an autobiography /ˌɔːtəbaɪˈɒgrəfi/ a book about a person's life, written by that person

a literary genre /ˌlɪtərəri ˈʒɒnrə/ literature which has the same style or subject

browse /braʊz/ walk around a shop looking at things, but without planning to buy anything

a paperback a book that has a cover made of thin card (opposite: **hardback**)

flick through look quickly at the pages of a book, magazine, newspaper, etc.

V4.3 Connecting words: reason and contrast

4C ❹ p35

giving reasons	because	due to	as	because of	since
expressing contrast	however whereas	apart from even though	instead of nevertheless	despite	

• *Because, however, whereas, as, since, even though* and *nevertheless* are followed by a clause (subject + verb + …): *… because people often play practical jokes on each other.*

• *Apart from, instead of, despite, due to* and *because of* are followed by a noun or verb+*ing*: *… apart from **one thing**. … instead of **coming** out of the left.*

• After *due to* and *because of* it is more common to use a noun than verb+*ing*: *… due to **a very mild winter**.*

TIPS! • We can also use these phrases for expressing contrast: *except for* (= *apart from*), *in spite of* (= *despite*), *although* (= *even though*).

• We use *however* and *nevertheless* to contrast two sentences. We usually put these words at the beginning of the second sentence.

• We use the other words/phrases in the table to contrast two clauses in the same sentence. We can put these words/phrases at the beginning or in the middle of the sentence: *Even though I was tired, I enjoyed myself. = I enjoyed myself, even though I was tired.*

V4.4 Ways of exaggerating (4D ❶ p36)

Match phrases 1–12 to meanings a)–l).

1. I'm speechless.
2. I'm dying for a drink.
3. I'm over the moon.
4. I'm scared stiff.
5. I'm starving.
6. I'm going out of my mind.
7. It costs a fortune.
8. It's a nightmare.
9. It's killing me.
10. It drives me crazy.
11. It takes forever.
12. It weighs a ton.

a) I'm very thirsty.
b) I'm very frightened.
c) I'm very worried.
d) I'm very happy.
e) I'm very hungry.
f) I'm very shocked, surprised or angry.
g) It's very painful.
h) It takes a very long time.
i) It makes me very angry.
j) It's very expensive.
k) It's very heavy.
l) It's a very difficult situation.

I'm dying for a coffee. Let's go to that café.

Good idea, I'm starving.

Yeah, and my feet are killing me!

Grammar

G4.1 Narrative verb forms; Past Perfect Continuous 4A **5** p31

Past Simple and Past Continuous

- We use the **Past Simple** for completed actions in the past. These tell the main events of the story in the order that they happened: *One day, one of the sailors **went** for a drive in the outback and accidentally **ran over** a kangaroo.*

- We use the **Past Continuous** for a longer action that was in progress when another (shorter) action happened: *While the sailor **was taking** some photos, the kangaroo **came round**.*

- We also use the **Past Continuous** for background information that isn't part of the main story: *In 1987 the world's best sailors **were competing** in the America's Cup yacht race off the coast of Fremantle.*

- Look at this sentence and the diagram: *While they **were flying** at 25,000 feet, one cow **broke free** and started running around inside the plane.*

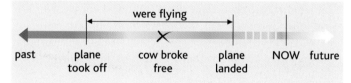

TIPS! • We also use the Past Continuous when two longer actions are happening at the same time: *While I was watching TV, Steve was making dinner.*
• We often use *when*, *while* and *as* with the Past Continuous: *Tony phoned me when/while/as I was getting ready to leave.* We don't usually use *while* or *as* with the Past Simple.

Past Perfect Simple and Past Perfect Continuous

- We usually use the **Past Perfect Simple** for an action that was completed before another action in the past: *Eventually the pilot of a Russian transport plane **told** the police what **had happened**.*

- We usually use the **Past Perfect Continuous** for a longer action that started before another action in the past (and often continued up to this past action): *The boat **had been sailing** in calm waters when a cow **fell** from the sky.*

- Look at this sentence and the diagram: *Before they took off from their Siberian airbase, the plane's crew **had stolen** some cows.*

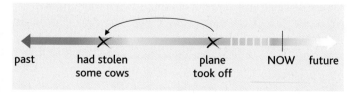

- Look at this sentence and the diagram: *The boat **had been sailing** in calm waters when a cow fell from the sky.*

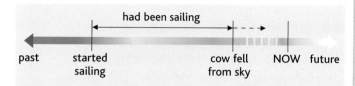

TIPS! • If the order of past events is clear, we don't usually use the Past Perfect: *I woke up, got dressed and made some breakfast.*
• When we're telling a story, we don't have to use the Past Perfect every time we refer to something further in the past. When we have established the time, we can use the Past Simple or the Past Continuous: *I started telling everyone about the wedding I'd **been** to in Italy two years earlier. My sister **was getting** married and I **arrived** late for the ceremony. When I **got** there I … .*

PAST PERFECT SIMPLE

- We make the Past Perfect Simple **positive** with: subject + *had* or *'d* + past participle.

  The police tried to work out why the boat **had sunk**.

- We make the Past Perfect Simple **negative** with: subject + *hadn't* + past participle.

  The accident **hadn't killed** the animal.

- We make Past Perfect Simple **questions** with: (question word) + *had* + subject + past participle.

  What **had** the crew **done** before they took off?

PAST PERFECT CONTINUOUS

- We make the Past Perfect Continuous **positive** with: subject + *had* or *'d* + *been* + verb+*ing*.

  The woman **had been trying** to get rid of the bugs for years.

- We make the Past Perfect Continuous **negative** with: subject + *hadn't* + *been* + verb+*ing*.

  She **hadn't been living** there for very long.

- We make Past Perfect Continuous **questions** with: (question word) + *had* + subject + *been* + verb+*ing*.

  Why **had** he **been driving** for so long?

TIPS! • We can use *by the time*, *when*, *because*, *so*, *before*, *after*, *as soon as* and *until* to make sentences with the Past Perfect: *By the time I got there, most people had gone home.*
• We don't have to use the Past Perfect with *because*, *so*, *before*, *after*, *as soon as* or *until* because the order of events is usually clear: *I (had) called her before I left the office. I waited until everybody (had) arrived.*
• We often use the Past Perfect after *knew*, *realised*, *thought*, *forgot* and *remembered*: *I knew that she'd been looking for a new job. I realised that I'd left my keys in the office.*

Language Summary 4

G4.2 Defining, non-defining and reduced relative clauses 4B ④ p33

Defining relative clauses

- Defining relative clauses tell you which person, thing, etc. the writer or speaker is talking about: *The granddaughter, Alba Trueba, finds some diaries <u>that her grandmother Clara wrote 50 years earlier.</u>*

- In defining relative clauses we use:

  who (or *that*) for people: *People who/that die early in the story often return as ghosts.*
  that (or *which*) for things: *'One Hundred Years of Solitude' is the novel that/which made magical realism popular around the world.*
  whose for possessives: *It tells the story of three generations of women whose lives are changed by their country's politics.*
  where for places: *This is a place where supernatural happenings are part of everyday life.*
  when for times: *The story takes place at a time when political groups are battling for control of the country.*

- We don't use commas with defining relative clauses.

TIP! • We can't use *what* in defining relative clauses: *Did you get the letter what I sent?* However, we can use *what* to mean 'the thing/things that': *Can you tell me what he said?*

LEAVING OUT WHO, THAT, WHICH, ETC.

- We can leave out *who, that* or *which* when these words aren't the subject of the defining relative clause.

- Compare the defining relative clauses in these sentences:

1 *It's the novel **that** made magical realism popular around the world.*

   In sentence 1 we must use *that* because it is the subject of the relative clause.

2 *She finds some diaries **(that)** her grandmother Clara wrote 50 years earlier.*

   In sentence 2 we can leave out *that* because it is the object of the relative clause (*her grandmother Clara* is the subject).

TIPS! • We never leave out *whose* in defining relative clauses.

• We can usually leave out *where* in defining relative clauses if we add a preposition at the end of the relative clause: *That's the house **where** I was born.* = *That's the house I was born **in**.*

• We can only leave out *when* if the time reference is clear: *Tomorrow is the day (when) I get my exam results.*

Non-defining relative clauses

- Non-defining relative clauses add extra non-essential information: *It tells the story of seven generations of the Buendía family, <u>who live in an isolated South American village called Macondo.</u>*

- We don't use *that* in non-defining relative clauses.

- We can't leave out *who, which, whose*, etc. in non-defining relative clauses.

- We must use commas with non-defining relative clauses.

TIPS! • In non-defining relative clauses we also use *whose* for possessives, *where* for places and *when* for time.

• In non-defining relative clauses *who* or *which* can also refer to a whole clause: *The book has dozens of characters, which can make the plot difficult to follow.* (*which* refers to 'the fact that the book has dozens of characters').

• Non-defining relative clauses are more common in written English than spoken English, particularly in stories and more formal types of writing.

Reduced relative clauses

- When a defining relative clause contains a continuous or passive verb form, we can often leave out *who, that* or *which* and the auxiliary. These reduced relative clauses are very common in spoken English.

- Look at the <u>underlined</u> reduced relative clauses in these sentences. Notice which words we can leave out:

1 *... everyone (who **is**) <u>**living** in the village</u> suffers from both insomnia and amnesia.* (*is living* = Present Continuous)

2 *... the first novel (that **was**) <u>**written** by the Chilean author Isabel Allende.</u>* (*was written* = Past Simple Passive)

Real World

RW4.1 Saying you're surprised or not surprised 4D ③ p36

saying you're surprised	saying you're not surprised
I don't believe it!	I'm not surprised, to be honest.
You must be joking!	I bet you were.
You're kidding!	Well, no wonder (you've got a virus).
Why on earth (doesn't he listen to me)?	Well, he would say that, wouldn't he?
Wow, that's fantastic news!	Yes, I can imagine.

TIPS! • We can also say *You're joking!* and *You must be kidding!*
• We can also say *What/Who/Where/How on earth ... ?*

QUESTIONS WITH NEGATIVE AUXILIARIES

- We often use negative auxiliaries in questions when we think we know the answer. The answer we expect can be *yes* or *no*, depending on the context.

- Look at Steve's questions from his conversation with his wife, Ellen:

a) *Hadn't they promised to be here today?*

   In sentence a) Steve thinks the answer will be *yes* because he knows that Ellen made the appointment.

b) *Didn't you install that anti-virus software?*

   In sentence b) Steve thinks the answer will be *no* because Ellen has a virus on her computer.

Vocabulary

V5.1 Animals 5A ❶ p38

Match animals 1–15 to pictures a)–o).

1	a tiger /ˈtaɪgə/	9	a spider
2	an eagle /ˈiːgəl/	10	a parrot
3	a crocodile	11	a goldfish
4	a leopard /ˈlepəd/	12	a mosquito
5	a bee		/məˈskiːtəʊ/
6	a rabbit	13	a shark
7	a snake	14	a bear /beə/
8	a butterfly	15	a whale /weɪl/

bite (bit, bitten) use your teeth to cut into something

a mammal an animal which has babies, not eggs (a bear, etc.).

an insect a very small animal which has six legs and sometimes wings (a bee, etc.).

a reptile an animal that produces eggs and uses the sun's heat to keep its blood warm (a snake, etc.)

poison /ˈpɔɪzən/ kill or make very ill by putting something harmful into an animal's or a person's body

lay (laid, laid) produce eggs (by a chicken, bird, snake, etc.)

sting (stung, stung) if an insect stings you, it produces a painful injury by making a small hole in the skin

hunt try to catch or kill an animal or a bird for food, sport or money

silk very strong, thin material produced by spiders and silkworms

a pet an animal you keep in your home

TIPS! • Skin, fur and silk are uncountable nouns.
• Bite, poison, sting and hunt can be verbs and nouns.
• an insect (UK) = a bug (US)

V5.2 Plants and gardens 5B ❶ p40

Match words/phrases 1–18 to things a)–r) in the pictures.

1	a herb /hɜːb/ a)	10	a lawn /lɔːn/
2	seeds	11	a greenhouse
3	a bulb	12	an orchard /ˈɔːtʃəd/
4	petals /ˈpetəlz/	13	a flower bed
5	pollen	14	a tree trunk
6	a pot	15	roots
7	a vine	16	a branch
8	a bush	17	leaves /liːvz/
9	a hedge /hedʒ/	18	a twig

TIP! • The singular of leaves is a leaf.

Language Summary 5

Vocabulary

V5.3 Back referencing (5C **6** p43)

- When we speak or write, we often use words like *them, where, one*, etc. to refer back to people, places or things that we have mentioned earlier.
- Look at the article 'The history of flowers' on p43. Notice what words/phrases 1–20 refer to.

TULIPS		ROSES	
1	which → tulips	11	they → roses
2	They → tulips	12	his → the Chinese emperor
3	where → Turkey	13	those → the roses
4	that period → the time of the Ottoman Empire	14	it → the oil
5	there → in Holland	15	who → the Romans
6	them → the bulbs	16	where → the botanical garden near Paris
7	At that time → in 1634	17	at that time → in the 18th century
8	them → the bulbs	18	they → roses
9	did so → became tulip growers	19	ones → roses
10	one → tulip	20	These → red roses

TIPS! • We use *it* to refer back to a specific thing:
A *Where's my mobile phone?* B *Sorry, I haven't seen* **it**.

• We use *one* to refer back to 'one of many':
A *Can I borrow your mobile phone?* B *Sorry, I haven't got* **one**.

• We often use *at that time* to refer back to a period of time:
I lived in Brazil in the eighties. **At that time** *I wasn't married.*

V5.4 Adjectives for giving opinions (5D **1** p44)

inevitable /ɪˈnevɪtəbəl/ certain to happen: *I think climate change is inevitable.*

damaging /ˈdæmɪdʒɪŋ/ causing harm: *Many chemicals have a damaging effect on the environment.*

disturbing making you feel worried, shocked or upset: *There's been a disturbing increase in crime in the city.*

wasteful using things in a way that doesn't use them efficiently or completely: *Throwing food away is so wasteful.*

moral behaving in a way that is thought by most people to be honest and correct: *It can be hard to make moral judgments when you're in business.* (opposite: **immoral**)

ethical /ˈeθɪkəl/ connected to beliefs of what is right and wrong or morally correct: *I don't think it's ethical to do experiments on animals.* (opposite: **unethical**)

legal /ˈliːgəl/ allowed by the law: *It's legal to drive in the UK if you're 17 or over.* (opposite: **illegal**)

sustainable able to continue for a long time: *We need a sustainable transport policy.* (opposite: **unsustainable**)

justifiable /dʒʌstɪˈfaɪəbəl/ acceptable or correct because you are able to see a good reason for it: *Is it justifiable to cut down forests to make paper?* (opposite: **unjustifiable**)

TIP! • *Damage* /ˈdæmɪdʒ/ and *waste* are both verbs and uncountable nouns.

Grammar

G5.1 Ways of comparing (5A **3** p38)

COMPARATIVES, (*NOT*) *AS ... AS*

a big difference	far (more addictive) than nowhere near as (high) as considerably (less) than not nearly as (beautiful) as a great deal (cheaper) than
a small difference	almost as (much) as nearly as (expensive) as slightly /ˈslaɪtli/ (bigger) than not quite as (enthusiastic) as
no difference	as (beautiful) as not any (nicer) than no (harder) than

- We use comparatives with *than*: *They're slightly* **bigger** *than the ones I've got.* not *They're slightly big than the ones I've got.*
- We use adjectives with *as ... as*: *The normal price is nowhere near as* **high** *as that.* not *The normal price is nowhere near as higher as that.*

TIPS! • We can also use *much/a lot* with comparatives to talk about a big difference and *a bit/a little* to talk about a small difference: *Koi are* **much/a lot more expensive than** *goldfish. This one's* **a bit/a little cheaper than** *all the others.*

• We can use *just* with *as ... as* to add emphasis: *They're* **just** *as beautiful as mine.*

• We can also use *more* and *less* with nouns: *There are* **far more people** *here than I expected.*

• We usually use *less* with uncountable nouns and *fewer* with countable nouns: *I have* **less free time** *and* **fewer days off** *than I used to have.*

• We can say *I'm not nearly as rich as* **he/she is**. or *I'm not nearly as rich as* **him/her**.

OTHER WAYS OF COMPARING

- We can use *twice/three times/four times*, etc. + *as ... as* to compare two things: *The koi were only about twice as big as my goldfish.* (= the goldfish were half the size of the koi).
- For long adjectives, we can use *get* + *more (and more)* + **adjective** to describe something that continuously changes: *Koi are getting more and more expensive.* (= the price is increasing all the time).
- For short adjectives, we can use *get* + **comparative** + *and* + **comparative** to describe something that continuously changes: *The survival rate was getting better and better.*
- We can use *the* + *comparative/more* ... , *the* + *comparative/ more* ... to say that one thing depends on the other: *The bigger they are, the more they cost.* (= how much they cost depends on how big they are).
The more I learned about koi, the more interested I became. (= every time I learned something new about koi, I became more interested in them).

TIP! • *the sooner, the better* = as soon as possible:
A *When do you want that report?* B *The sooner, the better.*

Grammar

G5.2 Future verb forms; Future Continuous
5B ⑤ p41

Future verb forms

- We use **be going to** to talk about a personal plan or intention: *We're going to take Katy to the Eden Project.*
- We use the **Present Continuous** to talk about an arrangement with other people or organisations: *We're staying in a small hotel in Padstow for a week.*
- We use **will** to talk about a decision that is made at the time of speaking: *No, don't worry, I'll take a day off.*
- We use the **Present Simple** to talk about a fixed event on a timetable, calendar, etc.: *It's on BBC2 and it starts at seven thirty.*
- We use **be going to** to talk about a prediction that is based on present evidence (something we know or can see now): *She's been working really hard and I think she's going to pass them all.*
- We use **will** to talk about a prediction that is not based on present evidence: *Oh, I'm sure he'll have a great time.*

TIPS! • When we use the Present Continuous for the future, we usually know exactly when these arrangements are happening: *I'm meeting Bill at four thirty.*
• We can also use *be going to* to talk about arrangements with other people or organisations: *What time are you going to see the doctor?*
• There is often very little difference between a prediction with *will* and *be going to*: *I think Chelsea will/are going to win the Champions League this year.*
• We often use *definitely* and *probably* with *will/won't*. Notice the word order: *Tony **will definitely/probably** get promoted. Gary **definitely/probably won't** get promoted.*
• We also use *will* to talk about future facts and for offers: *I'll be 50 next birthday. I'll give you a hand with the washing-up.*

Future Continuous

- We use the **Future Continuous** for something that will be in progress at a point of time in the future.
- Look at this sentence and the diagram: *This time next week **we'll be walking** around the Eden Project together!*

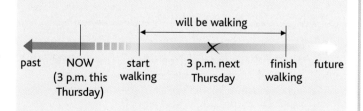

| past | NOW (3 p.m. this Thursday) | start walking | 3 p.m. next Thursday | finish walking | future |

- Compare these sentences:
  We're playing tennis at 2.30. (= the match **starts** at this time).
  We'll be playing tennis at 2.30. (= the match will be **in progress** at this time).

- We also use the **Future Continuous** for something that will happen in the normal course of events, without any particular plan or intention: *Actually, we'll be driving through your village so we can pick you up on the way.* (this is the best route). *Come round whenever you like, I'll be looking after the kids all day.* (this is what I normally do during the day).
- For this meaning there is often very little difference between the Future Continuous and the Present Continuous: *Don't call me in the morning, I'll be working/I'm working then.*

POSITIVE AND NEGATIVE

- We make the **positive** and **negative** forms of the Future Continuous with:
  subject + 'll (= will)/won't + be + verb+ing.

  This time tomorrow I**'ll be lying** on a beach.
  We **won't be going** there again for a while.

QUESTIONS

- We make **questions** with the Future Continuous with:
  (question word) + will + subject + be + verb+ing.

  When **will** you **be seeing** Fiona again?
  Will he **be working** that day?

TIP! • As with other continuous verb forms, we don't usually use state verbs with the Future Continuous: *This time tomorrow I'll know my exam results.* not ~~This time tomorrow I'll be knowing my exam results~~.

Real World

RW5.1 Discussion language (2): opinions
5D ④ p44

giving opinions

It'd be (much) better if (everyone bought ...)
I just don't think it's right that ...
One argument in favour of (being vegetarian) is that ...
I think people should (have the right to) ...

giving the opposite opinion

Maybe, but I don't see how (we) can ...
Fair enough, but I still think that ...
Yes, but then again, ...
Well, some people would argue that ...

clarifying your position

No, that's not what I'm trying to say.
What I meant was ...
No, that's not what I meant.
All I'm saying is that ...

giving yourself time to think

That's an interesting point.
I've never really thought about that.
Um, let me think.
It's hard to say.

Language Summary 6

Vocabulary

V6.1 Phrases with *take*   6A ❶ p46

take a risk do something that you know might be dangerous or have negative consequences: *You're taking a risk by going there on your own.*

take sb for granted expect that somebody will always be there and never show them any special attention or care: *My children take me for granted – I never get a word of thanks.*

take responsibility (for sth) say that you are responsible for something that has happened: *I take full responsibility for the accident.*

take advantage /əd'vɑːntɪdʒ/ **of sb** treat somebody badly or unfairly in order to get something from them: *Mark's always borrowing money – I think he's taking advantage of you.*

take notice (of sb/sth) pay attention to somebody or something and let them influence you (usually used in the negative with *any, no,* etc.): *I asked him to be quiet, but he didn't take any notice.*

take (my, your, etc.) time do something slowly and carefully without hurrying: *There's no hurry, just take your time.*

take sides support one person or group against another in an argument: *My mother never takes sides when my sister and I argue.*

TIP! • We can also *take something for granted*: *In this country we take clean water for granted.*

V6.2 Compound adjectives describing character
6B ❶ p48

Strong-willed people are determined to behave in a particular way, even if other people disagree with them. (P = positive)

Self-conscious /ˌself'kɒnʃəs/ people are shy and easily embarrassed because they think that everybody is looking at them and judging them. (N = negative)

Laid-back people are relaxed and appear not to be worried about anything. (P)

Open-minded people are happy to accept ideas and ways of life that are different to their own. (P)

Self-centred people are only interested in themselves and their own activities. (N)

Narrow-minded people don't want to accept new ideas or opinions that are different from their own. (N)

Easy-going people aren't easily upset, worried or annoyed by problems or other people's actions. (P)

Big-headed people think they are more important or cleverer than they really are. (N)

Bad-tempered people are often annoyed, angry or impatient. (N)

Absent-minded people tend to forget things. (N)

Level-headed people are calm and able to make sensible decisions in difficult situations. (P)

Self-assured people have confidence in their own abilities. (P)

TIPS! • Notice these opposites: *strong-willed* ≠ *weak-willed*; *narrow-minded* ≠ *open-minded* (or *broad-minded*); *bad-tempered* ≠ *good-tempered* (or *even-tempered*).
• On most compound adjectives the stress is on the second part of the adjective: *strong-willed, self-conscious,* etc.

V6.3 Guessing meaning from context   6C ❸ p50

● Sometimes you can guess the meaning of a word by:
a) deciding what part of speech it is (verb, noun, adjective, adverb, etc.).
b) recognising a similar word in your language, or another language you know.
c) understanding the rest of the sentence and the text in general.

● Look at the encyclopaedia extract 'Codes through the ages' on p50–p51. Notice the meaning of these words in context.

1 **decipher** /dɪ'saɪfə/ (verb) work out what something means
2 **wind** /waɪnd/ (**wound** /waʊnd/, **wound**) (verb) turn something repeatedly
3 **make sth out** or **make out sth** (phrasal verb) see something with difficulty
4 **reveal** (verb) show something that was hidden
5 **strip** (noun) a long, thin piece of material
6 **stick** (noun) a long, thin piece of wood
7 **straightforward** (adjective) simple

TIPS! • We usually use *make sth out* with words like *can't, couldn't, hard, difficult* and *impossible*: *What's that over there? I can't make it out.*
• We can also say *make out what/who* + clause: *It was impossible to make out what the message said.*

countless (adjective) too many to be counted: *Human beings have used countless ingenious ways of sending secret messages.*

scalp (noun) the skin on top of your head where your hair usually grows: *They shaved a messenger's head and wrote the message on his scalp.*

scrunch sth up or **scrunch up sth** (phrasal verb) press or squeeze paper or material into a small ball: *The silk was scrunched up into a tiny ball.*

swallow (verb) move something from your mouth to your stomach: *The message was swallowed so it couldn't be found.*

courier /'kʊrɪə/ (noun) a person who carries important messages and documents from one person to another: *The message was hidden in the courier's stomach.*

conceal (verb) hide something: *Porta described how to conceal a message within a hard-boiled egg.*

shell (noun) the hard part outside an egg, nut, etc.: *The message is written on the shell.*

Grammar

G6.1 Uses of verb+*ing* 6A ❸ p46

● We use verb+*ing* …

a) as part of a continuous verb form: *As an Englishman, I* **was laughing** *out loud* …

b) after prepositions: *Apart* **from asking** *for information* …

c) after certain verbs: *We also* **avoid talking** *about money.*

d) after certain verbs + object: *It's absolutely normal for commuters to* **spend years travelling** *on the same train* …

e) as an adjective: *This highly* **entertaining** *book looks at* …

f) in reduced relative clauses: *… people* **standing at a bus stop** *will often break an uncomfortable silence by* …

g) after *despite* or *in spite of*: *However,* **despite not wanting** *to engage in conversation* …

h) as the subject (or part of the subject) of a verb: *…* **talking to strangers on trains** *just isn't done!*

TIPS! ● We often use verb+*ing* after these verbs + object – *hear, see, watch, feel, imagine, stop, love, like, don't mind, dislike, hate*: *I often hear her* **playing** *the piano.*

● We can also use verb+*ing* as a noun: *I usually do the* **cooking** *and my husband does the* **cleaning**.

● We often use verb+*ing* when there isn't a noun that describes a particular idea: **Working at home** *can be rather lonely.*

● We also use verb+*ing* after these fixed phrases: *There's no point (in)* … ; *It's a waste of time* … ; *It's (not) worth* … ; *It's no use* … : *There's no point in telling her. She'll just get upset.*

G6.2 Modal verbs (1); levels of certainty about the future
6B ❹ p49

MODAL VERBS

● We often use *'ll* (= *will*) and *won't* to express future certainty: *I'll miss him in some ways. I* **won't** *be sad to see him go.*

● We often use *might, could* and *may* to express future possibility: *I* **might** *go for a bit. He* **could** *improve things. He* **may** *not want to give up his house.*

LEVELS OF CERTAINTY ABOUT THE FUTURE

● We use these phrases when we think something will definitely happen:
be bound to do sth: *He's bound to upset people.*
be sure to do sth: *But you're sure to get the job.*

● We use these phrases when we think something will probably happen:
be likely to do sth: *He's likely to be there for at least a year.*
may well do sth: *But Frieda may well apply.*
I dare say: *I dare say they'll promote him.*

● We use these phrases to say that we think something probably won't happen:
be unlikely to do sth: *He's unlikely to change his personality overnight.*
I don't suppose: *I don't suppose he'll worry about being popular.*
I doubt if: *I doubt if Lynn will go for it.*
I shouldn't think: *I shouldn't think they'll employ an outsider.*

● We use this phrase when we think something definitely won't happen:
I can't imagine: *I can't imagine they'll like him.*

+ infinitive	+ subject + *will* + infinitive
be bound to	I dare say
be sure to	I don't suppose
be likely to	I doubt if
may well	I shouldn't think
be unlikely to	I can't imagine

TIPS! ● We can also use these phrases to talk about present situations or states: *He's bound to be home by now. She's unlikely to be awake at this time. I don't suppose you know where my wallet is.*

● We can also say *I'm sure (that)* + clause: *I'm sure (that) he'll be here on time.*

Real World

RW6.1 Polite interruptions 6D ❷ p52

asking for permission to interrupt

Sorry to bother you, but have you got a minute?
Is this a good time?
Sorry to disturb you.
I was wondering if I could see you for a moment.
Are you busy?
Can I have a word?

refusing permission to interrupt

Sorry, this isn't a good time.
I'm really up against it at the moment.
I'm afraid I'm a bit tied up just now.
I'm rather pushed for time at the moment.
I'm really rather busy right now.

TIPS! ● If we are refused permission we often say:
Don't worry, *it's not important/it can wait/it's not urgent/I'll catch you later/some other time.*
When would be *a good time/a better time/more convenient?*

● When we want to give permission to the person interrupting us, we often say: *Yes, of course. What can I do for you? How can I help? What's the problem?* or *What's up?* (informal).

I was wondering if I could see you for a moment.

Sorry, this isn't a good time.

Don't worry, it can wait.

Language Summary 7

Vocabulary

V7.1 State verbs 7A ❶ p54

respect have a good opinion of somebody because of their character or their ideas: *I respect my boss because he's very honest.*

deserve have earned something because of your good or bad actions or behaviour: *After all that hard work, you deserve a holiday.*

involve include something as a necessary part: *My job involves visiting customers abroad.*

trust believe that somebody is honest and will not cheat you or harm you: *I trust my husband completely.*

suspect think or believe that something is true or probable: *We suspected that an employee was stealing from the company.*

realise understand a situation, sometimes suddenly: *He realised that he'd left his wallet at home.*

envy /'envi/ wish that you had somebody else's abilities, possessions, lifestyle, etc.: *I envy people who can make friends easily.*

recognise know somebody or something because you have seen or heard them before: *I hadn't seen Louise for 20 years, but we recognised each other immediately.*

adore really love: *My grandmother absolutely adores cats.* (opposite: **detest**)

realise

envy

recognise

adore

TIPS! • *Respect*, *trust* and *envy* are also uncountable nouns.

• *Deserve* is often followed by the infinitive with *to*: *He deserves **to be** promoted.*

• *Involve*, *adore* and *detest* are often followed by verb+ing: *My course involves **doing** a lot of research.*

• We don't usually use state verbs in continuous verb forms.

V7.2 Business and trade 7B ❻ p57

noun for a person	noun for a thing/an idea	adjective
a politician	politics	political
a capitalist	capitalism capital	capitalist
an economist	the economy	economic economical
a developer	a developer development	developed developing
an investor	(an) investment	invested
an industrialist	(an) industry	industrial industrialised
a producer	a producer a product production	productive
a manufacturer	a manufacturer	manufactured
an environmentalist	the environment	environmental
a polluter	pollution	polluted

TIPS! • *Economise, develop, invest, produce, manufacture* and *pollute* are all regular verbs.

• Notice the difference between *economic* and *economical*: *Government ministers met yesterday to discuss **economic** policy.* (= relating to the economy of a country). *This car is very **economical**.* (= saves you money).

V7.3 The Internet 7C ❶ p58

a search engine a computer programme that finds information on the Internet by looking for words you have typed in (Google, etc.)

a chat room a part of the Internet where you can use email to chat with other people about any topic you choose

a forum a part of the Internet where you can discuss a specific subject (technology, computer games, politics, etc.)

an online encyclopaedia /ɪnˌsaɪklə'piːdiə/ a collection of articles about different subjects arranged in alphabetical order, which is available on the Internet (Wikipedia, etc.)

an online dating agency /'eɪdʒənsi/ an online company that helps people meet other people in order to start a romantic relationship

a blog (short for **weblog**) a website where a person regularly writes his or her ideas and thoughts so other people can read and comment on them

an online RPG (role-play game) a game on the Internet where players take the parts of characters in the game

a webcam a type of camera that records sound and moving pictures which are then broadcast live on the Internet

an MP3 file a computer file which stores high-quality sound in a small amount of space

a podcast an audio or video file that you can download and listen to on a computer or a digital audio player

anti-virus /ˌæntɪ'vaɪrəs/ **software** software that protects your computer from viruses

wireless or **Wi-Fi** /'waɪfaɪ/ a system that allows people to connect to the Internet by using radio waves

TIPS! • *Forums* can also be called *discussion groups, web forums, message boards* or *discussion boards*.

• Someone who writes a blog is called *a blogger*.

• *Wi-Fi* is also spelt *wi-fi* or *wifi*.

Vocabulary

V7.4 Word building (2): prefixes 7C ③ p59

prefix	meaning	examples
pro-	for	pro-hunting, pro-war, pro-government
anti-	against	anti-nuclear, anti-war, anti-government
pre-	before	preview, pre-war
post-	after	postgraduate, post-war
under-	not enough	undervalued, underqualified, underrated
over-	too much	overestimate, overqualified, overrated
multi-	many	multinational, multicultural, multimillionaire
re-	do something again	redefined, recalculate, redecorate, rebuild
mis-	do something incorrectly	misused, miscalculate, misunderstand
ex-	used to be	ex-vice-president, ex-colleague, ex-smoker, ex-wife
self-	of/by yourself	self-reliant, self-defence, self-discipline
non-	not	non-scientific, non-stop, non-smoker

TIP! • We always use hyphens with *pro-*, *anti-*, *ex-*, *self-* and *non-*. With the other prefixes, it depends on the word.

V7.5 On the phone 7D ① p60

pay-as-you-go a system where you pay money in advance to your mobile phone company, which is then used to pay for each call you make

a (mobile phone) contract a written agreement between a mobile phone company and a customer

a (mobile phone) network a system of phone lines or electronic signals that are connected together

reception the quality of phone signals that you receive

get cut off when you lose the connection with the other person during a phone conversation

run out of credit use all the money you have on your pay-as-you-go mobile phone so that you can't make any more calls

top up your phone pay in advance for more time on your pay-as-you-go mobile phone

a ring tone the sound or short piece of music that your mobile phone plays when somebody calls you

voicemail an electronic telephone answering system used by companies and mobile phone users

an answerphone a machine in your home that records phone messages

a payphone a public telephone

a landline a phone line that you have in your home

hang up end a conversation and put the telephone down

TIPS! • We can often say *reception* or *signal*: *What's the reception/signal like where you live? I can't get any reception/a signal. The reception/signal isn't very good here.*
• We can also say *hang up on somebody*: *I was trying to explain the problem when the sales assistant hung up on me!*

Grammar

G7.1 Simple and continuous aspects; activity and state verbs 7A ⑤ p55

SIMPLE AND CONTINUOUS ASPECTS

● We use **simple** verb forms to describe something that is:
repeated: *I usually **buy** a paperback and just go and sit somewhere quiet.*
completed: *I've also **called** my parents to say goodbye.*
permanent: *Luckily I only **live** ten minutes away.*

● We use **continuous** verb forms to describe something that is:
in progress at a specific point in time: *Once I got so involved in the book I **was reading** that I missed my plane.*
unfinished: *I've **been sitting** here for nearly five hours.*
temporary: *I'm **doing** a part-time business management course at the moment.*

ACTIVITY AND STATE VERBS

● **Activity verbs** talk about activities and actions. Typical activity verbs are: *play, fly, travel, listen, run, work, sit, study* and *wait.*

● We can use activity verbs in both simple and continuous verb forms: *I **play** tennis every weekend. Carla's **playing** tennis at the moment.*

● **State verbs** talk about states, feelings and opinions. We don't usually use these verbs in continuous verb forms: *I **want** a new car.* not ~~I'm wanting a new car.~~

● Learn these common state verbs:

'be and have' verbs	be have (got) own belong possess exist
'think and know' verbs	think know believe understand remember forget mean recognise suspect realise doubt imagine suppose
'like and hate' verbs	like hate love dislike prefer want adore detest wish
other verbs	hear seem need agree hope weigh contain suit fit respect cost smell consist of deserve involve trust envy include

VERBS WITH TWO MEANINGS

● Some verbs, such as *see, have, think* and *be*, can describe activities and states, but the meaning changes. Look at the different meanings of the verbs in these examples:

(pink = activity, blue = state)

I'm supposed to be seeing (= meeting) some clients as soon as I arrive, but I see (= with my eyes) the flight's been delayed.

I have (= possess) three kids and I never get time to shop for myself, so I'm having (= experiencing) a great time today.

I'm also thinking of (= considering) buying a camera, but I think (= have an opinion) they might be cheaper online.

My youngest is (= permanent characteristic) usually very good, but he's being (= behaving) very difficult today.

Language Summary 7

G7.2 Present Perfect Simple and Present Perfect Continuous 7B ③ p57

- We use the **Present Perfect** to talk about things that connect the past and the present.

- We often use the **Present Perfect Simple**:

  a) for experiences in our lives up to now: *I've visited many amazing cities over the years.*

  b) for states that started in the past and continue in the present: *Even Chinese people I've known for years are amazed at how fast things have changed.*

  c) for completed actions that happened recently, but we don't say exactly when: *I've just got back to my hotel room.*

  d) with superlatives: *Shanghai is the most spectacular city I've ever seen in my life.*

  e) to talk about change: *Many of China's biggest cities have become more polluted.*

- We often use the **Present Perfect Continuous**:

  a) for longer actions that started in the past and continue in the present: *Liu Zhang has been working in Shanghai for ten years.*

  b) for longer actions that have recently finished, but have a result in the present: *Today I've been walking around the Pudong area of the city, and I'm both exhausted and exhilarated by the experience.*

  c) for actions that happened repeatedly in the past and still happen in the present: *I've been coming to China for nearly 20 years.*

- Look at this sentence and the diagram: *Liu Zhang has been working in Shanghai for ten years.*

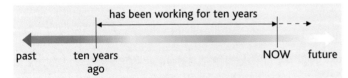

has been working for ten years

past   ten years ago   NOW   future

- We make the **Present Perfect Simple** with: subject + *have/'ve* or *has/'s* + past participle.

  I've known Rob for about ten years.
  He **hasn't called** me since Friday.
  What **have** you **done** today?

- We make the **Present Perfect Continuous** with: subject + *have/'ve* or *has/'s* + *been* + verb+*ing*.

  We've been living here since 2005.
  She **hasn't been working** very hard.
  Who **have** you **been talking** to?

SIMPLE OR CONTINUOUS?

- We often use the Present Perfect Continuous to emphasise the action we've been doing: *I've been doing my homework.* (we don't know if the homework is finished or not).

- We often use the Present Perfect Simple to say that we have completed something or that something has been completed: *I've done my homework.* (the homework is finished now).

- We often use Present Perfect Simple with verbs that describe short actions (*break, start, find, lose, buy, stop, finish,* etc.): *I've broken my glasses.* not *I've been breaking my glasses.*

- We often use the Present Perfect Continuous with verbs that describe longer actions (*learn, study, rain, try, play, read, wait,* etc.): *I've been learning English for six years.*

- With *work* and *live*, both forms are possible: *My sister's worked/been working here for ages. She's lived/been living in London since 2002.*

TIPS! • We often use these words with the Present Perfect Simple and Present Perfect Continuous: *for, since, just, yet, already, still, ever, never, recently, lately.*

• We also use the Present Perfect Simple with *this week/month,* etc. and *this morning/evening,* etc. if it is still that time of day.

• We can't use the Present Perfect with words/phrases that talk about a finished time period (*last year, in 1992, a week ago,* etc.).

HOW LONG OR HOW MANY?

- We usually use the Present Perfect Continuous to talk about how long something has been happening: *My company has been building skyscrapers here since 1993.*

- To make questions for this meaning, we use *How long*: *How long has your company been building skyscrapers here?*

- We usually use the Present Perfect Simple to talk about how many things have been completed: *This year we've built three new apartment blocks.*

- To make questions for this meaning, we use *How many* (+ noun): *How many new apartment blocks have you built this year?*

TIP! • For state verbs we must use the Present Perfect Simple with *How long: How long have you had your car?* not *How long have you been having your car?*

RW7.1 Problems on the phone 7D ③ p60

talking about phone problems

There's a bit of a delay on the line.
Sorry, you're breaking up a bit.
I didn't catch all of that.
I'm just about to run out of credit.
Sorry, it's a bad line.
You'll have to speak up a bit.
The reception isn't very good here.
Sorry, I didn't get any of that.
I keep losing you.
Sorry, we got cut off.
I think my battery's about to run out.

asking people to call you back

Shall I call you back on your landline?
Would you like me to phone you back?
Do you want me to give you a ring later?

TIP! • *Break up* = lose part of the signal; *speak up* = speak louder.

Vocabulary

V8.1 Dealing with money 8A ❶ p62

invest money in something*	≠	spend money on something
be in credit*	≠	be overdrawn*
get into debt*	≠	get out of debt
buy/get something on credit*	≠	pay cash for something
get a loan*	≠	repay a loan
have a good credit rating*	≠	have a bad credit rating
get a high interest rate*	≠	get a low interest rate
have a current account*	≠	have a savings account*
be well off*	≠	be short (of money)
take/get money out of an account	≠	put money into an account

*invest (money) in sth put money in a bank account, business, etc. in order to make more money

*be in credit have money in your bank account

*be overdrawn /ˌəʊvəˈdrɔːn/ when you have spent more money than is in your bank account

*debt /det/ money which is owed to another person or organisation

*buy/get sth on credit a way of buying something now and paying for it in the future

*a loan /ləʊn/ an amount of money that is borrowed, often from a bank, which must be paid back in the future

*a credit rating a measure of somebody's ability to pay back money, based on their financial history

*an interest rate the amount of money charged by a bank, credit card company, etc. for borrowing money, or the amount of money you earn when you keep your money in a bank account

*a current account a bank account that you can get money from at any time

*a savings account a bank account which earns a good rate of interest

*well off having a lot of money

TIPS! • We can also say be in debt: Mark's terrible with money – he's always in debt.

• In more formal situations we often use withdraw money (= take money out of your account) and deposit money (= put money into your account): I'd like to withdraw £100 and I'd also like to deposit this cheque.

V8.2 Phrasal verbs (2): money 8B ❶ p64

pay sb/sth back or pay back sb/sth pay somebody the money that you owe them: Can I borrow £10? I'll pay you/it back tomorrow.

pay sth off or pay off sth pay back money that you owe on a loan, etc.: I've finally paid off my student loan.

a mortgage /ˈmɔːgɪdʒ/ the amount of money you borrow from a bank or a similar organisation in order to buy a house: We've got a £250,000 mortgage.

take sth out or take out sth arrange to get a loan, mortgage, etc. from a bank or other financial company: We took out a loan to buy a car.

go down become lower in price, value, amount, etc.: Prices have gone down.

come to sth be a total amount when some numbers are added together: The house repairs came to about £1,000.

put sth down (on sth) or put down sth (on sth) pay part of the cost of something and promise to pay the rest later: I've put £10,000 down on a new flat.

a deposit an amount of money that is given in advance as part of a total payment for something: I'll leave a £500 deposit and pay the rest next week.

property buildings, houses, flats, etc.: Property is very expensive here.

come into sth receive money or property from a relative who has died: Rosie came into a lot of money when her aunt died.

take sth off or take off sth reduce the price of something by a particular amount: The shop took £50 off the table because it was damaged.

save up (for sth) keep money so that you can buy something in the future: She's saving up for a new bike.

rip sb off or rip off sb cheat somebody by making them pay too much money for something: £10 for an ice cream? He's ripping people off.

TIP! • Rip somebody off is an informal verb. The noun is a rip-off.

save up for something   rip somebody off

V8.3 Synonyms 8C ❸ p67

• We often use synonyms to avoid repeating words or phrases when we are speaking or writing.

work out	figure out	simple	straightforward
exact	precise	especially	particularly
problem	dilemma	usually	generally
appropriate	acceptable	normal	customary
compulsory	obligatory	strange	odd
certainly	definitely	watch	observe
insulted	offended	extra	additional
chase	pursue	differ	vary
discover	find out	difficult	complicated
simply	just	for example	such as

Language Summary 8

G8.1 Wishes (1); *I hope …*; *It's time …* (8A ④ p63)

WISHES IN THE PRESENT

- We often use **I wish …** to talk about imaginary situations in the present. This is often used to talk about the opposite to what is true or real: *I wish I had my own car.* (I don't have my own car, but I would like to).

- We use **wish + Past Simple** to make wishes about states: *I wish I knew where your father was.*

- We use **wish + Past Continuous** to make wishes about actions in progress: *I wish you weren't chasing these impossible dreams.*

- We use **wish + could + infinitive** to make wishes about abilities or possibilities: *I wish I could spare the time.*

- We use **wish + would + infinitive** to make wishes about things other people, organisations, etc. do that we would like to change. This is often used to show annoyance or impatience about things that are outside our control: *I wish you'd take more care of your things.*

- We can't use *wish + would + infinitive* to talk about ourselves: *I wish I had a job.* not ~~I wish I would have a job~~.

TIPS! • We can say *I wish …* or *If only …* : *I wish I could spare the time. = If only I could spare the time.*

• We can use *wish + didn't have to* to make wishes about obligations: *I wish I didn't have to go to work.* not ~~I wish I hadn't to go to work~~.

• We often use the second conditional to give reasons for wishes (see G3.1): *If I didn't have to go to work, I'd help you.*

• We can say *I wish I/he/she/it was …* or *I wish I/he/she/it were …* : *I wish I was/were ten years younger.*

I HOPE …

- We use **I hope …** to talk about things that we think might happen in the future: *I hope you get something soon.*

- *I hope …* is followed by a clause (subject + verb + …): *I hope they enjoy themselves.*

- Compare these sentences:
  *I **hope** she calls.*
  The speaker thinks she might call. This is a real possibility.
  *I **wish** she'd call.*
  The speaker doesn't think she will call. This is an imaginary situation.

TIPS! • *I hope …* is often followed by *will* + infinitive: *I hope he'll understand.*

• We also use *I hope …* to talk about the past: *I hope you didn't tell Terry what happened.*

IT'S TIME …

- We often use **It's (about) time + subject + Past Simple** to say that we are annoyed or frustrated that something hasn't happened yet: *It's time you got your own car.* We use *about* to add emphasis: *It's about time you found yourself a proper job.*

- We use **It's time + infinitive with to** to say that something should happen now: *It's time to go.*

TIPS! • *It's time …* can also be followed by the Past Continuous: *It's about time we were leaving.*

• We can also say *It's time for me/you*, etc. + infinitive with *to*: *It's time for me to go to work.*

• We can say *It's about time …* or *It's high time …* : *It's high time you found yourself a proper job.*

G8.2 Wishes (2); *should have* (8B ⑤ p65)

- We often use **wish + Past Perfect Simple** to make wishes about the past. These wishes are used to express regret and are often the opposite of what really happened: JOSH *I wish the ad hadn't been so big.* (The ad on Josh's car was very big. He didn't like it.)

- We can also use **should/shouldn't have + past participle** to talk about regrets in the past: ZOË *I should have eaten before I went in.* (Zoë didn't eat before she went in. She regrets that.)

TIPS! • We can also use the third conditional for regrets (see G3.2): *If I'd known about this before, I'd have done it years ago.*

• We can use *I wish …* or *If only …* to make wishes about the past: *I wish I'd been there. = If only I'd been there.*

• We can also make sentences in the past with *wish* with *you/he/she/we/they*: *They wish they hadn't moved house.*

RW8.1 Apologising (8D ④ p68)

apologising

I'm sorry that I didn't get back to you sooner.
I'm really sorry. I'm afraid (I broke your vase).
I'm sorry about (this afternoon).
I'm sorry for (borrowing money off you all the time).

giving reasons for your actions or being self-critical

I didn't realise (the time).
I shouldn't have (said those things to you).
I can't believe (I said that).
I didn't mean to (upset you).
I thought (you knew each other) for some reason.
I had no idea (you'd need a script).

responding to an apology

Don't worry about it.
Never mind.
It doesn't matter.
Forget about it.
Oh, that's alright.
No need to apologise.

- After *I'm sorry (that)* we use a clause.

- After *I'm sorry about* we usually use a noun.

- After *I'm sorry for* we usually use verb+ing.

TIP! • Notice the difference between *I didn't mean it.* (I didn't mean something that I said) and *I didn't mean to.* (I didn't mean to do something that I did).

V9.1 The cinema 9A ❶ p70

a review an article in a newspaper, magazine or online that gives an opinion about a new film, book, play, etc.: *I read a great review of Jim Carrey's new film.*

a critic a type of journalist who gives his/her opinion about something, particularly films, books, plays, etc.: *My cousin's the theatre critic for The Times.*

subtitled /'sʌb,taɪtld/ when a film or a TV programme has a printed translation of what the actors are saying at the bottom of the screen: *Most foreign films in the UK are subtitled.*

dubbed /dʌbd/ when the voices you hear in a film or TV programme are actors speaking in a different language, not the original actors: *Most American TV programmes in my country are dubbed.*

a remake a film that has the same story, and often the same title, as one that was made earlier: *Have you seen the 1998 remake of Hitchcock's 'Psycho'?*

a sequel /'siːkwəl/ a film, book, etc. that continues the story of an earlier one: *'Godfather II' is probably the greatest sequel ever made.*

be set in take place in a particular place or period of time: *The film is set in New York in the 1930s.*

special effects pieces of action in a film, TV programme, etc. that are created by using special equipment or on a computer: *'The Matrix' has the most amazing special effects I've ever seen.*

be based on sth when a novel or a true story is used as the starting point to develop a film, play, idea, etc.: *The film is based on a novel by Zadie Smith.*

a cast all the actors and actresses in a film, play or TV programme: *The new Spielberg film has a fantastic cast.*

a performance the action of entertaining other people by acting, singing, dancing, etc.: *Judi Dench gave an amazing performance as Elizabeth I in 'Shakespeare in Love'.*

a role the character played by an actor or actress in a film, TV programme, play, etc.: *In 'Casablanca', Humphrey Bogart plays the role of Rick.*

a soundtrack the recorded music from a film, which you can buy on CD: *I often listen to the soundtrack of 'Moulin Rouge' when I'm driving.*

a scene /siːn/ a part of a film or play in which the action stays in one place for a continuous period: *The wedding was my favourite scene in the whole movie.*

TIPS! • The noun for *subtitled* is *subtitles*: *Does this DVD have subtitles?*

• We can also say that a film is *dubbed into* another language: *I couldn't understand a word – the film was dubbed into Chinese.*

V9.2 Entertainment adjectives 9B ❶ p72

far-fetched /,fɑː'fetʃt/ extremely unlikely to be true

predictable happening in a way that you expect, not in an interesting or unusual way

moving having a strong effect on your emotions, usually so that you feel sadness or sympathy

fast-moving when the plot of a film, TV drama, etc. develops quickly (opposite: **slow-moving**)

sentimental dealing with emotions such as love and sadness in a way that seems exaggerated and unrealistic

gripping so exciting that it holds your attention completely

memorable likely to be remembered because it is very good, enjoyable or unusual

overrated thought to be better than it is (opposite: **underrated**)

scary /'skeəri/ frightening

weird /wɪəd/ strange, unusual, unexpected or unnatural

hilarious /hɪ'leərɪəs/ extremely funny

V9.3 Homonyms 9C ❻ p75

• Homonyms are words with the same spelling and pronunciation, but different meanings (*light*, *last*, etc.).

state 1 (noun) the mental, emotional or physical condition that somebody or something is in. *He's in no state to go to work. He's very ill.* **2** (noun) a part of a country: *Which US state is Hollywood in?*

handle 1 (verb) deal with something: *He can handle most problems on his own.* **2** (noun) a part of an object that is used to hold, carry or move it: *I broke the handle on the window.*

case 1 (noun) a particular example or situation of something: *It was a typical case of food poisoning.* **2** (noun) a container for keeping things in: *Have you seen my camera case?*

point 1 (noun) an idea, opinion or piece of information that is said or written: *That was an interesting point John made.* **2** (noun) a particular time: *At that point I left the meeting.*

round 1 (prep) in every part or in various parts of a place: *I had to go all round the town to find a hotel.* **2** (adj) shaped like a circle or a ball: *I'd like to get a round table for the kitchen.*

examination 1 (noun) when somebody looks at a person or a thing carefully in order to discover something about him, her or it **2** (noun) a set of medical tests

mind 1 (noun) the part of a person that enables them to think **2** (verb) be unhappy, upset or annoyed if something happens

sense 1 (noun) a general feeling or understanding of something **2** (noun) a clear meaning that is easy to understand

sack 1 (noun) a large bag made of strong material **2** (verb) tell somebody to leave their job, usually because he/she has done something wrong

change 1 (countable noun) when something becomes different **2** (uncountable noun) money that is in coins rather than notes

Language Summary 9

G9.1 The passive (9A ④ p70)

PASSIVE VERB FORMS

- We usually use the passive when we are more interested in what happens to somebody or something than in who or what does the action: *The Academy Awards ceremony* **is held** *in Hollywood once a year, usually in March.*
- We often use the passive when we don't know who or what does the action: *55 Oscars mysteriously vanished while they* **were being driven** *from Chicago to Los Angeles.*
- To make the passive we use: subject + *be* + past participle.

passive verb form	be	past participle
Present Simple	am/are/is	held
Present Continuous	am/are/is being	shown
Past Simple	was/were	given
Past Continuous	was/were being	driven
Present Perfect Simple	have/has been	confirmed
Past Perfect Simple	had been	nominated
be going to	am/are/is going to be	awarded

TIPS! • In passive sentences we can use '*by* + the agent' to say who or what does the action. We only include the agent when it is important or unusual information: *52 of the Oscars were found in some rubbish* **by a man called Willie Fulgear.**
• We don't use the Present Perfect Continuous and Past Perfect Continuous in the passive: ~~He has/had been being arrested.~~

OTHER PASSIVE STRUCTURES

- After certain verbs (e.g. *enjoy*) we use *being* + past participle: *Everyone* **enjoys being told** *they are good at what they do.*
- After certain verbs (e.g. *want*) we use *to be* + past participle: *Most of us* **want to be rewarded** *in some way.*
- After prepositions we use *being* + past participle: *Every actor* **dreams of being nominated** *for an Oscar.*
- After *the first/second/last* (+ noun) we use *to be* + past participle: **The first** *Academy Awards ceremony* **to be televised** *was in 1953.*
- After *have to* and *used to* we use *be* + past participle: *The ceremony* **had to be postponed** *in 1938 because of a flood. Newspapers* **used to be given** *the winners' names in advance.*
- After modal verbs we use *be* + past participle: *The names* **wouldn't be published** *until afterwards.*

TIP! • We can use all modal verbs (*can, must, will, could, might*, etc.) in passive verb forms: *He can't be trusted. All bags must be checked in at reception.*

G9.2 as, like, such as, so, such (9B ③ p72)

AS, LIKE, SUCH AS

- We use **such as** or **like** to introduce examples: *Critics* **such as** *Amis Jones loved it. Even though it has actors* **like** *Sy Harris and May Firth?*
- We use **as + noun** to say that somebody has a particular job: *I don't like Amis Jones* **as** *a critic.*

- We also use **as + noun** to say what something is used for: *There were just some black boxes which were used* **as** *tables and chairs.*
- We use **like + clause** to say that things happen in a similar way: *Well, Jones was wrong,* **like** *he usually is.*
- We use **like + noun (or pronoun)** to say that something is similar to something else: *The whole thing was* **like** *a bad dream.*

TIP! • We can also use *as* + clause to say that things happen in a similar way: *Well, Jones was wrong,* **as** *he usually is.*

SO, SUCH

- We use **so** and **such** to give nouns, adjectives and adverbs more emphasis.
- We use **so** + adjective: *The plot was* **so** *far-fetched.*
- We use **such** (+ adjective) + noun: *It had* **such** *a good cast.*
- We use **so** + *much* or *many* + noun: *I can't understand why it's getting* **so much** *attention. I've no idea why* **so many** *critics liked it.*

TIPS! • With *so* and *such* we often use '(*that*) + clause' to say what the consequence is: *The play was so slow* (**that**) *I* **actually fell asleep.**
• We often use *a lot of* with *such*: *There was* **such a lot of** *noise.*

RW9.1 Making and responding to suggestions (9D ③ p76)

asking if the person is free

Are you doing anything (this evening)?
Have you got anything on (this Saturday)?
What are you up to (on Sunday)?

making a suggestion

I thought we could give (that new club) a try.
I wouldn't mind (going to that). How about you?
Do you feel like (having an Indian)?
Do you fancy (going to hear them play)?

politely refusing a suggestion

I'm sorry, but I don't feel up to (going to a club).
Some other time, perhaps.
I'd rather give (that) a miss, if you don't mind.

saying you have no preference

I'm easy. Whatever you like.
I really don't mind. It's up to you.
I'm not bothered either way.
It's all the same to me.

- *Wouldn't mind, feel like, fancy* and *feel up to* are followed by verb+*ing*, a noun or a pronoun: *I wouldn't mind* **going** *to that.*
- *I'd rather* is followed by the infinitive: *I'd rather* **give** *that a miss, if you don't mind.*

Vocabulary

V10.1 **Household jobs** 10A **1** p78

a plug   a light bulb   shelves

a lock   a fence   a burglar alarm

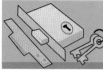

a duvet /ˈduːveɪ/   a leak   a roof

tyres /taɪəz/   oil   a boiler

put sth up or **put up sth** put something on a wall or build something: *I'm useless at putting up shelves. My neighbour put up a new fence last weekend.*

put sth in or **put in sth** put a piece of equipment into your home so that it is ready to use: *Bill's putting in some new lighting in the kitchen.*

fix repair something that is broken or not working properly: *When are you going to fix the roof?*

decorate make the inside of a building more attractive by painting the walls, putting up wallpaper, etc.: *I'm going to decorate the bathroom next.*

replace get something new to put in the place of something that has been broken, stolen, etc.: *I think it's time to replace the boiler, it's over 15 years old.*

dry-clean clean clothes with chemicals instead of water: *This skirt needs to be dry-cleaned.*

service examine a car, boiler, etc. and fix it if necessary: *My boiler is serviced every year.*

TIPS! • The singular of *shelves* is *a shelf*.
• *Leak* is also a verb: *Oh, no! The roof is leaking!*
• We can say *fix*, *repair* or *mend*: *I'll fix/repair/mend the roof.*
• *DIY* /diːaɪˈwaɪ/ = do it yourself (making or repairing things yourself instead of buying them or paying somebody else to do them): *My husband is very good at DIY.*
• The shop where you take clothes to be dry-cleaned is called *a dry cleaner's*.
• *Service* is also a noun: *When did your car last have a service?*

V10.2 **Male, female and neutral words** 10B **1** p80

male	female	neutral
a landlord*	a landlady	–
a chairman	a chairwoman	a chairperson
–	–	a soldier /ˈsəʊldʒə/
a widower	a widow*	–
a headmaster	a headmistress	a head teacher
a steward	a stewardess	a flight attendant
a groom*	a bride	–
a fireman	–	a firefighter
an actor	an actress	an actor
–	–	an author
a spokesman	a spokeswoman	a spokesperson*
a nephew /ˈnefjuː/	a niece /niːs/	–
–	–	a cousin /ˈkʌsən/
a hero* /ˈhɪərəʊ/	a heroine /ˈherəʊɪn/	a hero
a manager	a manageress	a manager
a salesman	a saleswoman	a salesperson

*a landlord a man who owns a house, flat, etc. and charges people rent to live in it
*a widow a woman whose husband has died and who has not married again
*a groom (or a bridegroom) a man who is about to get married or who has just got married
*a spokesperson somebody who is chosen by a group or organisation to speak officially to the public for them
*a hero a person who is admired for having done something very brave or achieved something great

TIP! • In modern usage we prefer to use neutral words/phrases which can refer to both men and women.

V10.3 **Compound nouns and adjectives** 10C **3** p83

high-powered (adj) having a very important and powerful job: *Anne's a high-powered accountant in the city.*
hard-earned (adj) deserving something because you have worked very hard for it: *He spent his hard-earned cash on a new bike.*
income tax (uncountable noun) a tax that you pay on the money you earn: *I think people pay too much income tax.*
a cutback when something is reduced in order to save money: *The company had to make some cutbacks.*
a drawback a disadvantage or the negative part of a situation: *One of the drawbacks of working in a hotel is the unsocial hours.*
time-consuming (adj) taking a long time to do: *Writing a book is very time-consuming.*
a breakdown when something stops working: *There's been a breakdown in communication.*

Language Summary 10

Vocabulary

TIPS! • The verb for *a cutback* is *cut back (on sth)*: *We need to cut back on the amount of paper we use.*

• The verb for *a breakdown* is *break down*: *It seems that communication has completely broken down.*

● Compound nouns are usually made from:
noun + noun: *a housewife, a workplace, income tax,* etc.
verb + preposition: *a cutback, a drawback,* etc.

● Compound nouns are usually written as one word or two words: *a babysitter, a human being,* etc.

● Compound adjectives are usually spelt with hyphens: *part-time, freshly-prepared, badly-cooked,* etc.

STRESS ON COMPOUND NOUNS AND ADJECTIVES

● The stress on compounds nouns is fixed and is usually on the first part of the compound noun: *housewife, workplace, food poisoning, income tax, cutback, drawback, babysitter, washing machine, breakdown.*
But: *human being, school lunch.*

● The stress on compound adjectives can sometimes change, depending on whether they come before a noun or not: *This is homemade bread. This bread is homemade. He's got a full-time job. He works full-time.*
But: *It's a time-consuming project. The project is very time-consuming.*

Grammar

G10.1 *have/get something done, get somebody to do something, do something yourself* 10A ❹ p79

have/get something done

● We use **have/get something done** when we pay somebody else to do a job: *We usually **have** the decorating **done** professionally. I still **get** my car **serviced** at the local garage.*

TIP! • *Get something done* is usually more informal than *have something done*.

POSITIVE

● We make the **positive** form of *have/get something done* with:
subject + *have* or *get* + something + past participle.

● We can use *have* or *get* in any verb form, for example:
Present Continuous: *Now I'm **having** the bathroom **redecorated**.*
Present Perfect Simple: *I've **had** lots of things **done** recently.*
Past Simple: *The roof was leaking so I **got** that **fixed**.*
Past Perfect Simple: *I'd never **had** any kitchen appliances **serviced** before.*
will + infinitive: *I'll **get** the door lock **replaced** as soon as I can.*

NEGATIVES AND QUESTIONS

● We make the **negative** and **question** forms of *have/get something done* by using the correct form of *have* or *get*. Look at these examples:
*Jan **doesn't have** her car **serviced** regularly.*
not ~~Jan hasn't her car serviced regularly~~.
***Does** Jan **have** her car **serviced** regularly?*
not ~~Has Jan her car serviced regularly?~~
*Donna **didn't have** her hair **cut** yesterday.*
***Did** Donna **have** her hair **cut** yesterday?*
*Sheena **isn't getting** her boiler **replaced**.*
***Is** Sheena **getting** her boiler **replaced**?*

get somebody to do something

● We use **get somebody to do something** when we ask somebody that we know to do the job. If it's a friend or family member, we probably don't pay them: *I **get** my husband **to do** most things round the house.*

POSITIVE

● We make the **positive** form of *get somebody to do something* with:
subject + *get* + somebody + infinitive with *to* + something.

● We can use *have* or *get* in any verb form, for example:
Past Simple: *I **got** my dad **to teach** me how to do things.*
be going to: *I'm going to **get** my brother **to check** they're safe.*

NEGATIVES AND QUESTIONS

● We make the **negative** and **question** forms of *get somebody to do something* by using the correct form of *get*:
*I **didn't get** anyone **to help** me.*
***Are** you **going to get** somebody **to fix** it?*

TIP! • We can also say *pay somebody to do something*: *I usually pay somebody to do the garden.*

do something yourself

● We use **do something myself**, **yourself**, etc. when we do the job without any help from other people: *I do most things round the house myself.*

● The reflexive pronouns are: *myself, yourself, himself, herself, itself, ourselves, yourselves, themselves.*

TIP! • We often use reflexive pronouns to emphasise that we do something instead of somebody else doing something for us: *I actually put some shelves up myself last weekend.*

He's having his hair cut.   She's decorating the kitchen herself.

Grammar

G10.2 Quantifiers 10B ④ p81

DIFFERENCES IN MEANING

- *Both of* and *either of* refer to two things or people: *I've got two older brothers and both of them do most of the cooking.*
- *Everyone, every, any of, anyone, all of* and *anything* refer to more than two things or people: *Back in the 1980s, everyone was talking about the 'new man'.*
- *Each* can refer to two or more things or people: *I've read two articles on the subject recently, and each article suggests … . And each time I read about how selfish men are … .*
- *No one, neither of, none of* and *no* refer to a zero quantity.
- *Neither of* refers to two things or people: *Neither of them spend hours in the pub.*
- *No one, none of* and *no* refer to more than two things or people: *… none of my friends do.*

DIFFERENCES IN FORM

- *Every* and *each* are followed by a singular countable noun: *Every **magazine** was full of pictures of him holding babies.*
- *Both of, neither of* and *either of* are followed by *the, my*, etc. + a plural countable noun, or the pronouns *you, us* or *them*: *Both of **them** do most of the cooking. I don't think either of **my brothers** want the lifestyle our father's generation had.*
- *Any of, all of* and *none of* are often followed by *the, my*, etc. + a plural countable noun: *All of **my married friends** … .*
- *No* is always followed by a noun. This noun can be plural, singular or uncountable: *No **newspapers** report that. No **newspaper** reports that. There's no **electricity**.*
- We can also use *any of, all of, all* and *none of* with uncountable nouns: *Don't touch any of the **food**.*
- *Everyone, every, no one, each* and *anything* are followed by a singular verb form: *No one **seems** to think the division of labour has really improved.*
- *All of, both of, neither of, either of* and *none of* are followed by a plural verb form: *All of my married friends **are** new men.*

WHEN TO USE *OF*

- We must use *of* with *any, both, either, neither* and *all* when they are followed by a pronoun: *I spoke to both of them.* not *I spoke to both them.*
- We can leave out *of* with *any, both, either, neither* and *all* when they are followed by *(the, my*, etc.) + a plural countable noun: *Both (the) places were lovely.* or *Both of the places were lovely.* not *Both of places were lovely.*

EVERY OR EACH?

- We use *every* when we think of people or things as **part of a group**: *Every employee has an ID card.* (= all the people).
- We use *each* when we think of people or things **separately**: *Check each person's ID.* (= check their IDs one by one).
- We usually use *every* for a **large** number and *each* for a **small** number: *I've been to every country in Europe. They have three children and each child has green eyes.*

ALL OR ALL (OF)?

- We use *all* + a plural countable noun to refer to **a group in general**: *All women are capable of being the breadwinner.*
- We use *all (of) my, the*, etc. + plural countable noun to refer to **a specific group**: *But all (of) my married friends are new men.*

EITHER (OF), NEITHER (OF), NONE OF AND NO

- We can use *either of* in positive and negative sentences: *Either of these places are fine. I don't like either of them.*
- We must use a singular noun after *either* and *neither* without *of*: *Neither match was very good.* not ~~Neither matches was very good~~.
- We can use a singular verb form after *either of, neither of* and *none of*: *Neither of his parents has visited him this month.*
- We must use a positive verb form after *neither (of), none of* and *no*: *None of my friends have a car.* not ~~None of my friends doesn't have a car~~.

ANY, ANYTHING, ANYONE, ETC.

- We usually use *any (of), anything, anyone*, etc. with negative verb forms: *I **haven't got** any money. They **didn't do** anything.*
- We can also use *any (of), anything, anyone*, etc. with a positive verb form to mean 'it doesn't matter which': *Read **any of** the articles* (= it doesn't matter which article) *written today on the subject and **anyone** (= it doesn't matter who) would think that men haven't changed.*

Real World

RW10.1 Adding emphasis 10D ③ p84

- Notice these common patterns for introductory phrases that add emphasis:

The thing One thing What	I	(don't) like love hate admire	about …	is …

The thing I don't like about this flat **is** the kitchen.
One thing I love about you **is** you always laugh at my jokes.
What I like about the flat **is** it's so light.

The thing that One thing that What	amazes annoys worries upsets	me about …	is …

The thing that amazes me about your mother **is** she still can't read a map.
One thing that annoys me about you **is** you never give me time to look at a map.
What worries me about the size of the kitchen **is** I can't help Polly with the cooking.

TIP! • We can also say *What irritates/bothers me about … is … : What irritates me about her is she's always late.*

Language Summary 11

V11.1 Work collocations 11A ❶ p86

make a living*	have a lot of work on*
do sth for a living	be on the go*
work freelance*	get down to* work
be made redundant*	work on an interesting project*
be out of work*	give a talk

*make a living earn the money that you need to live

*freelance doing work for several different companies rather than for just one company

*be made redundant lose your job because your employer doesn't need you any more

*be out of work be unemployed

*have a lot of work on have a lot of work that you need to do

*be on the go be very busy and active

*get down to sth finally start doing something that needs a lot of attention

*a project /ˈprɒdʒekt/ a piece of work which is completed over a period of time

TIPS! • We can say make a living or earn a living.
• We usually use do something for a living in questions: What does your brother do for a living?
• We can give a talk, give a lecture or give a presentation.

V11.2 Business collocations 11B ❶ p88

close a branch*	do business with somebody
take over* a company	set up* a new company
go out of business*	go bankrupt*
make a profit* or a loss*	import* products from another
expand* the business	country
go into business with	export* products to another country
somebody*	run a chain* of restaurants

*a branch a shop, office, etc. that is part of a larger company

*take sth over or take over sth to get control of a company, business, etc.

*go out of business stop doing business because your company has been unsuccessful

*a profit money that you make when doing business (opposite: a loss)

*expand become larger in size, number or amount

*go into business with sb start a business with somebody

*set sth up or set up sth formally start a new business, company, system, etc.

*go bankrupt become unable to pay your debts

*import buy or bring in products from another country (opposite: export)

*a chain a number of shops, hotels, restaurants, etc. owned or managed by the same person or company

V11.3 Verb patterns (2): reporting verbs 11C ❸ p91

	+ that + clause
mention explain	(subject + verb + ...)
point out* admit claim*	
agree promise recommend	
insist suggest	
agree offer promise	+ (not) + infinitive with to
threaten refuse claim	((not) to do)
remind advise persuade	+ object + (not) + infinitive with to
warn invite	(sb/sth (not) to do)
deny* recommend	+ verb+ing
suggest admit	(doing)
apologise (for) insist* (on)	+ preposition + (not) + verb+ing
blame* (sb for)	+ object + preposition + (not) +
accuse* (sb of)	verb+ing

Rob mentioned **that the profits were up 20% last month.**
He agreed **to run** the shop on his own for the first year.
I reminded **him to sort out** the staff wages.
He denied **doing** anything wrong.
He apologised **for not telling** me sooner.
He blamed **me for not letting** him hire enough staff.

TIPS! • The reporting verbs in blue in the table show the form of the verbs in blue in Mike'e email on p90.
• The reporting verbs in **bold** in the table have more than one verb pattern.
• Deny has a negative meaning. We say He denied stealing the money. not He denied not stealing the money.

*point out tell somebody some information, often because you think they have forgotten it or don't know it

*claim say something is true, even though you can't prove it and other people might not believe it

*deny say that something is not true, usually because somebody has said that you've done something wrong

*insist say repeatedly that something is true or that you want something to happen, often when other people disagree with you

*blame say that somebody is responsible for something bad that has happened

*accuse say that somebody has done something wrong

V11.4 Advertising 11D ❶ p92

advertising the business of trying to persuade people to buy products or services

publicity the attention somebody or something gets from appearing in newspapers, on TV, etc.

a slogan a short, memorable phrase used in advertising

a logo a design or symbol used to advertise something

an advertising campaign /kæmˈpeɪn/ a series of advertisements for a particular product or service

Vocabulary

an advertising budget /'bʌdʒɪt/ the amount of money available to spend on an advertising campaign

the press all the newspapers and magazines in a particular place or country

the media /'miːdɪə/ all the organisations that provide information to the public (newspapers, TV stations, etc.)

a leaflet a piece of paper that advertises something or gives you information

a free sample a small amount of a product that is given away free to the public

design /dɪ'zaɪn/ make or draw plans for a new product, building, car, etc.

launch /lɔːntʃ/ make a new product, book, etc. available for the first time

She's handing out leaflets.

He's giving away free samples.

TIPS! • We can say *an advertisement*, *an advert* or *an ad*.
• We say *the press/media* not *a press/media*.
• *Launch is also a noun: When is the product launch?*

Grammar

G11.1 Describing future events; Future Perfect

11A ③ p86

Describing future events

● We use the **Present Continuous** to talk about an arrangement in the future: *I'm having lunch with my boss tomorrow.*

● We make the Present Continuous with: subject + *am/are/is* + verb+*ing*.

● We use the **Future Continuous** to talk about something that will be in progress at a point in time in the future: *Sorry, I'll be interviewing people for our graduate trainee programme then.*

● We make the Future Continuous with: subject + *'ll* (= *will*) + *be* + verb+*ing* (see G5.2).

● We can use **will be in the middle of something** to describe an action that will be in progress at a point of time in the future: *I'll be in the middle of a meeting at four.*

● We can use **will be on my, his, etc. way to somewhere** to say that a person will be travelling at a point of time in the future: *I'll be on my way to Southampton at eleven.*

TIP! • We can also use *be in the middle of something* and *be on my, his, etc. way to somewhere* to talk about the present: *I can't talk now, I'm in the middle of cooking.*

Future Perfect

● We use the **Future Perfect** to talk about something that will be completed before a certain time in the future: *I'll have arrived by lunchtime.* (= some time before lunchtime).

● Look at this sentence and the diagram: *I'll have finished giving the talk by three thirty.*

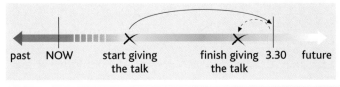

| past | NOW | start giving the talk | finish giving the talk | 3.30 | future |

POSITIVE AND NEGATIVE

● We make the **positive** and **negative** forms of the Future Perfect with:
subject + *will* or *'ll/won't* + *have* + past participle.

I'll have done it by midday.
I won't have done it by ten o'clock.

QUESTIONS

● We make **questions** in the Future Perfect with:
(question word) + *will* + subject + *have* + past participle.

What time **will** you **have finished**?

TIPS! • We often use *by* with the Future Perfect to mean 'before this time': *I'll have left the office by six o'clock.*

• We also use *by the time* + clause, *by this time next week, month*, etc. and *by the end of the day, week*, etc. with the Future Perfect: *Hurry up! The film will have started by the time we get there.*

G11.2 Reported speech   11B ④ p89

REPORTED SENTENCES

● Look at these pairs of sentences. Notice the way the second speaker reports what the first speaker said.

MIKE → DAISY "**I have** something interesting to tell you."

DAISY → MIKE "You said that **you had** something interesting to tell me."

ROB → MIKE "**I'm planning** to set up my own business."

MIKE → DAISY "Rob told me that **he was planning** to set up his own business."

ROB → MIKE "**I've been looking** for a good location since August."

MIKE → DAISY "He said **he'd been looking** for a good location since August."

Language Summary 11

Grammar

● We usually change the verb form in reported speech.

verb form in direct speech	verb form in reported speech
Present Simple I have an idea.	Past Simple He said he had an idea.
Present Continuous I'm leaving.	Past Continuous He said he was leaving.
Present Perfect Simple I've done it.	Past Perfect Simple He said he'd done it.
Present Perfect Continuous I've been working.	Past Perfect Continuous He said he'd been working.
Past Simple I woke up late.	Past Perfect Simple He said he'd woken up late.
Past Continuous I was sleeping.	Past Perfect Continuous He said he'd been sleeping.
Past Perfect Simple I'd seen it before.	no change possible He said he'd seen it before.
Past Perfect Continuous I'd been waiting.	no change possible He said he'd been waiting.
am/is/are going to I'm going to do it.	*was/were going to* He said he was going to do it.
will I'll call them.	*would* He said he'd call them.
can I can do it.	*could* He said he could do it.
must I must go.	*had to* He said he had to go.

TIPS! ● The modal verbs *could*, *should*, *would*, *might* and *ought to* don't change in reported speech.
● *Say* doesn't have an object: *I said (that)* not ~~I said her (that)~~.
Tell must have an object: *I told him (that)* not ~~I told (that)~~.
● The Past Simple doesn't have to change to the Past Perfect Simple. It can stay in the Past Simple.
● We don't have to change the verb form if the reported sentence is about something general or is still in the future: *"I've got a car."* → *He said he's got a car. "I'm going to Africa next year."* → *She said she's going to Africa next year.*
● We sometimes change time expressions in reported speech: *tomorrow* → *the next day*; *next Monday* → *the following Monday*; *this week* → *last week*; *last month* → *the month before*, etc.

REPORTED QUESTIONS

● Look at these pairs of sentences. Notice the way the second speaker reports the first speaker's question.

ROB → MIKE "**Do you want** to go into business with me?"

MIKE → DAISY "Rob asked me **if I wanted** to go into business with him."

ROB → MIKE "**Can you** come up with the other half?"

MIKE → DAISY "He wanted to know **whether I could** come up with the other half."

MIKE → ROB "How long **will it** take for the business to make a profit?"

MIKE → DAISY "I asked how long **it would** take for the business to make a profit."

● We make reported questions with:

(He) asked (me) (He) wanted to know	question word *if/whether*	+ subject + verb

● In reported questions the word order is the same as in positive sentences: *I asked where he was.* not ~~I asked where was he.~~

● We use *if* or *whether* when we report questions without a question word.

● We don't use the auxiliaries *do, does* and *did* in reported questions: *"What do you think?"* → *He asked me what I thought.* not ~~He asked me what I did think.~~

TIPS! ● The changes in verb forms are the same as in reported sentences.
● We sometimes use an object with *ask: He asked …* or *He asked me … .*

REPORTED IMPERATIVES AND REQUESTS

● To report **imperatives**, we use:
told + object + (*not*) + infinitive with *to*.

ROB → MIKE "**Don't talk** to anyone else about it."

MIKE → DAISY "Rob **told me not to talk** to anyone else about it."

● To report **requests**, we use:
asked + object + (*not*) + infinitive with *to*.

ROB → MIKE "**Can you meet me** in Brighton on Saturday?"

MIKE → DAISY "He **asked me to meet him** in Brighton on Saturday."

Real World

RW11.1 Discussion language (3)   11D ❹ p92

putting forward new ideas

One thing we could do is (use …)
I wonder if it'd be a good idea (to have …)
I know! Why don't we (give …)?
I've got an idea. How about (giving …)?

reacting positively to ideas

That sounds like a good idea.
Well, it's worth a try.
Yes, that makes sense.
Yes, that could work.

reacting negatively to ideas

Personally, I'd rather we didn't (use a celebrity).
OK, maybe we should avoid (using celebrities).
The main problem with (TV ads) is that …
I'm not sure that's such a good idea.

summarising and recapping

So what you're saying is that …
Am I right in thinking that … ?
Are you saying that … ?
Can we just go over this again?

Vocabulary

V12.1 Colloquial words/phrases (12A ① p94)

What's up? What's the matter/problem?: *You look worried. What's up?*

stressed out worried and anxious: *I'm very stressed out about work.*

bug sb annoy or worry somebody: *Getting junk mail really bugs me.*

crazy stupid or silly: *You must be crazy to leave your job.*

chuck sth out or **chuck out sth** throw something away: *I've chucked out all my old records.*

hang on a sec (= second) wait for a short time: *Hang on a sec, I can't find my keys.*

pop into somewhere go to a particular place for a short time: *She's just popped into the library.*

mess sth up or **mess up sth** do something wrong or badly: *I really messed up that exam.*

chill out relax: *Adela's chilling out in the garden.*

telly television: *I've just got a new telly.*

a quid (plural: **quid**) a British pound: *My jacket only cost twenty quid.*

the loo the toilet: *Excuse me, where's the loo?*

trendy fashionable: *He lives in a trendy area of Bristol.*

a mate a friend: *Mark's my best mate.*

pretty quite, but not extremely: *I thought the film was pretty good.*

fancy sb find somebody attractive: *I really fancy her – she's gorgeous.*

a guy a man: *Who was that guy you were talking to?*

a hassle something that is annoying because it causes problems or is difficult to do: *Changing banks is a hassle.*

TIP! • We can also say *pop out* (= go out) and *pop over/round* (= go and visit somebody): *I'm just popping out. Tom's just popped over to say hello.*

V12.2 News collocations (12B ① p96)

troops (plural noun) soldiers in large organised groups: *The government sent in troops to control the situation.*

spread (**spread, spread**) increase to cover a larger area or affect a larger number of people: *The virus spread rapidly through the population.*

flee (**fled, fled**) escape by running away because you think you are in danger: *During the war, many people were forced to flee the country.*

sue sb (**for sth**) take legal action against a person or organisation, especially for money, because you have been harmed in some way: *She sued the newspaper for £1 million.*

damages /'dæmɪdʒɪz/ (plural noun) money that is paid to a person or organisation by somebody who has caused them some harm or loss: *The company paid £500,000 damages to victims of the accident.*

a crisis /'kraɪsɪs/ (plural: **crises** /'kraɪsiːz/) a moment or period of great difficulty, uncertainty or danger: *The Prime Minister's resignation caused a political crisis.*

an outcry a strong expression of anger, made by a group of people or the public in general: *The early release of the prisoners caused a public outcry.*

attack use violence against somebody: *He was attacked on his way home from work.*

release allow somebody or something to move about freely: *He was released from prison last week.*

a hostage /'hɒstɪdʒ/ somebody who is taken prisoner by a person or group in order to force other people to do what the person or group want: *The hostages were released safely when the police took control of the building.*

invade enter a country or area with an army in order to take control of it: *England was invaded in the 11ᵗʰ century.*

TIPS! • We say *take somebody hostage*: *Three journalists were taken hostage over a week ago.*

• The noun for *invade* is *an invasion* /ɪn'veɪʒən/.

V12.3 Idioms (12C ③ p98)

• An idiom is an expression (usually informal) which has a meaning that is different from the meanings of the individual words. The words are in a fixed order.

be a far cry from sth be completely different from something

keep an eye out for sb/sth watch for somebody or something to appear

take sth with a pinch of salt not believe something to be accurate or true

pull sb's leg tell somebody something that isn't true as a joke

be a piece of cake be very easy to do

recharge sb's batteries do something to get new energy and enthusiasm

in the middle of nowhere a long way from any towns, villages or other houses

out of the blue completely unexpectedly

give sb food for thought make you think seriously about a topic

break the ice make people more relaxed in a new situation

make sb's day make somebody extremely happy

sleep like a log sleep very well without waking

make somebody's day   sleep like a log

Language Summary 12

G12.1 Modal verbs (2): deduction in the present and the past 12A 4 p95

- We often use the modal verbs *must*, *could*, *might*, *may* and *can't* to make deductions in the present and the past.
- When we believe something is true, we use **must**.
- When we think something is possibly true, we use **could**, **might** or **may**.
- When we believe something isn't true, we use **can't**.

TIPS! • When we know something is definitely true or is definitely not true, we don't use a modal verb: *Then we **popped into** that trendy new café for a coffee. OK, so you **didn't leave** it in the café.*

• We don't use *can* or *mustn't* to make deductions: *It must be true.* not *It can be true. He can't have gone home yet.* not *He mustn't have gone home yet.*

DEDUCTIONS IN THE PRESENT

- To make deductions about a state in the present we use:
  modal verb + infinitive.
  It **might be** in the bathroom.
  Yeah, of course, but it **must be** switched off.
- To make deductions about something happening now we use:
  modal verb + *be* + verb+*ing*.
  But someone **might be using** it to phone Australia!

DEDUCTIONS IN THE PAST

- To make deductions about a state or a completed action in the past we use:
  modal verb + *have* + past participle.
  Or someone **could have taken** it from your bag.
  So you **may have left** it on the table.
  You **can't have left** it at the restaurant.
  That guy in the club **must have stolen** it.
- To make deductions about a longer action in the past we use:
  modal verb + *have* + *been* + verb+*ing*.
  He **might have been waiting** for a chance to steal my phone.

TIP! • We can also use *couldn't* instead of *can't* to make deductions in the past: *You couldn't have left it at the restaurant.*

They must have been waiting for ages!

G12.2 Past forms of modal and related verbs 12B 4 p97

WOULD HAVE, COULD HAVE, SHOULD HAVE

- We use **would have** + **past participle** to imagine something in the past that didn't happen: *It's hard to say whether you or I would have reacted differently.*
- We use **should have** + **past participle** to criticise people's behaviour in the past: *The citizens of America should have realised they were listening to a play.*
- We use **could have** + **past participle** to say something was possible in the past, but didn't happen: *They could have listened to other radio stations to see if the story was real.*

TIPS! • We often use *would/could have* + past participle as part of a third conditional (see G3.2): *If you'd told me about the meal, I would/could have gone.*

• We also use *should have* + past participle with *I* to talk about regrets (see G8.2): *I should have listened to your advice.*

NEEDN'T HAVE, DIDN'T NEED TO

- We use **needn't have** + **past participle** to talk about things people did in the past that weren't necessary: *Of course, they needn't have worried.* (= the people worried, but this wasn't necessary).
- We usually use **didn't need** + **infinitive with to** to talk about things people didn't do in the past because they weren't necessary: *Fortunately the troops didn't need to fight an army of Martian invaders!* (= the troops didn't fight because it wasn't necessary).

TIP! • It is also possible to use *didn't need* + infinitive with *to* to talk about things people did in the past, but weren't necessary. Usually the context makes it clear whether the person did the action or not.
Compare these sentences:
He didn't need to wait for her, so he went straight home. (He didn't wait for her.)
He didn't need to wait for her, but he had nothing better to do. (He waited for her.)

COULD, WAS/WERE ABLE TO

- We usually use **could** to talk about a general ability in the past: *Orson Welles could broadcast any play he wanted.*
- We usually use **was/were able to** to talk about ability at one specific time in the past: *Welles was able to avoid a lengthy court case.*

TIPS! • We usually use *could* with verbs of the senses (*see*, *hear*, etc.): *They could see a cloud of poisonous gas approaching New York.*

• *Was/Were able to* is similar in meaning to *managed to*: *Welles was able to/managed to avoid a lengthy court case.*

• In the negative form, *couldn't* and *wasn't able to* can both be used in all situations, although *couldn't* is more common: *I couldn't find my wallet.* = *I wasn't able to find my wallet.*

Recording Scripts

R1.1

ANSWERS 2 went 3 'd never been 4 was travelling 5 picked up 6 was told 7 was 8 decided 9 recommended 10 've been going 11 always enjoy 12 is taught 13 think 14 've learned 15 'm studying

R1.2

TIM Hi, er, my name's Tim.

MIA Hi, I'm Mia. Nice to meet you.

T You too. You went to Professor Lee's geography lecture yesterday, didn't you?

M Yeah, but I didn't understand very much.

T Neither did I. But don't worry about it, it's only the first one.

M Yeah, I suppose so.

T Anyway, er, how's your first week going?

M Oh, it's just been crazy. I haven't stopped since I got here.

T No, me neither. And it's a huge campus – I keep getting lost!

M Yes, so do I. Yesterday I was walking around for ages looking for the bookshop.

T Did you find it?

M Yes, eventually, but it took me about half an hour.

T Well, at least you found it in the end. Maybe you should get a map.

M I did have a map! I just couldn't work out where I was to start with!

T So, um, what are you studying?

M I'm doing a degree in Environmental Science.

T Are you? My brother's done that course. He graduated last July.

M Did he? Has he found a job yet?

T Yes, he has, actually. He's just started working for an environmental charity in London. He doesn't get paid very much, but it's a start.

M Well, that's encouraging. And what are you studying?

T Geography and economics. Most people think economics is really boring, but I don't. I do find it quite difficult, though!

M Yeah, I'm not surprised. I'd be completely confused.

T Yeah. Anyway, do you live here on campus?

M No, I don't. I was told it was really expensive, so I'm living in a shared house about two miles from here. It seemed the cheapest option and, um, I don't want to borrow too much money.

T No, neither do I. I've, um, I've already got a student loan and I've spent quite a bit of it already.

M Yeah, I know what you mean.

T Right, I have to go. I've got a lecture at two.

M So have I. Maybe see you again soon.

T Yeah, I hope so. And try not to get lost again!

M I'll do my best. Bye!

R1.3

ANSWERS 1b) 2a) 3b) 4b) 5a) 6b)

R1.4

1 He hasn't decided which college he's going to yet.
2 When I've finished my degree, I'd like to do a PhD.
3 She's waiting to hear if she's passed her exams.
4 I'd been to a private school, but I didn't like it.
5 She doesn't think she'll go to the tutorial today.
6 I've started a Master's and I'm really enjoying it.

R1.5

ANSWERS 2 have 3 did 4 was 5 didn't 6 did 7 's 8 hasn't 9 has 10 do 11 are 12 do 13 'm 14 Are 15 do 16 did 17 did 18 didn't

R1.6

A

HENRY My worst exam moment happened when I was caught cheating by my mum after a history exam. I really liked history classes, but I didn't have a very good memory. So on the morning of the exam I wrote loads of important facts and figures on the insides of my shirt cuffs. I made sure that I got to the exam room really early so I could sit at the back. I managed to answer quite a few questions using the stuff I'd written on my shirt. I was terrified that I was going to get caught, but luckily the teacher never noticed what I was doing. Stupidly, though, when I got home I, er, I was so happy the exam had finished that I just got changed out of my school clothes and left them on my bed. Anyway, while I was playing football with my friends in the park, my mum came to get my dirty clothes so that she could do some washing. She found the shirt and immediately realised what I'd done – she was absolutely furious, of course, and stopped my pocket money for three months. It taught me a lesson though, and, um, and I've never cheated at anything since.

B

YVONNE My worst exam nightmare was definitely my French O Level oral exam. When I was at school – this was, um, over twenty years ago now – kids weren't taught how to actually speak French, we just did loads of grammar exercises and translated texts and stuff. So I knew quite a lot of grammar and my written French wasn't too bad, but I didn't have a clue how to have even the most basic conversation. I think I did quite well on the written papers, but when it came to the oral exam, I, um, I couldn't understand a word the examiner was saying to me. He seemed to be speaking incredibly fast, and I just got so nervous I couldn't think. The only thing I knew how to say was 'Je ne comprends pas' – which means 'I don't understand', of course. So every time the examiner asked me a question, I just said, "Je ne comprends pas". That was all I said in the whole exam! The examiner probably thought I was an idiot, but at the end of the exam he did tell me that I had very good pronunciation. I still failed though, obviously!

R1.7

KIM Sue, over here!

SUE Hi, Kim, great to see you! It's been ages, hasn't it?

K Yeah, a couple of months at least. How are things?

S Oh, pretty good, thanks. What about you?

K Yeah, I'm fine. I'm still working at that new place I told you about.

S Yes, I remember. How's it going?

K Oh, er, well, things are really busy at the moment, lots of meetings and deadlines and stuff. And at the moment this is my only free evening during the week.

S Why's that?

K I'm, er, I've started doing loads of evening classes.

S Really? Like what, exactly?

K Well, last night I did creative writing. It sounds fun, but actually it's quite challenging.

S How do you mean?

K Well, we have to write something in class every week, like, er, yesterday I had to imagine I was an animal and write a story about a typical day – things like that.

S Yeah, I see what you mean. What's the teacher like?

K Oh, he's great, very enthusiastic and supportive. He's, um, he's written two novels, so I guess he knows what he's talking about.

S I'm sure he does. What else are you doing?

K Well, on Mondays I do a photography course. I got a digital camera for my birthday and there are lots of things I don't know how to do.

S Such as?

K Er, things like taking close-ups, getting the photos to print out properly, that sort of thing. Oh, and I'm doing a computer course as well. It's really difficult, actually.

S Is it? How come?

K Well, we're doing website design, and everyone else seems to know a lot more than I do. I'm in the, um, the intermediate class, but I might change to beginners.

S Wow, you are busy, aren't you?

K Yes, I am, but being out almost every night is actually helping me relax more.

S In what way?

143

Recording Scripts

K Well, you know, I used to work late most evenings, but now I have to be at my classes by 6.30. And if I force myself to do something different in the evenings, it helps me sleep better.

S Right. Maybe I should start doing some.

K Well, you could always come to my dance class tomorrow night.

S What sort of dancing?

K Salsa. I go every week.

S Really? Who with?

K A few people from work. We're all, um, we're all beginners, but it's great fun. You should come, you'd love it.

S Well, I'll see if I'm free and let you know.

K Great! Anyway, enough about me, what are you up to at the moment?

S Well, um, I'm off to the USA on Sunday.

K Are you? How long for?

S Two weeks.

K Is this work or holiday?

S Holiday. First I'm going to my cousin's wedding in Seattle …

R1.8 R1.9

1 A Gary called me this morning.
  B What about?
2 A We're going on holiday tomorrow.
  B Where to?
3 A I'm going to the cinema tonight.
  B Who with?
4 A We've borrowed £10,000 from the bank.
  B What for?
5 A I've just got an email.
  B Who from?
6 A I've just sent an email.
  B Who to?
7 A Pete's staying with me at the moment.
  B How long for?
8 A I've just been told to go home.
  B Who by?

R1.10

SUE First, I'm going to my cousin's wedding in Seattle.

KIM Are you? Who with?

S My brother, Frank. I'm rather nervous about the whole thing, though.

K Really? How come?

S Frank and I don't really get on particularly well.

K How do you mean?

S Er, we tend to argue quite a lot.

K Yes, families can be difficult, can't they? And what else are you doing?

S After the wedding I'm going on a trip that my friend Brad's organised.

K Are you? What sort of trip?

S We're going walking in the Rockies.

K How long for?

S Five days. Oh, I can't wait!

R2.1

CASSY I resent the government telling me what I should and shouldn't eat.

And, um, anyway, they keep changing their minds about what's good and bad for you. You don't know what to believe. For example, I'm … we're always hearing stuff about fat being bad for us. Er, it causes heart attacks and all that, but I heard on the radio only this morning that the French eat a high fat diet and they have fewer heart attacks than we do in America, so where, er, where does that leave us? As for me, well I don't care about how much fat I eat. Every day when I get home from work, I'll have a coffee and half a packet of chocolate cookies. That's a lot of fat. But, um, I know what I like and I eat what I like. I've always been like that. Tonight I'll probably have a burger and fries for dinner – even more fat! And you know what? My mom's always telling me what I should and shouldn't eat, and the joke is, I never get ill and she's ill all the time.

TED Most of the time I watch what I eat, but, er, sometimes I'll eat things that I know are unhealthy like ice cream or pizza. But when I was a teenager I'd get up in the morning and go straight to the cookie jar. I used to be addicted to chocolate chip cookies – my mom used to hide them from me. And then I read a lot of books about health and nutrition, and I knew I had to change. One of the big killers is fat, so I'm always reading food labels to see what the fat content is. It drives my girlfriend crazy. And did you know that, er, Japanese people have far fewer heart attacks than Americans? That's because they have a very low fat diet, you know, stuff like sushi, rice, that sort of thing. They don't, er, they don't add fat to anything, well, that's what I heard anyway.

R2.2

I'm used to getting up at 5 a.m. every day. | I'm slowly getting used to it. | It takes a while for a foreigner to get used to them. | I wasn't used to people driving so close to me. | I still haven't got used to being a pedestrian here. | I'll never get used to doing that.

R2.3

prefer preference preferable preferably | originate originality origin original originally | realism reality realistic realistically | responsibility responsible responsibly | recognise recognition recognisable recognisably

R2.4

NANCY I've been running a sandwich delivery service in the centre /r/ of the city for /r/ over /r/ a year. When I first started I wasted loads of time because I wasn't at all organised.

After /r/ I'd started making the sandwiches I'd realise that I hadn't got everything I needed for /r/ all the different fillings. That meant I'd have to spend another /r/ hour /r/ in the supermarket or /r/ even a couple of hours sometimes! So then I was late with all the deliveries. But four /r/ or five months ago I did a time management course. It was rather /r/ expensive, but I got a lot from it. They taught me simple things like, um, how to write good lists. Now I have a file on my computer for /r/ all the food I buy, so, er, when I go shopping I just print the list off. They also suggested timing how long it takes to get from one place to another and that means I can be more realistic about how long I need to deliver /r/ all the sandwiches. And my regular customers all order /r/ in advance now, so that means I can, um, get all the food at the same time and nothing's wasted. Yeah, um, things are /r/ a lot more /r/ organised now. And I've also stopped trying to make the perfect sandwich. People don't notice the difference between excellent and perfect. Yes, the business is improving, and I'm sure /r/ it's all due to that course I did.

JAKE As part of the introductory week at university we had to do a time management course. I was dreading it, but actually some of it was, um, yeah, really helpful. I learned how to prioritise things, you know, really think about what was important or urgent, er, deadlines for coursework and stuff like that, which helps me to keep things in perspective. And doing two things at once was another good suggestion. So if I'm travelling I'll, um, I'll listen to my taped notes, or while I'm in the shower I'll try to remember things from my last lecture. But some of their suggestions were, um, totally unrealistic – like how long you have to study for each subject. So if a subject is difficult, they recommended you study four hours for every hour in class. That means I should be studying maths for 20 hours a week outside of class! No way am I going to do that! But, er, one thing that really surprised me was they told us, er, not to be perfectionists. You can't be perfect, so you only disappoint yourself. I think that's right. As the course leader said, there will always be people weaker and stronger than you – just learn to live with it. Yeah, it was a good course, I, er, I think I learnt a lot.

R2.6

JAMES Jenny, you haven't touched your sandwich. Look, Liam has nearly finished his. (Don't want it.) OK, go and play with Harriet then. Oh dear, she's hardly eaten anything.

HAZEL Don't worry about it. It's best just to let kids eat when they want.

LILY I don't know about that. I think it's important for kids to get used to good eating habits as early as possible. That's what I did with my kids, and when I look after Liam that's what I do with him. Right from the word go, you should make them stay at the table until they finish their food.

H I can't really see the point of forcing kids to eat. I think that just makes kids hate meal times and food becomes a bigger problem.

L Oh, do you think so? I think if kids aren't allowed to play until they've eaten their food they soon learn to empty their plates. You have to be strict right from the beginning or they just get into bad habits.

J I see what you mean.

H Oh, I wouldn't say that. I've never been strict with Harriet and she eats anything. All you have to do is make it fun, like, for example letting them help when you're getting food ready.

J I see your point. I must admit we always send Jenny out of the kitchen when we're cooking.

L Quite right too. It's dangerous in a kitchen for a five-year-old.

J I suppose that's true, actually.

H But life's dangerous for a five-year-old. They're always falling down and stuff. And I don't mean ... I'm not suggesting you leave the kid alone in the kitchen to make the meal. You're there supervising everything.

J I should imagine it slows everything down if they're helping you.

H OK yes, but on the other hand they're learning valuable life lessons.

J Mmm. You might be right there. That's a good point.

L Well, I'm still not convinced. What can a five-year-old do to help in the kitchen?

H Little things like letting them get things for you out of the fridge or the cupboards. Or let them wash the vegetables for you. Just simple things.

J You mean, sort of make it a game.

L But Harriet's a girl.

H Well, I can't argue with that.

L No, I mean I don't think little boys are interested in that kind of thing, do you?

J Oh, I don't think that's necessarily the case at all.

H Yes, and you'll never find out if he's interested unless you give it a go. Anyway it's important that boys learn how to cook, don't you think?

L I suppose you've got a point there. Right, Liam, time to go. You're doing the cooking this evening.

R2.7

LILY I think children_under /r/ eight should go to bed_at seven.

HAZEL Do you think so? Why not let them go to bed when they're tired?

JAMES I don't know_about that. Kids never_/r/_admit they're tired.

H That's_a good point.

L Yes, I think seven_o'clock is_a good bedtime for /r/ all young kids.

J You might be right there.

H Well, I can't really see the point_of forcing kids to go to bed.

J But_if you don't, parents never have_any time_on their /r/_own.

L I see what you mean.

H Well, I'm still not convinced. If my kids were /r/_all_in bed_at seven, I'd never see them.

L But_if they're /r/_up late, they get bad-tempered.

J Yes, you can't_argue with that.

R2.8

ANSWERS 2d) 3b) 4a) 5f) 6h) 7e) 8g) 9k) 10i) 11j) 12n) 13o) 14m) 15l) 16q) 17s) 18p) 19r) 20v) 21t) 22u)

R3.1

ARNIE Three more coffees, please, Sam.

SAM Coming right up.

JOANNE Did you hear what happened at the parking lot near here yesterday?

CHUCK No, what?

J Apparently a woman had been shopping and when she went back to the parking lot she saw four men in her car. So she took a gun out of her purse and threatened to shoot them.

A Whoa! What did they do?

J Well, they got out of the car and just ran away. But then – get this – when the woman got into the car she realised it wasn't hers. Her car looked identical, but it was parked nearby.

C So what happened next?

J Well, of course she was horrified at what she'd done so she went to the police department to explain.

C Well, that's something, I guess.

J Yes, and when she arrived, the four men were there, complaining about this crazy woman who'd threatened to shoot them.

A So, she hasn't been charged with anything?

J No. No one was hurt, and she had a licence for the gun. But if the woman had shot the men, she'd have been in serious trouble.

A That's ridiculous. If the men hadn't run away, she could have killed them.

C Yes, but no one was hurt.

J That's really not the point. The point is there are just too many people carrying guns these days.

S Here you go.

A Thanks, Sam.

S You're welcome.

A That reminds me – a guy in our street was arrested recently for shooting the tyres of a car which was parked outside his house, just, er, well, just because the alarm kept going off at night. He was charged with vandalism – lost his gun licence and had to pay a fine.

C I have to say, I wouldn't have been too happy if the alarm had woken me up. Those car alarms drive you crazy going off night after night.

J Sure, but you wouldn't have shot the tyres!

C Course not, no. If it had been me, I might have left a note on the car, or something.

J What would the owner of the car have done if he'd seen him? I mean, the guy with the gun was seriously angry.

A Yeah, well, we'll never know. So what sentence would you have given him?

J Well, a lot more than just a fine and losing his gun licence, that's for sure. He's a danger to society. I mean, I think we've got to do something about all this, all this violence. There were, er, about 450,000 violent crimes involving guns in this country last year. We've ... I mean, we've got to do something ...

R3.3

1 If I hadn't gone to the party, I wouldn't have met her.

2 I'd have come round earlier if you'd asked me to.

3 If Sue had been more careful, she might not have got hurt.

4 He wouldn't have known about it if you hadn't told him.

5 If Dave had known when your flight was, he could have picked you up.

R3.4

I wouldn't have /əv/ met her → If I hadn't gone to the party, I wouldn't have /əv/ met her. | if you'd asked me to → I'd have /əv/ come round earlier if you'd asked me to. | she might not have /əv/ got hurt → If Sue had been more careful, she might not have /əv/ got hurt. | if you hadn't told him → He wouldn't have /əv/ known about it if you hadn't told him. | he could have /əv/ picked you up → If Dave had known when your flight was, he could have /əv/ picked you up.

R3.5

LAWYER Good afternoon, Ms Mead. Come in and /ən/ take a /ə/ seat. Firstly I'd like to /tə/ say how sorry I am that /ðət/ this has /həz/ happened.

BONNIE Well, thank you /jə/ for /fə/ seeing me so quickly. I've been trying to /tə/ get some /səm/ legal advice for /fə/ ages, but I was /wəz/ getting nowhere.

L Glad I can /kən/ be of /əv/ help.

B No one seems to understand what's happening, except my sister.

My friends can't understand why I'm so anxious and /ən/ why I can't just get on with my life.

L Well, if people haven't experienced identity theft, they can't imagine what it's like, or how much time it takes to /tə/ deal with everything.

B Yes, I know. I've had to /tə/ take unpaid leave from /frəm/ work. It, um, it takes hours to /tə/ make phone calls, write letters and, and /ən/ see people. No one realises that bit.

L No, they don't. So you, um, you're not working at /ət/ the /ðə/ moment?

B No, but I'm due back in a /ə/ couple of /əv/ weeks.

L Right. So tell me, how did it all start?

B Well, I didn't, um, I didn't know anything was /wəz/ wrong until I got a /ə/ letter from /frəm/ a /ə/ credit card company about four months ago, asking if I'd tried to open a /ə/ new account. I hadn't, of /əv/ course. So I, um, I decided to /tə/ check into things further and /ən/ found that /ðət/ there were /wə/ six new credit cards and /ən/ two new bank accounts in my name. This other person had /həd/ run up huge bills on the /ðə/ credit cards and /ən/ both bank accounts were /wə/ overdrawn.

L So what did you /jə/ do?

B I went to /tə/ the /ðə/ police. They took all the /ðə/ details, but basically they said that /ðət/ they couldn't do anything until I, um, till I showed them some /səm/ evidence that /ðət/ I hadn't spent all the money.

L Yes, well, that's where I can /kən/ help. So, er, who have /həv/ you been in touch with so far?

B Obviously the /ðə/ credit card companies, but it hasn't stopped this other person using the credit cards. I also, er, I told my bank to /tə/ close the accounts that /ðət/ weren't mine, but as /əz/ soon as /əz/ one account was /wəz/ closed, she opened another.

L Yes, once this woman was /wəz/ in the /ðə/ system as /əz/ you, she could do just about anything.

B So it seems. Anyway, I also called my mobile phone company to /tə/ tell them to /tə/ close a /ə/ new account that /ðət/ had /əd/ been opened in my name, and /ən/ they said that /ðət/ they had to /tə/ check with the other Bonnie Mead.

L And what happened?

B They believed her and /ən/ closed the /ðə/ case!

L So no one believed you?

B No. I even asked the /ðə/ credit card companies to /tə/ send me copies of /əv/ documents that /ðət/ I hadn't actually signed. And /ən/ they did send them, but they sent them to /tə/ her! It was /wəz/ unreal, I couldn't believe it was /wəz/ happening.

L Right ... , um, let's see what we can /kən/ do to /tə/ get your /jə/ life back. First I'll need, er, I'd like a /ə/ copy of /əv/ all your /jə/ bills, then if you could ...

R3.6

	strong	weak		strong	weak
can	/kæn/	/kən/	of	/ɒv/	/əv/
was	/wɒz/	/wəz/	to	/tuː/	/tə/
were	/wɜː/	/wə/	from	/frɒm/	/frəm/
has	/hæz/	/həz/ /əz/	as	/æz/	/əz/
have	/hæv/	/həv/ /əv/	and	/ænd/	/ən/
are	/aː/	/ə/	that	/ðæt/	/ðət/
do	/duː/	/də/	some	/sʌm/	/səm/
you	/juː/	/jə/	a	/eɪ/	/ə/
at	/æt/	/ət/	the	/ðiː/	/ðə/
for	/fɔː/	/fə/	your	/jɔː/	/jə/

R3.7

BONNIE Hello?

HELEN Hi, Bonnie. I got your message. I called back, but you were out. You sounded in a terrible state. Would you like me to come round?

B No, it's OK, but thanks for offering. I feel much better now I've spoken to a lawyer.

H Oh, yes. How did it go?

B Well. I was there for about an hour and he was very helpful. However, there was another threatening letter waiting for me when I got home.

H Oh no! Who from this time?

B It's another one from, er, Hillard's department store, would you believe, saying I still owe them £1,000 for that sofa I never ordered. I mean, I wouldn't mind, but I spent two hours on the phone to them about it last week.

H Let me give them a ring for you.

B No, thanks. I'd better phone them myself. If you called them, it might get even more confusing.

H Yes, it probably would. Anyway, what did the lawyer say?

B Well, he wasn't impressed with my filing system, with everything in one file. The first thing he wants me to do is to, er, to put it all in different files, one for each company, and order all the bills by date. I'm not looking forward to doing that.

H Would it help if I sorted it out for you?

B It's a really boring job. Are you sure you wouldn't mind?

H Of course not. I'm good at things like that.

B Thanks. That'd be a great help. Don't think I can face going through all those letters again. Anyway, enough about me. How are things with you? You're, um, you're off to see Meg in Paris soon, you lucky thing.

H No, I can't go now. Nigel can't look after the kids because he's got to go to Rome for work.

B Well, why don't I look after the kids?

H Are you serious?

B Of course I am.

H Well, it'd be wonderful if you could.

B Right, that's settled then.

H Thanks. Do you want to come and stay here? I'll make a bed up for you, if you like.

B No, don't worry. It'd be easier if I brought the kids back here.

H I could get our babysitter to come and help you in the evenings – you know, put them to bed and stuff.

B No, that's OK. I can manage. So when are you off?

H The Eurostar leaves, er, let me see ... at 6 o'clock on Thursday evening.

B What if I picked the kids up from school and brought them straight here?

H As long as you don't mind.

B No, not at all.

H That'd be great. Thanks.

B So how long do you want me to look after them?

H Oh, I thought I could leave them with you until they're all eighteen!

B Oh yes, right!

R3.8

Would you like me to come round? | No, it's OK, but thanks for offering. | Let me give them a ring for you. | No thanks, I'd better phone them myself. | Would it help if I sorted it out for you? | Are you sure you wouldn't mind? | Why don't I look after the kids? | Well, it'd be wonderful if you could. | I'll make a bed up for you, if you like. | No, don't worry. It'd be easier if I brought the kids back here. | What if I picked the kids up from school? | As long as you don't mind.

R3.9

1

NIGEL Would you /jə/ like me to /tə/ help you /jə/ move tomorrow?

BONNIE Are /ə/ you /jə/ sure you /jə/ wouldn't mind?

N No, of /əv/ course not.

B Thanks. That'd be a /ə/ great help.

N Why don't I come over this evening and /ən/ help you /jə/ pack?

B It'd be wonderful if you /jə/ could.

2

N Let me help you /jə/ pack those files.

B No, don't worry. I'd better do those myself.

N Well, what if I carried these heavy things downstairs for /fə/ you?

B As /əz/ long as /əz/ you /jə/ don't mind.

N Not at /ət/ all. Then I'll pack up the /ðə/ computer and /ən/ printer, if you /jə/ like.

B No, that's OK. It'd be easier if I sorted those out.

R4.1

THE DEAD KANGAROO STORY

In 1987 the world's best sailors were competing in the America's Cup yacht race off the coast of Fremantle, in Western Australia.

One day, one of the sailors went for a drive in the outback and accidentally ran over a kangaroo. The sailor got out and leaned the dead kangaroo against the side of the car. Then he decided to put his America's Cup team jacket on the animal and take a few pictures to show his friends. However, it turned out that the accident hadn't killed the animal, it had only knocked it out. While the sailor was taking some photos, the kangaroo came round. Realising that something was wrong, the animal immediately ran away – taking the sailor's jacket, his passport, three credit cards and $1,000 in cash with it.

THE FALLING COW STORY

In 1997 the crew of a Japanese fishing boat were rescued after their boat had sunk in very unusual circumstances. According to the fishermen, the boat had been sailing in calm waters when a cow fell from the sky and crashed through the boat. Unfortunately the police thought the crew had made the whole story up and arrested them. They remained in prison while the police tried to work out why the boat had sunk. Eventually, the pilot of a Russian transport plane told the police what had happened. Before they took off from their Siberian airbase, the plane's crew had stolen some cows from a nearby field. While they were flying at 25,000 feet, one cow broke free and started running around inside the plane. The crew managed to push it out of the door and into the sea – or so they thought.

THE EXPLODING HOUSE STORY

A woman from California had been trying to get rid of all the bugs in her home for years, but without success. Then, in December 2001, she bought nineteen 'bug bombs', which are designed to spread insecticide over a wide area. She put all the bug bombs in her house, but unfortunately she hadn't read the instructions, which warned that no more than one bomb should be used at any one time, and they should never be used indoors. All nineteen bug bombs went off at the same time, completely destroying the building and causing over $150,000 worth of damage. A number of bugs were also hurt.

R4.2

The boat had /əd/ been /bɪn/ sailing in calm waters. | The police thought the crew had /əd/ made the whole story up. | The pilot told the police what had /əd/ happened. | The plane's crew had /əd/ stolen some cows. | A woman had /əd/ been /bɪn/ trying to get rid of all the bugs for years. | She hadn't read the instructions.

R4.4

KEVEN Dave, have you ever played an April Fool's Day joke on anyone?

DAVE Um, no, not really – but my brother Alan told me a great story about a practical joke from his university days.

K He went to, er, Bristol, didn't he?

D Actually, it was Birmingham.

K That's right. I knew it began with B. When was he there?

D This was back in the mid-eighties.

K Oh, right.

D Anyway, this story happened during Rag Week – you know, when students do all sorts of silly things to raise money for charity, like, er, race each other down the main street on beds, or walk around the streets in strange costumes collecting money or whatever.

K Yeah, I know what you mean. We have the same sort of thing in Ireland.

D Well, one day Alan and his two flatmates were woken up at 7 a.m. by the sound of workmen drilling the road outside their house.

K Oh no!

D Yeah, what a nightmare! Apparently they'd all been to a big party the previous night and had got to bed at about four thirty, so they didn't, um, they weren't too happy about being woken up first thing in the morning.

K Yes, I can imagine. So what did they do?

D Well, one of Alan's flatmates went out to a payphone across the road and called the police.

K Really? What did he say?

D According to Alan, his friend told the police that some university students were digging up the road outside their house, you know, as a Rag Week stunt.

K You're joking!

D No, really. He said that the students were dressed as workmen from the local council, and asked the police to come round and make them stop. Obviously he, um, he gave a false name and house number.

K Right.

D Meanwhile, Alan's other flatmate went out to tell the workmen that some students dressed as policemen were going round telling people what to do as part of a Rag Week stunt.

K So what happened?

D Well, about ten minutes later, two policemen turned up and told the workmen to stop drilling, obviously because they, um, they thought they were students. And of course the workmen just ignored them because they thought the policemen were students too!

K Ha ha, what a great idea!

D Yeah, I know. In the end they managed to work out what had happened and realised they were all victims of a practical joke. Apparently they thought it was quite funny.

K And, um, what about Alan and his friends?

D Er, they were all secretly watching the whole thing from their window. Alan said it was absolutely hilarious.

K I bet it was.

D Luckily, nobody ever found out who'd called the police, otherwise they'd have, um, they'd have been in big trouble.

K That's a brilliant story!

D Yes, it is, isn't it?

K Oh, by the way, have you heard from Sally recently? She lives in Birmingham now, doesn't she?

D Yes, she does, although, um, we haven't been in touch for a while. I think she's still working at the same place, but ...

R4.5

STEVE Hi, I'm home. Have you had a good day?

ELLEN No, not really. Actually, it's been a bit of a nightmare.

S Oh, dear. What's happened?

E Well, um, first I waited in all morning for the new TV to be delivered, but they never turned up.

S Oh, I don't believe it! Hadn't they promised to be here today?

E Yeah, but I'm not surprised, to be honest. They didn't turn up last week either. I was pretty angry, though.

S I bet you were.

E Anyway, I called them and they said that they'd definitely be here next Wednesday.

S Next Wednesday? You must be joking!

E That's, er, that's the earliest they could do, they said. I told them if they didn't turn up next time, I'd cancel the order.

S Quite right too. That TV cost a fortune!

E And then, er, well, my laptop crashed while I was on the Internet. I think it's got a virus.

S Didn't you install that anti-virus software?

E Um, well, not exactly, no.

S Well, no wonder you've got a virus. Oh I'll have a look at it later, if you like.

E Thanks. What else ... er, oh, Jack got sent home from school.

S Oh no, not again! What did he do this time?

E He was, um, he was caught fighting during the break.

S You're kidding! Oh that boy drives me crazy sometimes. I keep telling him to stay out of trouble. Why on earth doesn't he listen to me?

E He said that the other boy started it.

S Well, he would say that, wouldn't he?

E I don't know what to do with him, Steve, I really don't.

S Don't worry, we'll work it out. I'll, er, go and talk to him in a bit.

E Oh, there was one piece of good news. My brother Derek called. Guess what? He's finally found a job.

S Wow, that's fantastic news! What sort of job?

Recording Scripts

E It's, um, it's in a department store, selling furniture. Poor Derek, he's been unemployed for so long. I'm really pleased for him.

S Yes, I can imagine. Did you ask him round this weekend?

E No, I forgot. I'll call him again later.

S Anyway, I'm dying for a cup of tea. Want one?

E Mmm. Yes, please.

S And is there anything to eat? I'm starving.

E Dinner's in the oven. So, how was your day?

S Well, er, I had quite a good day, actually. Guess what? ...

R4.7

STEVE Guess what? I've been promoted!

ELLEN Wow, that's fantastic news!

S Yes, I'm over the moon about it.

E I can imagine. No wonder you look so happy. I'm really pleased for you.

S Thanks. And I get a forty per cent pay rise.

E You're kidding! Anyway, weren't they going to give the job to Stuart?

S Yes, they were. But I'm not surprised they didn't, to be honest. He was really angry when he found out, though.

E I bet he was.

S And we're going to Florida this weekend to celebrate.

E You must be joking! That'll cost a fortune!

R4.8

ANSWERS 2 plans 3 knew 4 the two 5 love 6 must 7 yesterday 8 supposed 9 tears 10 Losing 11 that 12 could 13 love 14 half 15 hear 16 confused 17 true 18 plan 19 loved

R5.1

They're /r/ as /əz/ beautiful as /əz/ butterflies. | The more /r/ I learned about them, the more /r/ interested I became. | Koi are getting more /r/ and more /r/ expensive. | That's almost as /əz/ much as /əz/ I paid for my house. | The normal price is nowhere near /r/ as /əz/ high as /əz/ that. | The bigger they are, the more they cost. | They're slightly bigger than /ðən/ the ones I've got.

R5.2

DIANE Hello?

EMMA Hi, Diane. It's me.

D Oh, hello, Emma. How are you doing?

E I'm fine, thanks.

D And how are Katy and Paul?

E Oh, they're fine. Katy's doing her GCSEs at the moment.

D How are they going?

E Very well, I think. She's been working really hard and I think she's going to pass them all.

D Oh, that's good.

E Anyway, the reason I'm calling is that we're heading down to your part of the world next week on holiday.

D Really, you're coming to Cornwall?

E Yeah, we're staying in a small hotel in Padstow for a week. Paul got a very cheap deal on the Internet.

D Great! Well, we'll have to meet up sometime.

E Yes, definitely.

D Have you got any plans?

E Well, we're going to take Katy to the Eden Project. She's thinking of doing environmental studies next year.

D Oh, right.

E So I thought she'd enjoy it. Paul's not too keen, though, it's not really his thing.

D Oh, I'm sure he'll have a great time. It's supposed to be really interesting.

E Actually, we were wondering if you'd like to come with us.

D Yes, I'd love to. Which day are you going?

E We're not sure yet. What do you think?

D Well, I've heard it's less busy towards the end of the week.

E How about Thursday, then? That's a week today. Or will you be working that day?

D No, don't worry, I'll take a day off. That shouldn't be a problem. Actually, there's a programme on TV about the Eden Project on Saturday evening.

E Really? When?

D Let me have a look. It's on BBC2 and it starts at ... seven thirty.

E Thanks, we'll try to watch it.

D So how will you be getting to the Eden Project?

E By car. Actually, we'll be driving through your village so we can pick you up on the way.

D Sure you don't mind?

E Course not. It'll be great to see you.

D You too. It's been a long time.

E Yes, it has, hasn't it? Just think, this time next week we'll be walking around the Eden Project together!

D Let's hope it doesn't rain!

E Yes, absolutely. Anyway, what else have you been doing lately?

R5.3

We'll be driving through your village. | We'll be walking around the Eden Project together. | How will you be getting to the Eden Project? | Will you be working that day? | I'll be seeing them tomorrow. | He won't be coming to the party.

R5.4

ANSWERS 2 are we going 3 We'll be having 4 I'll record 5 we'll watch 6 I'm going to buy 7 she'll let 8 I'll give 9 I'll be seeing 10 I'll ask 11 starts 12 We're going to miss 13 she'll be

R5.5

Although we still don't really know how our sense of smell works, our love of perfume goes back a very long way. The Ancient Egyptians used to put perfumed oils in their hair, and the oil found in Tutankhamun's tomb was still fragrant when it was opened, 2,000 years after he'd been buried there. And at feasts in Roman times, white birds with their wings soaked in perfume flew around the room so that the air was filled with a sweet scent. In fact, all through history, kings and queens have shown a passion for perfumes. In 1573, Queen Elizabeth I of England was given a pair of perfumed gloves. She wore them all the time, and loved them so much that she had a coat and a dress made which had the same scent.

In Paris there's a perfume museum called *Osmothèque*, which has an amazing 1,100 perfumes. Next to the museum is a school where perfumers are taught how to create new fragrances. It takes eight years to become a fully-qualified perfumer, and there are only about 400 in the world. To make a single perfume you need between 400 and 500 ingredients, which are often extremely expensive. One of the ingredients in Chanel N° 5 for example, costs $40,000 for half a kilo and smells like burnt candle wax. Incidentally, Chanel N° 5 got its name because it was the fifth perfume offered to Coco Chanel by her perfumer, Ernest Beaux.

And just in case you think perfumes are only for women, it's worth pointing out that men have always worn 'perfumes' in one form or another. The French Emperor Napoleon Bonaparte loved perfume, and apparently used one or two bottles a day! These days many men wear perfumes designed for both men and women, such as CK1, or even perfumes just for men like Michael Jordan Cologne, named after the famous American basketball player.

How do you decide whether a perfume is right for you? Well, the first rule is, never buy a perfume that you haven't tried on your skin. Different skin types react differently to each perfume – what smells wonderful on a friend may well smell terrible on you. And secondly, keep perfume in a dark place at a temperature of no higher than 15°C. Heat and light are the enemies of perfume.

R5.6

1 White birds with their wings soaked in perfume flew around the room.

2 All through history, kings and queens have shown a passion for perfumes.

3 Queen Elizabeth I of England was given a pair of perfumed gloves.

4 She wore them all the time.

5 She had a coat and a dress made which had the same scent.

6 Perfumers are taught how to create new fragrances.
7 And there are only about 400 in the world.
8 Many men wear perfumes designed for both men and women.
9 How do you decide whether a perfume is right for you?
10 Never buy a perfume that you haven't tried on your skin.

R5.7

RACHEL George, have you ever worked out your ecological footprint?

GEORGE No, but it sounds complicated.

R Oh, you can do it online in 5 minutes. I, er, I did it today.

G And?

R Well, it was a bit disturbing, actually. It told me that if everyone in the world had a lifestyle like me, we'd need 2.3 planets to survive!

G Wow!

R Yeah, makes you think, doesn't it? Our lifestyle simply isn't sustainable.

G Maybe, but I don't see how we can really change it. I mean, I recycle newspapers, turn off the TV at night, that kind of thing. Are you suggesting we all, um, go and live in caves or something?

R No, that's not what I'm trying to say. What I meant was that there are lots of other things we can do, not just recycling or saving energy.

G Like what?

R Er, well, take food shopping, for example. Do you ever wonder how far the food you buy has travelled to get to your local supermarket?

G Hmm, that's an interesting point. I've never really thought about that.

R Well, a lot of it's flown halfway around the world, which you know causes greenhouse gases, so it'd be much better if, er, if everyone bought food that's produced locally.

G But if we all stopped eating, say, bananas, then the economies of some Caribbean countries would collapse overnight. How moral or ethical would that be?

R Fair enough, but I still think that we should eat more locally produced food and avoid stuff that has too much packaging.

G Yes, but then again, the packaging keeps the food fresh. We're not going to ... nobody's going to buy food that's gone off, are they?

R No, of course not, but I just don't think it's right that the food industry produces so much rubbish.

G OK, then, how else could I reduce my ecological footprint?

R Um, let me think ... well, you could become a vegetarian.

G Really? Why do you say that?

R Well, one argument in favour of being vegetarian is that farming animals is so wasteful and uses so much energy. Did you know that, er, one hectare of land can produce enough soya beans to feed 600 people, but only enough beef to feed 20 people?

G Really? Wow!

R Yeah, and, um, and you need 100 times more water to produce a kilo of beef than a kilo of wheat. It's just ridiculous and completely unjustifiable ...

G I don't know about that. I think people should have the right to eat whatever they want. I mean, are you saying that human beings shouldn't be allowed to eat meat?

R No, that's not what I meant. All I'm saying is that meat production is very damaging to the environment.

G Well, some people would argue that it's the customers' fault, not the farmers'.

R That's exactly my point. It's up to us to change things. Anyway, we'd better order. What do you fancy?

G Er, well, it's hard to say ... I was going to have a burger, but now I think I'll just have a salad.

R Good choice!

R5.8

RACHEL I think people should leave their cars‿at home more /r/ often.

GEORGE Maybe, but I don't see how you can‿ask‿everyone to give‿up their cars.

R No, that's not what‿I'm trying to say. What‿I meant was people should use public transport‿if they can.

G Fair‿/r/‿enough, but I still think‿a lot‿of people prefer to drive.

R All‿I'm saying‿is that cars‿are /r/ a big‿environmental problem.

G Yes, but then‿again, public transport is‿often more /r/ expensive.

R I know, but‿it'd be better‿/r/ if we thought‿about how much transport costs the planet, not just‿ourselves.

G That's‿an‿interesting point. I've never really thought‿about that.

R6.1

The section of Kate Fox's book **explaining** the rules of queuing is fascinating and the English obey these rules without **thinking** about it. **Jumping** a queue will certainly annoy those people **queuing** properly. However, despite **feeling** intense anger towards the queue-jumper, the English will often say nothing – **staring** angrily is more their style.

Then there are the rules for **saying** please and thank you. The English thank bus drivers, taxi drivers, anyone **giving** them a service. In fact the English spend a lot of time **saying** please and thank you, and they hate not **being** thanked if they think they deserve it. Not **saying** thank you will often cause a person to sarcastically shout out, "You're welcome!".

R6.2

BRUCE I don't care how long it takes. I want it right!

MAN OK. Sorry. I'll have it for you by the end of the day.

LUCY Look. Bruce is having a go at someone again. By the way, are you going to his leaving party?

DON I might go for a bit.

L Yes, me too. You know, I'll miss him in some ways.

D Well, you don't have much contact with him, but I do. And I won't be sad to see him go. He's, um, he's extremely difficult to work with – he doesn't listen to anyone.

L Yeah, I was in a meeting with him once and nobody could get a word in. And he's so bad-tempered. If he's like that in the Leeds office, he's bound to upset people.

D Well, he's unlikely to change his personality overnight. But the Leeds office isn't doing well, and you know, he could improve things there.

L Yes, he probably will, although I can't imagine they'll like him.

D I don't suppose he'll worry about being popular. He's just ... he's not that kind of person, is he? I remember him saying, "I'm not here to make friends, I'm here to sort out the company's problems." And to be fair, he has.

L Sure, no question about that. Is he, um, taking his family with him, do you know?

D Well, he's likely to be there for at least a year so I'll be surprised if he doesn't. He's a real family man.

L But commuting's a possibility, I suppose. He may not want to give up his house here. Anyway, er, are you applying for his job?

D Maybe. Do you know who else is going for it?

L Well, Patrick certainly won't. He knows he doesn't stand a chance of getting it. And I doubt if Lynn will go for it, she's not that ambitious.

D But Frieda may well apply. And if she does, they might give it to her.

L But you're sure to get the job, you could do it with your eyes closed.

D Hmm, no. They don't think I'm very well organised. And they could be looking for someone from outside.

L I shouldn't think they'll employ an outsider, just for a year.

D Yes, but surely Bruce won't come back to the same job.

L You're right, he probably won't. I dare say they'll promote him if he's successful in Leeds. Uh oh, here he comes.

B Don, if you've finished, can I see you in my office?

D Right. No, I definitely won't miss him.

L Good luck.

D Thanks. See you later.

Recording Scripts

R6.4

MICHAEL Hello /w/ and welcome to the programme. With us today /j/ in the studio /w/ is Joe /w/ Allen, who's a professor /r/ of mathematics, and Sally /j/ Evans, who /w/ actually worked for the British Secret Service for /r/ over twenty years. They're both here with me to discuss the /j/ importance of secret codes throughout history.

JOE Good afternoon.

SALLY Hello.

M Sally, now /w/ I understand that a code invented during the reign of Roman Emperor Julius Caesar was used for hundreds of years after his death.

S Yes, amazingly /j/ it was. It was quite a simple code, really. All the letters of the /j/ alphabet simply moved three places. So, um, A became D, B became E, etc.

M How /w/ is it possible that the code remained unbroken for /r/ all that time?

S Well, we /j/ often forget that back in those days not many /j/ ordinary people knew how to read, so that's probably one of the main reasons why /j/ it lasted so long.

M When did people start working out how to break codes?

S Well, one of the /j/ earliest people to /w/ ever break coded messages was an Arab mathematician called al-Kindi, who lived in the 9th century. He was an extremely /j/ intelligent man and he wrote 290 books, on medicine, linguistics, astronomy /j/ and mathematics. He /j/ even wrote one or two /w/ on music. At the time he was known as the philosopher /r/ of the /j/ Arabs and, um, in fact his book on deciphering codes was only rediscovered relatively recently in Istanbul in 1987.

J Yes, and actually /j/ it was, um, it was because he knew /w/ a lot about maths and languages that he was able to /w/ understand how /w/ a code could be broken. He did it by working out how frequently each letter was used in a language.

M Can you /w/ explain that in a little more detail?

S Yes, for /r/ example, let's take the /j/ English language. If you take any general text in English, you'll find that the letter /r/ E /j/ is the most frequent. And when you've worked out how /w/ often each letter /r/ appears, then you have a way /j/ of breaking the code.

M Ah, I see. So you look for the most common letter /r/ and you /w/ assume that letter represents the letter /r/ E.

J That's right. And letters in the code that have a very low frequency will probably represent Q /w/ and Z because they /j/ only /j/ occur very rarely /j/ in English.

M Hm, that's very /j/ interesting. But do /w/ all codes use letters of the /j/ alphabet?

S No. Some use symbols, which just means that you, um, you look for the most frequent symbol instead of the most frequent letter. In fact the /j/ author Sir /r/ Arthur Conan Doyle, who wrote the Sherlock Holmes books, used stick men as a code in his book *The /j/ Adventure of the Dancing Men*. In that story, Sherlock Holmes manages to break the code when he realises that the dancing men represent letters of the /j/ alphabet.

M So, er, it seems that Conan Doyle knew /w/ about al-Kindi's way /j/ of deciphering codes.

S Definitely.

M And is al-Kindi's way /j/ of breaking codes still being used today?

R6.5

Well, one of the /j/ earliest people to /w/ ever break coded messages was an Arab mathematician called al-Kindi. | Yes, for /r/ example, let's take the /j/ English language. | So you look for the most common letter /r/ and you /w/ assume that letter represents the letter /r/ E.

R6.6

1

LUCY Come in. Hello, Angus.

ANGUS Sorry to bother you, but have you got a minute?

L Sorry, this isn't a good time. I'm really up against it at the moment. Is it urgent?

A No, not really. I just wanted to go over these figures. Er, don't worry, some other time.

L Yes, give me an hour or so.

A OK. See you later. Thanks.

2

LUCY Hello. Lucy Baker speaking.

MARTIN Hi, it's me. Is this a good time?

L Oh, not really. I'm afraid I'm a bit tied up just now. Is it important?

M No, don't worry. I just wanted to ask you about house insurance, but I'll catch you later.

L Thanks. Oh, oh, and Martin, can you pick something up for dinner?

M Sure. See you later. Bye.

L Bye.

3

LUCY Come in. Hello, Clare.

CLARE Sorry to disturb you, Ms Baker. I was wondering if I could see you for a moment.

L Er, I'm rather pushed for time at the moment. Can it wait?

C Um, yes, it's not urgent. It's just about the report you asked me to type up. When would be convenient?

L Try me again in a couple of hours.

C Right.

4

LUCY Yes?

TINA Hello, Lucy. Are you busy?

L I'm afraid I am a bit, Tina.

T Just a quick question. When would be a good time to install some new software on your computer?

L Er, tomorrow?

T Fine by me. I'll do it first thing tomorrow morning.

L Thanks.

5

LUCY Yes?

JULIAN Lucy, can I have a word?

L I'm really rather busy at the moment, Julian, but what's the problem?

J Er, I don't suppose I could use your office any time today. It's just that I get so many interruptions out there I can't get any work done. (laughter) What have I said? What's so funny?

R6.7

1 Sorry to bother you, but have you got a minute? **a)**

2 Is this a good time? **b)**

3 Sorry to disturb you. **b)**

4 I was wondering if I could see you for a moment. **a)**

5 Are you busy? **a)**

6 Can I have a word? **b)**

R6.8

A Sorry to bother you, but have you got a minute?

B Sorry, this isn't a good time.

B I'm really up against it at the moment.

A I'll catch you later, then.

A Is this a good time?

B I'm afraid I'm a bit tied up just now.

A I just wanted to ask you about house insurance.

A Sorry to disturb you.

A I was wondering if I could see you for a moment.

B I'm rather pushed for time right now.

A When would be a good time?

A Can I have a word?

B I'm really rather busy right now.

A Don't worry, it's not important.

R6.9

Listening Test (see Teacher's Book)

R7.1

DAN A new survey out today has revealed that we're spending more time than ever waiting in airport departure lounges. So we sent our reporter Nicole Watson to Heathrow to find out how people are passing the time there.

NICOLE Thanks, Dan. Excuse me, madam, where are you flying to today?

WOMAN 1 Er, I'm going to Madrid.

N And can I ask how you normally spend your time while you're waiting for your flight?

W1 I usually buy a paperback and just go and sit somewhere quiet.

N So you just read until your flight is called?

W1 Yes, that's right. Once I got so involved in the book I was reading that I missed my plane.

N Really?

W1 Yes, it was quite embarrassing, actually.

N And what about you, sir? How long have you been here today?

MAN 1 I've been sitting here for nearly five hours.

N Wow, that's a long time!

M1 Yes, there's a problem with the plane or something.

N Oh and how have you been spending your time?

M1 Well, I really love people-watching and airports are just brilliant for that. So that's all I've been doing, really. Oh, I've also called my parents to say goodbye.

N Right. And the gentleman sitting next to you. How do you feel about waiting at airports?

M2 I absolutely detest it, to be honest. Luckily, I only live ten minutes away, so I usually check in as late as I can.

N And how are you spending your time here today?

M2 I'm doing a part-time business management course at the moment, so I'm trying to catch up on my coursework.

N And why are you travelling today?

M2 I'm flying to Hamburg for some meetings. I'm supposed to be seeing some clients as soon as I arrive, but I see the flight's been delayed. Just my luck, eh?

N And how about you, madam?

WOMAN 2 Well I've been looking round all the shops. I have three kids and I never get time to shop for myself, so I'm having a great time today.

N Have you bought anything?

W2 Yes, a handbag and some perfume. I'm also thinking of buying a camera, but I think they might be cheaper online.

N And where are your kids now?

W2 They're with my husband in that restaurant over there having lunch. My youngest is usually very good, but he's being very difficult today. So we've decided to take it in turns to look after them.

N Thanks very much. So that's how people are passing the time at Heathrow today, Dan. Back to you in the studio.

D Thanks, Nicole. Now, these days many people seem to ...

R7.2

CLIVE Ah, here's Ian.

IAN Hi, everyone. Sorry I'm late.

MOLLY No problem. Clive and I have only just got here ourselves.

OLIVIA So, er, so how was your first day back at work?

I Well, um, it was a bit of a nightmare, actually.

O Oh, why's that?

I Well, I've only ... I'd only been away from the office for like a week, but there were over 300 emails in my inbox this morning!

C Yeah, that always happens to me too.

M Well, I love getting emails. It's ... it's about the only thing I use the Internet for these days.

C Apart from shopping, of course.

M Yeah, that's true, I do do a bit of shopping online.

C A bit? Molly, please ...

M Well, you see, it's so easy, isn't it – you just kind of like click on a few icons and that's that. You don't ... it doesn't feel like you're spending money at all!

C It does when the credit card bill arrives ...

O Yeah, I generally, um, I buy a lot of things online too, especially, er, books and CDs and you know things like that.

C Oh, I don't buy CDs any more, I just download music straight onto my MP3 player.

O Do you have to pay for it?

C If it's new stuff, yeah, you like have to pay for each song you download, but it's, er, it's very cheap. And I go to ... there are some other websites where you can like download songs by new bands for free.

O Um, we should start doing that, Ian.

I You see, it's ... it's just that I've never sort of found the time to work out how to do it.

O That's because you're usually too busy, um, playing that role-play game of yours. Honestly, every time I ... I often come home and find that he's been sitting in the study for hours, you know, fighting some evil monster or something.

I That's only when your mother comes to stay.

O Ha ha, very funny.

C They're, er, they're very addictive though, those role-play games, aren't they?

I Yeah, and incredibly popular too. Any number of people can play. Some of them have like about half a million people playing at the same time.

M Really? Wow!

WAITER Excuse me, are you ready to order?

M Oh, er, no, sorry, we've been chatting. Can we have, um, can you give us a few more minutes?

W Of course.

O Well, the thing I love most about the Internet is our webcam.

M Really? Do you, um, do you use it much?

O Yeah, I do, actually. Most of ... a lot of my family live in the States, and we kind of, er, use the webcam to keep in touch – you know, for birthdays and, er, that kind of thing.

M Um, that sounds fun.

O Yes, it's wonderful.

C Right, let's order. Is there, er, anything you'd recommend?

R7.3

1

TONY Hello.

GREG Hi, is that Tony?

T Yes ...

G Hi, it's Greg. Greg Robertson.

T Greg! Hey, I haven't heard from you for months! How are you?

G I'm good, thanks. Listen, I'm calling from Sydney on my mobile, so I can't be long – it's probably costing me a fortune!

T So what's going on in ...

G Anyway, the reason I'm ... Sorry. There's a bit of a delay on the line.

T Shall I call you back on your landline?

G No, don't worry. This is just a quick call to ... I'm flying ... Tuesday ... I ... you'd like to meet ... evening.

T Sorry, you're breaking up a bit. I didn't catch all of that.

G Is that any better?

T Yes, I can hear you now.

G I said I'm flying to London next Tuesday.

T Really? Wow, that's brilliant news!

G Yeah, and I was wondering if you'd, you know, like to meet up in the evening.

T Yes, course, that'd be great. Actually, why don't I, um, come and pick you up from the airport?

G Well, it'd be great if you could, thanks a lot. I get into Heathrow at, er, let me see ... 3.20 in the afternoon, your time.

T What's your flight number?

G Let me see. Er, I'm just about to run out of credit. I'll, um, I'll email you the flight details.

T Great. See you on Tuesday, then. Bye.

G See you later.

2

TONY Hello, Harry.

HARRY Hello, Tony. How are things?

T Oh, not bad, thanks. I was, um, I'm just about to go and see those new clients, you know, the software company.

H Good, hope it goes well. Anyway, the reason I'm calling is that we're having a planning meeting next ...

T Sorry, it's a bad line. You'll have to speak up a bit.

H Would you like me to phone you back?

T No, it's OK, I can hear you now. What were you saying?

H We're having a big planning meeting next, er, er, Tuesday afternoon, and I'd like you to be there.

T Next Tuesday?

H Yes. We'll be discussing plans for this year's sales conference and we want your ideas. Why, is there a problem?

T No, it's fine. I'll be there.

H Good. It's in, let me see, er, Meeting Room B and we'll be starting at 2.30. See you then.

T Right.

H Oh, and, er, good luck with the new clients.

T Thanks.

3

JENNY Hello?

TONY Hello, Jenny?

J Oh hi, Tony. How's your day going?

T Fine, what about you?

J Oh not too bad, thanks. Busy, as usual.

T I can't hear you very well. Where are you?

J I'm on the train.

T Oh, OK, that's why.

J Yeah, the reception isn't very good here. Do you want me to give you a ring later?

T No, it's OK. I just wanted to ask you if you're, um, free on Tuesday afternoon. Greg's flying in from Aus ...

J Sorry, I didn't get any of that. We just went through a tunnel.

T I said Greg's flying in from Australia on Tuesday.

J Greg Robertson? Wow, great!

T Yeah. The thing is, I have to, um, I've got to go to a meeting that afternoon. Can you pick Greg up from Heathrow?

J Yes, sure, no problem. I'm not working that day.

T Great. Maybe that evening we ... people round ... you want.

J Oh, I keep losing you. Say that again?

T I said that maybe that evening we could, er ...

T Sorry, we got cut off.

J Yeah, another tunnel, sorry. What were you saying?

T I was saying that maybe we could have some people round that evening, you know, for dinner or something.

J Fine, good idea. Let's talk about it later. I think my battery's about to run out.

T OK, have a good journey. Speak soon. See you tonight.

R7.4

1

A Why don't we meet outside the /ðə/ cinema at /ət/ seven?

B Sorry, I didn't get any of /əv/ that. It's a /ə/ bad line.

A I said let's meet outside the /ðə/ cinema at /ət/ seven.

B I keep losing you. Shall I call you /jə/ back on your /jə/ landline?

A Yes, if you /jə/ don't mind. I think my battery's about to /tə/ run out.

2

A The meeting's at /ət/ three thirty in Room F.

B Sorry, I didn't catch all of /əv/ that. You're breaking up a /ə/ bit.

A I said, the /ðə/ meeting's at /ət/ three thirty in Room F.

B OK ... Oh dear, I'm just about to /tə/ run out of /əv/ credit.

A Would you /jə/ like me to /tə/ phone you /jə/ back?

B That'd be great, thanks.

R7.5

ANSWERS 2 time 3 sentence 4 crime
5 mistakes 6 few 7 face 8 friend 9 fighting
10 end 11 time 12 losers 13 world
14 taken 15 fame 16 thank 17 roses
18 cruise 19 whole

R8.1

EDDY Hi, Mum.

MOTHER Oh, hello, Eddy.

E Brought the car back. Thanks.

M Did you put any petrol in it?

E Sorry, I couldn't. I'm a bit short of money. In fact, I'm £50 overdrawn and the rent's due on Friday. You couldn't, er, lend me a couple of hundred, could you?

M It's about time you found yourself a proper job.

E Acting is a proper job.

M So you keep telling me.

E Please, Mum. I'll pay you back, I promise.

M Oh, alright. £200 you say?

E Yeah, that'd be great. Thanks.

M Er, I'll have to see how much I've got in my savings account first. But this is the last time, Eddy.

E Yeah, yeah, you always say that, Mum.

M No, I'm serious. It's about time you grew up. If you had a job, you wouldn't have to borrow money from me all the time.

E I wish I could spare the time, Mum, but, you know, it's all these auditions I have to go to.

M Yes, well, I hope you get something soon. But still, I wish you weren't chasing these impossible dreams.

E What impossible dreams?

M Oh, you know, dreams about becoming a film star.

E Yeah, well, actually, I'm hoping to hear from my agent about an audition I did for a TV advert. She, er, she hasn't phoned, has she? I gave her this number.

M No, sorry, she hasn't.

E Oh, I hope she calls.

M What's wrong with your mobile, anyway?

E I, um, I lost it, that's why I gave her this number.

M Oh, I wish you'd take more care of your things. How many is that you've lost?

E Only two! And the first one was stolen.

M Yes, so you said. Anyway, what's the ad for?

E Norland Bank. I'd be a customer who's asking for a loan.

M Well, if you get it, you won't have any problem learning your lines then, will you? Oh, but I won't keep going on about it. Anyway, it's time to go. I have to be at work by six. Oh I wish I knew where your father was. He needs the car later tonight so he was going to give me a lift to work. Can you drive me and then bring the car back for Dad?

E It's time you got your own car, Mum.

M Yeah, well, when you pay me back all the money you owe me, I'll be able to afford one, won't I?

R8.3

1 I wish she lived a bit nearer.
2 I wish he'd bought chocolate instead.
3 I wish she'd visit more often.
4 I wish he worked for us.
5 I wish I'd had enough time to finish.
6 I wish I earned a bit more money.

R8.5

GRAHAM Good meal, Ruth?

RUTH Yes, it was excellent, I thought. Another glass of wine?

G No, thanks. Just some more water, please.

R Do you want coffee?

G No, I'm fine, thanks.

R Could we have the check, please, Jack?

JACK Certainly, ma'am.

G Look, this is on me.

R But Graham, you bought dinner yesterday.

G Don't worry, it's on expenses. By the way, do waiters here always introduce themselves?

R Well, Cornell University did a study on tipping and found that restaurant staff got much bigger tips if they introduced themselves.

G Really?

J Here's your check, ma'am.

G I'll take it, thanks. Right, er, oh, how much tip should I leave?

R Twenty per cent is about right – maybe more if they introduce themselves.

G Wow! It's half that in the UK.

R Half! No, 15% would be the absolute minimum here.

G Er, right. While we're on the subject, I was in the hotel bar last night and the guy next to me ordered a drink, got $2 change, which he left on the counter. Did he, um, did he just forget to pick it up?

R No, we tip bartenders here, a couple of dollars a drink or, er, if you pay at the end of the evening for everything, then 15 or 20% of the total.

G Mm. We British never tip bar staff. Some people, you know, offer them a drink, but not money.

R Wow, that's really strange. You'd never do that here!

G Yeah, I know.

J Thank you very much, sir.

G Thanks. Er, yeah, and, um, tipping New York taxi drivers – there's another thing I'm never sure about.

R Er, same rule as restaurants, 15 to 20%. But they wouldn't ... you'd never give less than a couple of dollars, even if it's for a short journey across town. Say it's a $6 fare, you'd give them a $10 bill and say "give me back two dollars and we're good".

G Taxi drivers in London generally expect to get a tip too.

R So, how much do you give?

G Oh, it varies. Some people just, um, just tell them to keep the change. Others give 10%.

R What about hotels in the UK? Do you tip the bellhops?

G Er, we call them porters. Yes, if they carry your bags to your room, we usually give them like a pound or two. And here?

R Yeah, you'd tip the bellhop here too, a dollar a bag and two dollars for every journey he makes to your room.

G And what if you want room service?

R Yes, we'd always give a tip for room service. A couple of dollars.

G We'd probably give them a couple of pounds or something.

R Yeah, knowing who and how much to tip is always a problem when you're in a different country. I remember when I was in Argentina last year ...

R8.6

1 Just a glass of water, please. (UK)
2 Do you want coffee? (US)
3 You bought dinner yesterday. (UK)
4 Twenty per cent is about right. (US)
5 You'd never give less than a couple of dollars. (US)

R8.8

1

EDDY Hello?

CYNTHIA Eddy. It's Cynthia. Look, I'm sorry that I didn't get back to you sooner. I didn't realise the time. It's been mad here today.

E Oh hi, Cynthia. Don't worry about it. I haven't been waiting that long. Well?

C Er, bad news about the Norland Bank advert, I'm afraid. You didn't get the part. However, they do want you to do a voiceover for a series of cat food ads. Could be quite good money.

E Oh, I wish I'd got the bank advert. But OK, what are they offering?

C Sorry, forgot to ask.

E Never mind. I'll take anything at the moment.

C They'll have a contract for you to sign at the recording studio. You need to go to the studio in ...

2

EDDY Hi. How was work?

MOTHER Oh, er, quite busy for a Monday evening. Not a great night for tips, though. What are you doing with those flowers?

E Oh I'm really sorry. I'm afraid I broke your vase. I'll get you another one.

M It doesn't matter. I never really liked it anyway. So, did you hear from your agent?

E Yes, I, um, I didn't get the Norland Bank ad, but I did get a voiceover job next week for some cat food ads.

M Well at least that's something. Look, I'm sorry about this afternoon. I shouldn't have said those things to you.

E Like telling me to grow up?

M Sorry, I can't believe I said that. I didn't mean to upset you.

E Oh, forget about it, Mum. It's OK. And I'm sorry for borrowing money off you all the time. But who knows, these cat food ads might lead onto other work.

M Let's hope so, eh?

3

JESS New improved Purr. The cat food no cat can resist. Mmm. New ... improved ... Purr. The cat food no cat can resist ...

EDDY Morning, I'm Eddy Daniels. I'm, um, I'm here to do the voiceover for the cat food ad.

PAULA Nice to meet you, Eddy. I'm Paula Evans, the producer. We're, er, running a bit late, so shall we make a start?

E Sure.

J Hi, I'm Jess, by the way. I'm working on the ad too.

P Oh, I'm sorry, I didn't introduce you. I thought you knew each other for some reason. I always assume everyone knows everyone in this business.

E Oh, that's alright. Nice to meet you.

J You too.

P OK. Shall we do a run through?

E Er, I haven't seen the script so could I just have a moment to, um, to read through it?

P Oh, sorry, I had no idea you'd need a script.

E No need to apologise. I only need to go over the lines a couple of times.

P Ah, well they're, um, they're not lines exactly. Didn't your agent tell you?

E Tell me what?

P Er, you're playing the part of the cat.

E The cat?!

R8.9

1

A I'm sorry that_I called you_/w/_an idiot. I can't believe I said that.

B Forget_about_it. You're /r/_under_/r/_a lot_of pressure.

A I didn't mean to_/w/_upset you.

2

A I'm really sorry_/j/_about last night. I shouldn't_have phoned so late.

B No need to_/w/_apologise. I went straight back to sleep_anyway.

A I had no_/w/_idea_/r/_it was that late. I thought_it was much_earlier for some reason.

3

A Sorry for losing my temper with you the_/j/_other day.

B Don't worry_/j/_about_it.

A I'd only had_about two_/w/_hours' sleep.

B Really_/j/_it doesn't matter. I could tell you were_/r/_absolutely_/j/_exhausted.

R9.1

ANSWERS 2 are watched 3 include 4 last 5 to be produced 6 were being made 7 produce 8 be seen 9 spends 10 is being forced 11 being transported 12 go

R9.2

GILLIE Hi, Nick! Fancy seeing you here!

NICK Hi. Yes, just been out for a meal with some friends from work. And you?

RICHARD Oh, we've just been to see *Another Monday*. Do you know it?

N I've read about it. What was it like?

R It was rubbish. It really was.

G But it got such great reviews. Critics such as Amis Jones loved it, but I really don't know why.

R Well, Jones was wrong, like he usually is.

N Well, you can never tell with reviews really, can you? And I must admit, I don't like Amis Jones as a critic. So, not a good production then.

G Oh, Nick, don't get us started.

N Even though it has actors like Sy Harris and May Firth? That's surprising. They're usually very good.

G It wasn't the actors' fault. Sy Harris was great, like he always is.

R The whole thing was like a bad dream – even the set. Well, I say set, but on the stage there were just some black boxes which were used as tables and chairs. That was it! Talk about minimalist!

G You can say that again.

R It had such a good cast, but I thought it was really difficult to follow.

G Impossible to follow, actually. The plot was so far-fetched and the ending was completely unrealistic.

R And honestly, the play was so slow that I, er, I actually fell asleep at one point. I've no idea why so many critics liked it – it's really overrated.

G Yeah, It was. It was dreadful. Probably the worst thing I've seen this year. I can't understand why it's getting so much attention.

N Well, I can tell you didn't like it.

G Whatever makes you think that, Nick?

R Yeah, what gives you that impression?

Recording Scripts

R9.3

GARY And how's work?

RITA Yeah, (it's) fine.

G And your mum? (Is) She any better?

R (She's) Much better, thanks.

G Did you go and see her last week?

R No, **I meant to**. (I'm) Going (on) Wednesday though. (I) Just couldn't get any time off work last week. **I tried to**, but we were too busy.

G Right.

R So what have you been up to this week?

G Oh, er, (I) went to see the Degas exhibition at Tate Modern. (Have) You seen it?

R No, (I) haven't had a chance to (see it) yet. But did you see the Rachel Whiteread sculpture there, you know, in the main entrance hall?

G Yes. 14,000 white plastic boxes all piled on top of one another. (It's) Such a load of rubbish and they call it art!

R Oh, I think her sculptures, such as the staircase or the bath, they're just so exciting. (Have you) Seen those?

G No, and **I don't want to**. I don't need to go to a Rachel Whiteread exhibition to see things I can see at home.

R Well, she says she's, er, caught the 'ghost of the lost object' … so you look at it differently, like you're, um, you're looking at something for the first time. Like Tracey Emin's bed.

G That wasn't even a sculpture, (it was) just her bed, with a load of dirty clothes and rubbish around it.

R Did you see it?

G (I) **Wouldn't want to**. Why (would I) give up a Saturday to look at her bed?

R She wasn't just showing her bed really, she was expressing her pain. Apparently she was so upset after her boyfriend left her that she stayed in that bed for weeks. It's the artist showing her feelings, her depression.

G Well, it depresses me, that's for sure. Just like those people that burnt a million pounds.

R The K Foundation.

G Whatever. They filmed themselves burning all that money and called it art. (That was) So disgusting. Think of all the people they could have helped with that money.

R Yes, (I) agree with you there. Interestingly, the K Foundation also gave £40,000 to Rachel Whiteread.

G Say no more! But seriously Rita, what is art, for you? (Is it) Paintings produced by computers like the AARON programme? (They) Got rave reviews from the public, but some of the critics said they weren't art.

R (I) Haven't seen them, but no, they're not art because there was no intention.

The computer didn't intend, or try to produce art. But Tracey Emin and Rachel Whiteread did.

G Yeah, maybe **they tried to**, but they didn't succeed.

R OK, let me ask you this. Did you like the Degas paintings – were they art?

G Yes, (of) course. (I) Loved the one called, er, what was it … , er, *Racehorses in Front of the Grandstand*.

R Well, in his time, he was laughed at. Now his paintings are considered masterpieces.

G What's your point? You can't seriously compare Degas with Tracey Emin?

R No, **I'm not trying to**. (I'm) Just trying to point out that attitudes change …

R9.4

GARY Hello?

RITA Hi, Gary, it's me.

G Oh, hi Rita. How are you doing?

R Fine, thanks. Listen, are you doing anything this evening?

G Nothing much. Why?

R Well, I thought we could give that new club a try. Do you want to go? It's supposed to be good.

G I'm sorry, but I don't feel up to going to a club. Got to get up early tomorrow. Some other time, perhaps. But they're showing *The Godfather* at the Arts Cinema. I wouldn't mind going to that. How about you?

R Er, I'd rather give that a miss, if you don't mind. Seen it so many times.

G Well, we could just go out for a meal then.

R Yes, that sounds good.

G Do you feel like having an Indian? Or we could go for Thai – or maybe Japanese?

R I'm easy. Whatever you like.

G Shall we give that new Indian a try?

R I really don't mind. It's up to you.

G Mmm, decisions, decisions. Actually, come to think of it, I've had Indian twice already this week. So Thai or Japanese?

R I'm not bothered either way. But if you don't make your mind up soon, they'll be closed!

G I'd prefer Thai, I think. That OK with you?

R It's all the same to me, I don't mind. Just make a decision.

G Of course. It's, er, it's so hard to find anywhere to park near the Thai place.

R Gary!

G No, I was just thinking, we'd be better off walking.

R It's pouring with rain out there.

G Oh, so it is.

R Look, on second thoughts, let's give tonight a miss and arrange something for the weekend.

G Oh, alright.

R Have you got anything on this Saturday?

G It's my mum's birthday.

R OK. Well, what are you up to on Sunday?

G I haven't got anything planned.

R Well, my youngest brother's got a new band. Do you fancy going to hear them play at The Junction on Sunday evening?

G Great. We could eat first. What do you fancy? Thai, Indian, Japanese or …

R Well, you've got three whole days to decide!

R9.5

JENNIFER Hello?

GARY Hi, Jennifer. Have you /jə/ got anything on this Sunday?

J No, I haven't. Why do /də/ you ask?

G Do you /dəjə/ fancy coming to /tə/ see Rita's brother's band?

J Er, I'd rather give that a /ə/ miss, if you /jə/ don't mind.

G No, don't worry, that's OK. So, what are /ə/ you /jə/ up to today?

J Nothing much. Do you /dəjə/ want to /tə/ do something?

G Well, I wouldn't mind going to /tə/ see *The /ðə/ Godfather*. How about you?

J Great. What time's it on?

G It's on at /ət/ five o'clock and eight twenty.

J Which do /də/ you prefer?

G I don't mind which one we go to. It's up to /tə/ you.

J Let's go to /tə/ the /ðə/ later one.

G OK. Eight twenty's fine. Do you /dəjə/ feel like having something to eat first?

J Sure, what kind of /əv/ food do you /dəjə/ fancy?

G I'm easy. Whatever you /jə/ like.

R10.1

JAN I do most things round the house myself and I even service my own scooter. Well, I, um, just got fed up with being ripped off all the time – like when I had my washing machine serviced. I'd never had any kitchen appliances serviced before. The guy charged me a £50 callout charge just for walking through the door. The service was on top of that. Crazy! So, er, I got my dad to teach me how to do things. I still get my car serviced at the local garage, but I'm, er, I'm going to start car maintenance classes soon, so then I'll be able to do that myself too.

DONNA Ask me to change a plug and I wouldn't know where to start. No, if I can't get my brother to do things for me, I pay to get them fixed. I've had lots of things done recently. Er, I had to get the boiler serviced because it wasn't working properly. Then the roof was leaking so I got that fixed. Then the leak left a stain on the bathroom wall so now I'm having the bathroom redecorated. I wish I were more practical. I'd have saved a fortune.

SHEENA My husband works away quite a lot so I've had to learn how to do a lot of things myself. In fact I'm getting better at doing DIY. I actually put some shelves up myself last weekend, but before I put any books on them I'm going to get my brother to check they're safe first. But there are still things I can't do. For example I've lost my back door key so I'll get the door lock replaced as soon as I can. I can't do that myself.

PENNY I can do a few things myself, like I can change plugs, but I can't do very much else. So, um, I get my husband to do most things round the house. He's really good at fixing things. He's, you know, he's very practical like that, but he does hate painting so, er, we usually have the decorating done professionally. But, um, he does pretty much everything else himself, and he's really good and a lot cheaper than a professional.

R10.3

ANSWERS 2 no 3 none of 4 anything 5 every 6 neither of 7 both of 8 either of 9 everyone 10 no one 11 all of

R10.5

NAOMI Did you read that article in today's *Independent*, saying women should give up work to become housewives?

POLLY Yes, but that's such a middle-class idea. Most couples these days can't live on one salary.

MATT They can. They just choose not to.

P No, they don't. We couldn't live on your salary, Matt.

M Yes, we could.

N Well, that's not the point. If women give up their careers to stay at home and look after the family, what do they do if things go wrong and they end up getting divorced? They're too old to start training for a job.

M Well, um, they usually get half the husband's money so they don't have to work.

P They do.

N No, women staying at home isn't the answer, Matt. Men should help round the house more.

P Speaking of which, have you read this? *Why Men Lie and Women Cry*.

N No. Any good?

M It's not bad.

P You haven't read it, have you?

M I have read it, actually.

P I bet you didn't agree with any of it.

M You're wrong, I did agree with it. Well, um, some of it anyway.

N I am surprised. Didn't think men read things like that.

M Ooh, that's a bit sexist, Naomi.

N It isn't sexist, it's a fact. You know, men don't usually read that stuff.

M Well, I did. Basically it says that when we ... if men and women want to live together successfully, they need to understand each other better. Not rocket science, is it?

N Understand what?

P Oh, you know, um, things like how men drive women crazy.

N How?

P Well, er, problem-solving for one. Apparently men like to, um, sort out their own problems. They only talk about problems when they want solutions. You know what women are like, we talk about our problems over and over again. We just want sympathy, but men think they have to give us solutions, and when we don't respond to their solutions they stop listening. Men do that all the time.

M No, we don't.

P Of course you do, it's classic.

M Yes, it says in the book that women use, er, use three times more words in a day than men. When a man gets home he's used up all his words for the day and just wants to sit in front of the TV.

P With the remote ...

M Yeah, but his wife still has, oh, er, about four or five thousand words left to say. And most of what she says is exaggerated.

N Meaning?

M Women say things like, "I've told you a *million* times." "I'll *never* speak to you again." "You *never* listen to me" ... that kind of thing, and because men deal in facts they say, "Well, I'm listening to you now" ... that kind of thing. Then the arguments start.

N Ooh, that would certainly start an argument in our family. But men exaggerate too.

M No, we don't.

N They do. They, oh, they go on about how good their car is, how gorgeous their latest girlfriend is, that sort of thing. That's exaggerating.

M But that's about facts, not emotions. Women say, er, you *always* do this, you *never* do that and ...

P But Matt, I *never* say ... , oh, things like that.

N So, you two newlyweds, how is married life anyway?

R10.7

1

POLLY We couldn't live on your salary, Matt.
MATT Yes, we could.

2

M Well, um, they usually get half the husband's money so they don't have to work.
P They do.

3

P You haven't read it, have you?
M I have read it, actually.

4

M Ooh, that's a bit sexist, Naomi.
NAOMI It isn't sexist, it's a fact.

5

N But men exaggerate too.
M No, we don't.

R10.8

POLLY Matt, where are you?
MATT In here.

P There you are. Can you tidy up the living room please, Matt?

M Uh huh.

P Thanks. You know, the thing I don't like about this flat is the kitchen. I can't move in there.

M Hmm.

P By the way, that was your Mum on the phone. She said they got a bit lost, but they'll be here soon. You're not listening, are you?

M I am listening, Polly.

P So what did I say?

M Oh no! My memory's gone! I can't remember a thing. Who are you? What are you doing in my flat?

P Oh Matt, you are an idiot.

M I'm not an idiot. I married you, didn't I?

P Ah.

M One thing I love about you is you always laugh at my jokes.

P Don't count on it. Hey, I thought you were tidying up. Come on, Matt, it's nearly one o'clock and this room is a complete mess. Oh, and where did you put the stuff for the salad?

M You didn't ask me to get any.

P Oh, Matt, I did ask you. I asked you this morning.

M Oh, sorry. I'll phone Mum's mobile and ask her to pick some up on her way.

P You can't do that.

M Yes, I can. She's my mother, she'll do anything for her son.

P Yeah, right. Go get the salad.

M Too late.

VAL Hello, darling. Sorry, we're late.

ALL Hello, hello ...

TOM The thing that amazes me about your mother is she still can't read a map.

V I can actually, Tom. One thing that annoys me about you is you never give me time to look at a map. Which way? Which way? Right or left? I just get flustered.

P Well, you're here now. Let me take your coats. Matt – salad.

M You don't want salad, do you, Mum?

P Matt! You do want salad, don't you, Val?

V Um ...

M OK, back in a moment.

Recording Scripts

T Is this apple pie homemade, Polly?

P It certainly is homemade.

V Oh, it's delicious, dear.

P Thank you.

V And your flat is so, um …

M Small?

V Mmm, no, I wasn't going to say that. I was going to say – what I like about the flat is it's so light.

P Mmm. But the kitchen is a bit small.

M Yes, what worries me about the size of the kitchen is I can't help Polly with the cooking – there's no room.

T Oh, how on earth do you put up with him, Polly?

P Well, it's early days – we've only been married for a month!

R10.9

is the kitchen → The thing I don't like about this flat is the kitchen. | you always laugh at my jokes → One thing I love about you is you always laugh at my jokes. | she still can't read a map → The thing that amazes me about your mother is she still can't read a map. | you never give me time to look at a map → One thing that annoys me about you is you never give me time to look at a map. | it's so light → What I like about the flat is it's so light. | I can't help Polly with the cooking → What worries me about the size of the kitchen is I can't help Polly with the cooking.

R10.10

VAL What I like about Sundays is I've got time to read the paper. Where is it?

TOM I haven't seen it.

V Yes, you have. You were reading it an hour ago.

T I wasn't. I was reading the TV guide.

V OK. No need to get angry.

T One thing that upsets me about you is you always contradict me!

V No, I don't.

T You do! You're doing it now!

V No, I'm not! And the thing that annoys me about you is you always have to be right.

T That's because I am!

R10.11

ANSWERS 2 all 3 really 4 exactly 5 Although 6 right 7 heard 8 burning 9 quite 10 have 11 just 12 that 13 today 14 bright 15 important 16 now 17 only 18 this 19 maybe 20 again 21 probably 22 supposed 23 here 24 Actually 25 long 26 home 27 so 28 just

R11.1

MIKE Mike Richards.

ROB Hello, Mike? It's Rob.

M Hi, Rob! Long time no hear. How are you doing?

R Er, not bad, thanks. How's life in the world of advertising?

M Oh, er, fine, I guess. I've got a lot of work on at the moment, but between me and you, I've been finding it hard to get down to things recently.

R Maybe it's time for a change.

M Yeah, maybe. So, is this just a social call, or, er, … ?

R Well, not exactly. I'd like to, um, talk to you about a new project I'm working on.

M Really? What kind of project?

R I'd prefer to tell you face to face, if that's OK.

M Sure. When?

R The sooner, the better, if possible. What about tomorrow? Are you free for lunch?

M Let me check … Sorry, I'm having lunch with my boss tomorrow. I can't really get out of that.

R No, course not. Er, OK, how about some time in the morning? I could get to your office by ten thirty.

M Sorry, I'll be interviewing people for our graduate trainee programme then. Actually, that'll probably take up the whole morning.

R OK, what about the afternoon? Say, four o'clock?

M No, sorry, I'll be in the middle of a meeting at four. Then I've got two more meetings I have to go to. Maybe I could meet you in the evening?

R Sorry, I can't do the evening, I've got to stay at home and look after the kids.

M Oh, OK.

R Well, how about Wednesday morning, say, eleven?

M No, I'll be on my way to Southampton at eleven. I'm giving a talk at a conference there.

R Well, Southampton's not far from me, maybe I can meet you there.

M OK, that might work.

R What time would suit you?

M Well, I'll have arrived by lunchtime … ah, but then I have to have lunch with some clients.

R You are on the go all the time, aren't you? So what time's your talk?

M It starts at two, so I'll have finished giving the talk by three thirty – but then I'll have to chat to lots of people – you know what conferences are like.

R Well, er, how about I buy you dinner?

M Yeah, fine. I'm staying in a hotel that night anyway and going straight to work the next morning.

R Great! Shall we say 7.30?

M Yes, fine.

R Let me know where you're staying and I'll pick you up.

M Will do. Er, Rob …

R Yeah?

M What's this all about?

R Tell you on Wednesday. See you then. Bye!

R11.3 R11.4

1 She'll have /əv/ moved out by the end of the week.

2 I bet he'll be watching TV when we get there.

3 At eight o'clock he'll be driving to work.

4 We won't have /əv/ seen everything by then.

5 They'll have /əv/ got home by the time we arrive.

6 This time next week I'll be lying on a beach.

R11.5

MIKE Oh, that was a hard day. It's good to be home.

DAISY So, how did the conference go? Did they like your talk?

M Er, yes, I think so. Nobody walked out, anyway.

D Well, that's good. So, um, you said that you had something interesting to tell me.

M Er, yeah. I had dinner with Rob last night.

D Yes, you said. How's he doing?

M Well, he's working freelance now – magazine articles, that sort of thing. But Rob told me that he was planning to set up his own business.

D Really? What kind of business?

M He wants to open a coffee shop. You know, with sofas, newspapers, good music, healthy food, Wi-Fi – somewhere you can really relax.

D Whereabouts?

M In Brighton.

D Oh, right.

M Yeah, he said he'd been looking for a good location since August, and now, um, now he reckons he's found the perfect place.

D And where's that?

M Between the seafront and the Lanes – you know, that nice old shopping area.

D That's a good spot. Lots of tourists and students.

M Yeah, that's what I thought. And here's the thing. Rob asked me if I wanted to go into business with him.

D But you've got a job.

M Yeah, but he'd like, er, do all the work, run the coffee shop and all that.

D So why does he need you?

M He's looking for someone to invest in the business. He said he could raise half of the money and he wanted to know whether I could come up with the other half.

D How much exactly?

M Twenty-five thousand.

D What?! Where on earth are we going to get that kind of money?

M Well, we've got ten thousand saved up, and we could, um, take out a bank loan for the rest.

D I'm not sure, darling. It's a huge risk.

156

M Well, I asked how long it would take for the business to make a profit. He thought about six months, maybe less.

D Does Rob know anything about setting up a business?

M I think so. Look, he's given me a copy of his business plan. We can go through it together this evening, if you like.

D Mmm, OK.

M Anyway, he asked me to meet him in Brighton on Saturday.

D Mike, I'm really not sure about this.

M I'm just going to talk to him, that's all.

D Have you discussed this with anyone at work?

M No. Rob told me not to talk to anyone else about it – except you, of course.

D OK, but promise that you'll discuss this with me before you do anything.

M Course I will. So, how was your day?

R11.6

MIKE Hello, Daisy. It's me.

DAISY Hi, where are you?

M I'm still in Brighton. Rob's just left. He told me to say hello to you.

D Thanks. So, how did the meeting go?

M Very well, actually. First Rob asked me what I thought of his business plan.

D You thought it was good, didn't you?

M Yes, I was very impressed, actually. He told me that the plan had already been approved by the bank – the one he wants to borrow £25,000 from.

D Oh, right.

M And he said that he'd been talking to an interior designer. You know, to redo the inside of the shop. It's, um, it's a restaurant at the moment.

D Yes, you told me.

M Also, he wanted to know if I'd help with the advertising, which, er, of course I'd be happy to do.

D Right. So, what do you think?

M Well, it looks an excellent investment. But of course I told him I couldn't say yes or no until I talked to you.

D Sounds like you want to go ahead with it.

M Well, to be honest, I think we'd be crazy not to. Oh, and I said I'd be talking to the bank on Tuesday. You know, about the loan.

D That shouldn't be a problem, though, should it?

M No, er, I don't think so. I asked Rob when he needed a decision by, and he said by, um, by next weekend.

D Really? That soon?

M Yes, apparently he's not the only person trying to buy the place. I asked him if he was talking to any other investors, and he said no. So it's up to us, really.

D Well, if you're sure, then let's just do it. It's only money, after all.

M I don't think we'll regret it. I did make one condition, though.

D What was that?

M I told him that he had to name the coffee shop after you!

R11.7

DAISY Your email was a bit of a shock – (1)Rob trying to sell the coffee shop to Café Pronto. I couldn't believe (1)it!

MIKE No, me neither.

D I bet (2)you were furious.

M You could say (2)that, yes. I've, um, I've calmed down a bit now, though.

D So what do you think we should do?

M Well, let's look at the options. Option one – we go along with Rob's plan and sell the shop.

D We'd, um, make some money, so it would have been worth it financially. Twenty-five thousand profit in a year isn't bad, is it?

M No, not at all. It's just that ... you know, I just don't want (3)our coffee shop to become another (4)branch of Café Pronto. (5)They're all the same, aren't (4)they?

D (5)That's true. I'm not keen on the idea either. You're very fond of (3)the place, aren't you?

M Of course. I know we don't go (3)there very often, but think of (6)all that work we did getting (3)it ready.

D How could I forget (6)it? (7)All the cleaning and painting and stuff we did with Rob. I quite enjoyed (7)that, actually.

M Yes, me too.

D So, what's option two?

M We, er, could just (8)refuse to sell – Rob wouldn't be able to sell without our agreement.

D But he said he'd (9)shut down the coffee shop if we did (8)that.

M Yes, but I don't think he (9)will. He still needs the money, doesn't he? What else is he going to do?

D I don't know, but he did sound pretty fed up with working (3)there.

M OK, so (8)that's probably not a good idea.

D Well, there is another option ...

M What's that?

D We could buy Rob's share of (10)the coffee shop and take over the business.

M But who'll run (10)the place while we're at work?

D We will. I could quit my job, and you're ... well, you're always saying how much you hate (11)working for that advertising agency.

M I don't hate (11)it exactly.

D Yes, you do. You're always going on about how bored you are there and how you can't wait to leave.

M Yeah, well, OK ... But where will we get the money from?

D Well, we can, um, sell (12)the house and move to Brighton. (12)It's probably worth twice what we paid for it anyway, and we'll easily be able to (13)buy Rob's share of the business with the profit.

M And what if Rob doesn't agree?

D Oh, he will – (14)he's only in it for the money now, you said (14)so yourself.

M Well, (13)it could work ...

D Definitely.

M Well, I really do need a change, and, er, the coffee shop is making money. As they say, you only live once.

D Absolutely!

M OK, let's do (13)it. And who knows, maybe in a few years we'll be running our own chain of coffee shops.

D Yes, and then Daisy's can start buying branches of Café Pronto!

R11.8

JUDY Hello everyone, thanks for coming. Firstly I'd like to welcome Roger Barnes, the product manager for *Go!*. Roger, this is Amanda, who's just taken over from Mike as the account executive for this product, and she'll be handling the launch. You've already spoken to each other on the phone, I think.

ROGER Yes, we have. Hello, Amanda. Nice to meet you finally.

AMANDA You too.

J And this is Colin, our creative director.

R Nice to meet you too, Colin.

COLIN And you.

J Right, let's see what ideas we've got for the *Go!* campaign. Amanda?

A Well, one thing we could do is use mobile phone ads. You know, send short video ads straight to people's mobiles.

J That sounds like a good idea. Colin?

C Well, it's worth a try. And it doesn't cost very much.

J OK, so that's one idea. Amanda, what about the press campaign?

A Well, we suggest full-page colour ads in all magazines with a healthy living section – women's magazines, Sunday supplements, sports magazines, that kind of thing. It's a healthy product, so this should be our target market.

J Mmm, yes, that makes sense.

R I wonder if it'd be a good idea to have a celebrity advertising the product.

A Well, it depends. If you like the celebrity, you might buy the product. But if you can't stand the person, you probably won't.

R So, what you're saying is that the wrong celebrity could actually damage the campaign?

A Um, yes, I think so.

J Colin, what do you think?

C Personally, I'd rather we didn't use a celebrity. For one thing, you never know what the media might find out about their private lives in the future. Then where would we be?

R OK, maybe we should avoid using celebrities.

J Am I right in thinking that we're not planning a TV ad at this point?

Recording Scripts

A Er, probably not, no. The main problem with TV ads is that they're incredibly expensive and our budget isn't very big.

R Are you saying that we won't be advertising *Go!* on TV at all?

A Not initially, no.

J I'm not sure that's such a good idea. We need to have some kind of TV ad, I think.

R I'll see what I can do about increasing the budget.

C I know! Why don't we give away free samples of *Go!* to commuters in the morning?

J Yes, that could work. Everyone likes free samples, and in the summer everyone's thirsty, especially if they're travelling.

R Absolutely!

C We could offer a choice of flavours too, you know, strawberry, pineapple ...

A I've got an idea. How about giving away a free glass with the *Go!* logo on? Then the *Go!* logo will be on their desk at work all day.

C Yes, I like that idea. Nice one.

J Right, can we just go over this again? Ideas we have on the table are – a mobile phone campaign ...

R11.9

AMANDA I know! Why don't we use cartoon characters?

COLIN I'm not sure that's such a good idea. I think we need some real people.

A Yes, maybe you're right.

C One thing we could do /w/ is show someone drinking the product.

A Yes, that makes sense. How /w/ about using some attractive models?

C Personally /j/ I'd rather we didn't use models. They /j/ always look so false.

A So what you're saying is that you want ordinary-looking people.

C Yes, exactly. The kind of people who might actually go /w/ out and buy *Go!*.

A Well, it's worth a try.

C I wonder /r/ if it'd be /j/ a good idea to show how much fruit is in it?

A Yes, that could work. OK, can we just go /w/ over this again?

R12.1

ANGIE Morning, Louise. Want some breakfast?

LOUISE No, thanks.

A What's up? You seem a bit stressed out.

L Yeah, I can't find my mobile.

A It might be in the bathroom. That's where you usually leave it.

L No, it's not there, I've looked. Oh, it really bugs me when I lose things.

A Did you, um, have you tried calling the number?

L Yeah, of course, but it must be switched off. It just puts me straight through to voicemail.

A Right.

L Oh, I've looked everywhere. It's not here. Maybe I lost it last night.

A Or someone could have taken it from your bag.

L Oh no, I hope not.

A Hey, don't panic, it's, um, oh, it's bound to be around here somewhere.

L But someone might be using it to phone Australia!

A Oh, chill out, Louise. Let's just try and work out where you left it. Then you can call and cancel it if you need to.

L Yeah, good idea.

A OK, um, let's see ... I met you after work, then we popped into that trendy new café for a coffee.

L And I definitely had my mobile then because I called my mate Jackie just after we left.

A OK, so you didn't leave it in the café. Where did we go next?

L Govinda's.

A Yeah, that's right. Oh, and someone called you in the middle of the meal, didn't they?

L Yeah, my sister.

A Do you remember what you did with your phone after that?

L Not really, no.

A So you may have left it on the table or something.

L Possibly, yeah. Maybe I should call the restaurant.

A It won't be open yet.

L Oh, yeah, you're right.

A Hang on a sec. You can't have left it at the restaurant, because someone texted you while we were queuing outside the club.

L That's right, yeah. Hey, do you remember that guy who, um, kept staring at us all the time? He might have been waiting for a chance to steal my phone.

A Maybe. He was a bit weird, wasn't he?

L Definitely. But did we phone for a taxi when we left?

A No, we just stopped one in the street. And you really fancied the driver, if I remember rightly.

L Well, he was quite good-looking, wasn't he?

A Yeah, not bad, I suppose. Anyway, I think that guy in the club must have stolen it. Call the phone company now and get the number stopped.

L Oh, what a hassle. This is really going to mess up my day.

A Here, use my phone. I'll go and see if there's any post.

L Thanks a lot. Now, what number do I call?

R12.3 R12.4

1 I think I must have /əv/ left it at home.

2 He could have /əv/ been /bɪn/ talking to someone else.

3 We might have /əv/ locked the keys in the car.

4 She can't have /əv/ been /bɪn/ working all night.

5 I may have /əv/ sent it to the wrong address.

6 Your father must have /əv/ been /bɪn/ trying to call you.

R12.5

ANSWERS 2 must be having 3 must have delivered 4 could be 5 can't be 6 must have been lying 7 must have found 8 might have written

LOUSIE Oh, yes. Oh, there is a note. It says, "Louise, you left this in the back of my cab last night. Give me a call sometime. Here's my mobile number. Patrick."

ANGIE Oh, wow, how interesting! Patrick must be that taxi driver you fancied. So, are you going to call him?

L Maybe – if I don't lose my phone again first!

R12.6

They needn't have /əv/ worried. | They should have /əv/ realised they were listening to a play. | They could have /əv/ listened to other radio stations. | I would have /əv/ reacted differently. | They shouldn't have /əv/ fled their homes. | We couldn't have /əv/ done anything else. | I wouldn't have /əv/ said that.

R12.7

TIP! ● Words in pink are weak forms.

LAURA Hi, Chris.

CHRIS Oh hi, Laura.

L Good day /j/ at work?

C Yeah, not bad, thanks. Is Mark here yet?

L Yes, he's just getting us some drinks.

MARK Hi, Chris. (Hi) Here you go.

C Oh, thanks.

M Cheers!

L AND C Cheers!

M So, Laura, how, um, how /w/ are you settling in to your new flat?

L Er, not very well, actually. I think it's haunted.

M Haunted? You're pulling my leg!

L No, /w/ I'm serious.

M But you live in a two-bedroomed flat in south London, not a castle in Transylvania!

C Er, that's vampires, not ghosts, you /w/ idiot. And anyway, there's no reason why her flat can't be haunted.

M Oh, so you believe in ghosts too, do you?

C Er, well, maybe. You can't say for certain they don't exist.

M So, tell us about your ghost, Laura. Does it, um, wear /r/ a white sheet and go wooooh?

L No /w/ it's, er, it's nothing like that. But I knew something was wrong as soon as I moved in. No wonder the previous owners were so keen to sell.

c What do you mean, wrong?

L Well, first_of_all, my /j/ old cat refuses to go /w/ into my bedroom. In my last flat she slept_on the /j/ end_of my bed every night, so /w/ I thought that was rather /r/ odd.

M Well, the previous_owners' cat might have slept_in that room. Or they could have had_a dog.

L They didn't have_a cat_or /r/ a dog. Anyway, the /j/ other night, while_I was lying in bed reading, I heard footsteps_outside my room.

M Could_have been the people next door, perhaps?

L No, /w/ it can't_have been them, they're /r/ away /j/ at the moment. Anyway, /j/ I went_and had_a look, but there was nobody there. And then one night_I saw /r/ it. Or rather, her.

c Wow! What did she look like?

L She was, er, let's see, she was_about forty, dressed_in clothes from the fifties_I'd say, and she was just standing there staring at me. Then she just, um, just vanished_into thin air.

c How spooky! You must_have been terrified.

L Yeah, I was, actually. Then_a couple_of days later /r/ I saw her /r/ again. I woke_up_and she was standing_in the corner. She was holding her hands_out, like this, as though she was_asking for help.

M I don't think she's the one who should be /j/ asking for help, Laura.

c Leave her alone, Mark. So /w/ is there /r/ anything_else unusual_about the flat?

L Let me think ... oh yeah, there's this, um, this part_of the kitchen that's_always freezing cold.

M That's called the fridge.

c Ignore him, Laura. He's the most sceptical person_on the planet.

L Anyway, I don't know what_to do.

M Well, I know /w/ a good psychiatrist_I can recommend.

c Yeah, I bet you do! So what options do you have?

L Well, I thought_I might try /j/ and get some help, but_I don't really know who to call_about this_sort_of thing ...

R12.8
Listening Test (see Teacher's Book)

Answer Key

2A ❶ b) p14

1 25%   2 50%   3 33%   4 70%

3A ❷ b) p22

1 a) 2 points	b) 1 point	c) 3 points
2 a) 1 point	b) 3 points	c) 2 points
3 a) 3 points	b) 2 points	c) 1 point
4 a) 1 point	b) 3 points	c) 2 points
5 a) 3 points	b) 1 point	c) 2 points

12–15 points You're an extremely honest and trustworthy person. You probably sleep very well at night!

8–11 points You're reasonably honest, but occasionally you think of yourself instead of doing the right thing.

5–7 points Where did you leave your morals? Perhaps you should try to be a bit more honest in the future!

3C ❽ p27

The judges in these real-life court cases handed down these sentences.
Student A The postman was sent to prison for six and a half years.
Student B The secretary who stole £4.3 million was sent to prison for 16 years.
Student C The man who illegally copied and sold DVDs was given a three-year prison sentence.
Student D The farmer was sent to prison for life. However, his sentence was later reduced to five years, and he was released from prison after three years.

4A ❹ b) p31

THE DEAD KANGAROO STORY Not true. There have been numerous versions of this urban legend over the years, the first appearing in 1902 (in this story the kangaroo was hit by a train). There are also different versions of this story told in other countries. In the USA, for example, the animal is usually a deer.

THE FALLING COW STORY Possibly true. This story was reported by the Reuters News Agency in April 1997 and appeared in newspapers all over the world. However, many urban legend websites now say that this story is false, as a very similar story had appeared in the *Moscow News* seven years earlier.

THE EXPLODING HOUSE STORY True. This story happened in December 2003 at the home of a woman named Aurelia Oliveras in San Diego, California. Luckily nobody was hurt in the explosion because Mrs Oliveras, her husband and her two-year-old daughter were in the back garden at the time.

8B ❸ b) p64

Pose as a live model The usual rate is £7–£10 an hour.
Invigilate exams Between £8 and £18 an hour.
Join a focus group Between £30 and £100 a session.
Take part in psychological research Between £10 and £60 a session.
Be a mystery shopper £8–£10 a visit, but could be as high as £100 a day.
Let companies advertise on your car Between £70 and £220 a month.

9C ❽ c) p112

1 Art *Convergence*, Jackson Pollock (1952)
2 Art *Black Bean*, from *Soup Can Series I*, Andy Warhol (1968) 3 Art *Untitled*, Mark Rothko (1960–1961) 4 Art *In Advance of the Broken Arm*, Marc Duchamp (1915) 5 Not art victim of the volcanic eruption, Pompeii, AD 79 6 Art *A Glimpse of Hope*, Rebecca Warren (2003) 7 Not art weathercock from a church, France 8 Not art model in a shop window, Goa, India
9 Art *Equivalent VIII*, Carl Andre (1966)
10 Not art section of the Millau bridge, France 11 Not art 'Split Apple Rock', natural rock formation, New Zealand
12 Not art picture painted by an elephant

Phonemic Symbols

Vowel sounds

/ə/ father ago	/æ/ apple cat	/ʊ/ book could	/ɒ/ on got	/ɪ/ in swim	/i/ happy easy	/e/ bed any	/ʌ/ cup under
/ɜː/ her shirt	/ɑː/ arm car	/uː/ blue too	/ɔː/ born walk	/iː/ eat meet			
/eə/ chair where	/ɪə/ near we're	/ʊə/ tour mature	/ɔɪ/ boy noisy	/aɪ/ nine eye	/eɪ/ eight day	/əʊ/ go over	/aʊ/ out brown

Consonant sounds

/p/ park soup	/b/ be rob	/f/ face laugh	/v/ very live	/t/ time white	/d/ dog red	/k/ cold look	/g/ girl bag
/θ/ think both	/ð/ mother the	/tʃ/ chips teach	/dʒ/ job page	/s/ see rice	/z/ zoo days	/ʃ/ shoe action	/ʒ/ television
/m/ me name	/n/ now rain	/ŋ/ sing think	/h/ hot hand	/l/ late hello	/r/ marry write	/w/ we white	/j/ you yes

CD-ROM/Audio CD Instructions

Start the CD-ROM

- Insert the *face2face* CD-ROM into your CD-ROM drive.
- If Autorun is enabled, the CD-ROM will start automatically.
- If Autorun is not enabled, open **My Computer** and then **D:** (where D is the letter of your CD-ROM drive). Then double-click on the *face2face* icon.

Install the CD-ROM to your hard disk (recommended)

- Go to **My Computer** and then **D:** (where D is the letter of your CD-ROM drive).
- Right-click on *Explore*.
- Double-click on *Install face2face to hard disk*.
- Follow the installation instructions on your screen.

Listen and practise on your CD player

You can listen to and practise language from these conversations in the Student's Book Real World lessons on your CD player at home or in the car:

R1.7	R2.6	R3.7	R4.5	R5.7	R6.6
R7.3	R8.8	R9.4	R10.8	R11.8	

What's on the CD-ROM?

- **Interactive practice activities**

Extra practice of Grammar, Vocabulary, Real World situations and English pronunciation. Click on one of the unit numbers (1–12) at the top of the screen. Then choose an activity and click on it to start.

- **My Activities**

Create your own lesson. Click on *My Activities* at the top of the screen. Drag activities from the unit menus into the *My Activities* panel on the right of the screen. Then click on *Start*.

- **My Portfolio**

This is a unique and customisable reference tool. Click on *Grammar, Word List, Real World* or *Phonemes* at any time for extra help and information. You can also add your own notes, check your progress and create your own English tests!

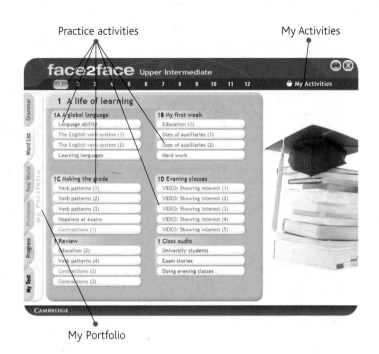

Practice activities | My Activities

My Portfolio

System specification
- Windows 98, NT4 with Service Pack 6, ME, 2000 or XP
- 128Mb RAM
- 500Mb hard disk space (if installing to hard disk)

Support

If you experience difficulties with this CD-ROM, please visit: www.cambridge.org/elt/cdrom

---

Acknowledgements

The authors would again like to thank everyone at Cambridge University Press for their support, enthusiasm and hard work, in particular: Dilys Silva (Senior Development Editor); Andrew Reid, Verity Cole and Keith Sands (Editorial team); Ruth Atkinson (Freelance editor); Laurie Harrison (Electronic Operations Manager); Nicholas Tims, Alison Greenwood and Nicholas Murgatroyd (CD-ROM team) and all the team at Pentacor (Book design). We would especially like to thank Sue Ullstein (Senior Commissioning Editor) for her enormous contribution to the *face2face* project over the last few years. We simply couldn't have done it without you, Sue.

Chris Redston would like to thank the following people for all their support and encouragement: Mark and Laura Skipper, Will Ord, Dylan Evans, Kari Matchett, Heidi Sowter, Karen Thomas, Natasha Muñoz, Steve Moore, Susanne Brunsch, Katy Wimhurst, Mat and Sarah Hunt, Polly Kirby, Margie Fisher, Joss Whedon, the Hilder family, his sisters, Anne and Carol, his dear father, Bill Redston, and of course his dear co-author, Gillie Cunningham. He would also like to offer very special and heartfelt thanks to Adela Pickles for all her patience, understanding and love, and for putting up with bookwriting guy for another year. It'll be funloving guy's turn soon, I promise!

Gillie Cunningham would like to offer special thanks to the usual suspects: Richard Gibb, Amybeth, Sue Mohamed and her dearco Chris Redston, for being their wonderful selves as always and for offering help and support whenever it was needed. Many thanks also go to Jan Bell for joining the *face2face* writing team – great to be working with you again, Jan.

The authors and publishers would like to thank the following teachers for the invaluable feedback which they provided:
Cesar Elizi, Brazil; Iris Grallert, Germany; Alison Greenwood, Italy; Madeline Hall, UK; Nancy Hulek, Germany; Malyina Kazue Ono Leal, Brazil; Ana Mercado, Spain; Alejandro Naveas, Chile; David Rea, UK; Gloria Isabel Torres, Spain; Jolanta Urbanik, Poland.

The authors and publishers are grateful to the following contributors:
pentacor**big**: cover and text design and page make-up
Hilary Luckcock: picture research, commissioned photography
Trevor Clifford: photography
Anne Rosenfeld: audio recordings

The authors and publishers are grateful to the following for permission to reproduce copyright material. All efforts have been made to contact the copyright holders of material reproduced in this book which belongs to third parties, and citations are given for the sources. We welcome approaches from any copyright holders whom we have not been able to trace but find that their material has been reproduced herein.

For the text in 1A: adapted from 'Who owns English?', *Newsweek*, 7th March 2005 © Newsweek Inc; for the text in 5A: based on 'The world according to carp' by Sally Weale, *Guardian*, 24th July 2002 © Guardian Newspapers Limited 2002; for the text in 5D: adapted from Ecological Footprint Quiz www.myfootprint.org © 2002 Redefining Progress; for the text in 10C: adapted from 'The last taboo' by Lucy Cavendish, *Independent*, 7th November 2005 © Independent News and Media Limited.